HEROES

HEROES

✦

A Year in Vietnam With The First Air Cavalry Division

Mike Larson

iUniverse, Inc.
New York Bloomington

HEROES

A Year in Vietnam With The First Air Cavalry Division

iUniverse books may be ordered through booksellers or by contacting:

iUniverse
1663 Liberty Drive
Bloomington, IN 47403
www.iuniverse.com
1-800-Authors (1-800-288-4677)

ISBN: 978-0-595-52521-8 (pbk)
ISBN: 978-0-595-51267-6 (cloth)
ISBN: 978-0-595-62574-1(ebk)

Printed in the United States of America

Dedication

A couple of years ago, I mentioned to a colleague at St. Cloud State University that I wanted to write a book about my year in Vietnam. Why would you want to do that—now? he asked. Well, I responded, mainly I want to write it for my family—and for those soldiers I met in Vietnam, in case any of their children would wonder, "What did you do in the war, Daddy?"

This book is dedicated to my wife, Kay, who showed incredible love and patience during those 12 months that I served in Vietnam; to our children, Christopher and his wife Angie; David and his wife Ricki; and Molly and her husband Joe; and to all of the wonderful grandchildren they have given us.

You are my legacy, and I am so proud of all of you.

Contents

Acknowledgements

I owe a great debt of gratitude to my wife, Kay, and to my parents, Leonard and Lois Larson, who saved every one of the letters I wrote home during my year in Vietnam. Even on those letters I failed to date, most of the postmarks are legible. Further, my parents began numbering my letters right away, starting with "Mike's first letter home," and they dated a number of them. By my count, I wrote nearly 200 letters to them. These letters, combined with notes I saved from during my tour, provided an invaluable record for me in detailing events during one year with the First Air Cavalry Division.

My sister, Jill Larson Sundberg, deserves my gratitude as well. She recruited me into the world of writing, editing and publishing books. Without her encouragement, it's very possible I never would have undertaken this project.

I am grateful to Donald Graham, chairman of the board for the Washington Post Co., and to the late John Root, former chairman of the Humanities Department at the Illinois Institute of Technology in Chicago, Ill. A few years ago, the three of us exchanged our copies of the *Cavalair*, the division newspaper of the First Air Cavalry. That exchange allowed all three of us to greatly enrich our personal archives of that newspaper.

In reading the *Cavalair,* it's difficult to know when specific events occurred. Our reports and our photographs from the field required weeks—and sometimes months—to be cleared by U.S. Army censors in Vietnam. For example, some articles I wrote in September and October of 1967 didn't see the light of day until early in 1968. So in preparing this record, I have relied primarily on my letters home and on notes I kept during my tour to describe events during my year in Vietnam.

I also owe a special thanks to my son Christopher's wife, Angie Larson. A couple of years ago, she said to me, "I consider any American soldier who went to war to defend this country a hero." Her comment stuck with me, and it gave me the courage to use her words of praise as the title for this book.

Introduction

The country of Vietnam stretches from the south some 1,025 miles to China on its north border, folded like a lazy capital "S" between Cambodia and Laos on the west and the South China Sea and the Gulf of Tonkin on the east.

A country of just over 125,000 square miles, with a population of 83 million people, modern-day Vietnam is controlled by a Communist regime based in Hanoi. The Communists gained control in 1975, barely two years after the last U.S. soldiers left Saigon.

Vietnam, an independent country for almost a thousand years, had fallen victim to French colonialism in the mid-19th century. During World War II, Japan took control. Following World War II, Communist leader Ho Chi Minh gained prominence, forming the Vietminh, an alliance of Communist and non-Communist nationalist groups.

An armed struggle brought independence for South Vietnam in 1954 and led to the partition of the country near its midsection. For nearly 20 years, soldiers from the South, aided by soldiers from the United States, Canada, South Korea, Australia, New Zealand, and the Philippines, would fight soldiers from the North, who were supplied in large part by China and the Soviet Union.

In 1975, after the fall of Saigon, Vietnam was reunited under the current Communist regime.

During the two-decade struggle between North and South, the Demilitarized Zone (DMZ) remained the demarcation that defined the two countries. In September of 1967, Robert McNamara, U.S. secretary of Defense, urged construction of an electric fence just below the DMZ, a barrier that would include electronic detection devices to help stem the flow of North Vietnamese Army troops and supplies into the South. McNamara envisioned a barrier stretching east and west some 40 miles across one of the narrowest parts of Vietnam's width.

But McNamara's plan never gained traction.

Instead, military leaders called upon elite forces from the Army of the Republic of Vietnam (ARVN), South Vietnamese Marines and South

Vietnamese Rangers, U.S. Marines, and the Army's First Air Cavalry Division to patrol South Vietnam's northernmost provinces.

The First Air Cavalry, boasting 16,000 soldiers and more than 400 helicopters, had been the first full division inserted into Vietnam. Elements of the division fought the first major engagement of the war, the November 1965 battle in the Ia Drang Valley in the Central Highlands, crushing North Vietnamese troops who threatened to cut South Vietnam in two.

The First Cav's airmobile concept unleashed the most helicopter firepower that had ever supported U.S. foot soldiers. This capability was enhanced by aerial observation by commanders, by logistical, supply and medical helicopter support, and by the ability to carry out fast-paced long-distance moves. The airmobile concept proved to be incredibly effective, and its success launched a new era in the history of land warfare.

Early in 1968, the First Air Cavalry Division would focus much of its attention near the DMZ, basing its activities around Quang Tri, Hue and Khe Sanh. For seven months, I would spend time with First Cav soldiers in all of those hot spots.

In this book, I have begun with the Battle of Hue, certainly one of the bloodiest, but also one of the most significant battles of the war. On January 31, 1968, the first day of the celebration of the lunar new year, Vietnam's most important holiday, the Vietnamese Communists launched a major offensive up and down South Vietnam. The Communist leaders targeted Saigon and Hue as two of the biggest prizes.

Since this was Tet, most ARVN units believed North Vietnamese Army and Viet Cong soldiers would abide by an unspoken truce during the holiday, and large numbers of ARVN troops had traveled home on leave when the first attacks occurred.

Nearly a month would pass before U.S. and South Vietnamese troops could retake all of the captured cities, including the former imperial capital of Hue. There, the allies would fight for 26 days to retake the city from NVA and VC soldiers.

Up and down Vietnam, the Tet offensive proved a major military defeat for NVA and VC forces. Despite some major early successes, all of the attacks ultimately failed. In Hue alone, NVA and VC forces numbering more than 12,000 were driven back. The South Vietnamese populace did not rise up to help the enemy soldiers; thousands of troops from the North were killed or wounded; overwhelming counterattacks by South Vietnamese and American troops sent NVA soldiers who did survive scurrying back across the DMZ. Many military analysts say the insurgent infrastructure was so damaged by the end of the Tet offensive that no large enemy offensives could be mounted for four years.

Yet analysts today agree that the offensive proved a huge political and psychological victory for North Vietnam. The unrest it created in the United States led to President Lyndon Johnson deciding not to run for reelection and led to President Richard Nixon ending the war and bringing his troops home.

After focusing for the first three chapters on the Battle of Hue, I return to July of 1967, my first days in country, and I attempt to provide a more easily followed chronology of my year in Vietnam.

In my first letter home from Camp Radcliff at An Khe, dated July 21, 1967, I described Vietnam as a "nice country—not jungles, but more like our Minnesota landscape—rolling hills, nice trees, and hot summer days." Little did I realize that I would find plenty of jungle during the rest of my tour. Almost one year later to the day, I would describe leaving Vietnam and returning to "The World," which is what we called the United States. The return flight would be quite a contrast to our flight in. In coming to Vietnam, we rode in a jet, but we ate sandwiches and drank sodas handed to us by U.S. Air Force enlisted men. On the ride home, we had real flight attendants, and all of them were women.

I also described the country in a letter to my sister: "South Vietnam's landscape resembles Minnesota. One kid said it looks just like Kentucky. Except for the war, it would be a nice place to visit—if you could just bring your family for a vacation."

I would be assigned to the Public Information Office (PIO) at Camp Radcliff. We were called public information specialists. However, many of us who spent time with the infantry called ourselves combat reporters and combat photographers. It was a badge of honor to differentiate us from those public information specialists who spent most of their time at the base, "in the rear," as we called it, editing our stories, dispatching our stories, and performing other duties that didn't usually draw enemy fire.

Combat reporters venturing into the field certainly had it better than the infantry. As reporters and photographers, we could jump into a departing helicopter whenever we wanted and fly back to base to write our stories and develop our film. That was a luxury the foot soldier did not share.

One infantry soldier I met early on said he had thought about injuring himself to get back home. "I first thought of shooting off my toe," he said. "I'd point an empty gun at it and pull the trigger. It looked so easy, but after I put in the first bullet, I'd chicken out."

This colorful soldier, who spoke with a distinct Brooklyn accent, entertained several of us with his stories as we sat around a little fire and dined on our C-rations. He had at least a couple of us in stitches.

He said he also had tried to injure himself by jumping out of a helicopter during an aerial assault, riding the skids and then leaping off about 20 feet above the ground. He didn't get injured then, either, because he landed perfectly in soft, muddy clay, and sank several inches into the ground. His sergeant ran up to him and shouted, "Boy, I'm proud to have you in my outfit. You really came out of that machine."

Finally, he said, he stopped taking his malaria pills, tablets that soldiers were supposed to pop every day. "I stopped taking them for a week, but do you think a mosquito would bite me? The flies bugged the hell out of me, but I couldn't *find* a mosquito."

My first mission while reporting on the infantry in Vietnam was a cordon-and-search of a village to flush out Viet Cong. The First Air Cavalry foot soldiers surrounded the village and moved in while a Vietnamese National Police Field Force (NPFF) swept through the village. I saw four young men dressed in black pajamas racing into a thatched hut, desperately trying to get away. I could see them through the open windows as members of the NPFF rounded them up. It was amazing to watch how they could pick out suspected members of the Viet Cong.

I was terrified. I was told later that a cordon-and-search operation was one of the safest things you could do in the field. I admitted to one infantry soldier how scared I had been during that first mission. He was "short," a term we used to describe a soldier who had been in Vietnam a long time, a soldier who was almost ready to return to The World. He told me not to worry, that such fear was typical early on. "You'll find that you'll be scared for your first month or two, then the fear will go away for the next few months. Then you'll be scared again when you're close to getting back to The World." He was totally on target, and that was my experience with fear.

One of the PIO reporters who served with me said near the end of his tour that there were times when he came under fire that he put down his camera and picked up his gun. Under fire, he wanted to be able to help the foot soldiers.

For me, the best option was to keep taking pictures. I tested my M-16 rifle early in my tour, squeezing off a few rounds at the Camp Radcliff firing range with other green soldiers during our initial orientation. But I never considered myself a seasoned member of the infantry. I had heard stories of green soldiers who somehow mistook U.S. troops for enemy soldiers and squeezed off a few rounds. With my lack of infantry experience, I had decided early on that I didn't want to make such a devastating mistake. Even though I religiously cleaned and oiled my M-16 rifle, I used my trigger finger to shoot photographs.

In my newspaper career following my year in Vietnam, I worked with many marvelous and talented people. But I never worked with any group that gave me greater pride than the men who documented activities of the First Cav. And I believe that those of us who worked in PIO would agree that no one gave us greater pride than the incredible soldiers whose exploits we covered. They showed deep dedication, unselfishness and courage under fire. These men, who put their lives on the line, were the real heroes of the Vietnam War, and they provided me with the inspiration for this book.

In the First Air Cavalry Division's Public Information Office, we often met other journalists covering the war. Many of us who spent time in the field became friends with John Olson, an enlisted soldier and an incredible photographer who traveled with many combat units. Still in his early 20s, Olson shot for *Stars and Stripes* newspaper and most of his work appeared there, but some of his photographs also ended up as centerspread packages in the *Cavalair*.

In reading and researching for this book, I found a recent interview with Olson, who talked about his wartime experiences. His words beautifully captured the essence of my feelings about Vietnam. I have to admit that sometimes, when I sit and daydream about my time overseas, I honestly do wish I could do it all over again.

I guess that's why Olson's words resonated so well with me. He summed up so perfectly the experience that was Vietnam.

"In many ways," he said, "Vietnam was destiny for me. I went there as a 19-year-old. I had my 20th and 21st birthdays there. It made me who I am, and in my life today in business, when somebody tells me what's possible, I have a good sense of what *is* possible. I can't imagine who I would be if I had not spent that time there. It was a period of time I wouldn't trade for anything and would never have the nerve to do again."

Cities in South Vietnam, circa 1967 and 1968.

Part One: Battle Of Hue

(January 31, 1968–February 25, 1968)

o o o o o o o o o o o o o o o o o o o o o o o o o o o o o o o o o o

"These soldiers did things that brought tears to my eyes. I've never seen such unselfishness. When you saw what these men did under murderous enemy fire, you know what kind of kids we have fighting over here, and you just don't worry about the United States anymore."

A commanding officer
from First of the Seventh,
Third Brigade
"Garry Owen" troops
following the Battle of Hue

Chapter 1
The Third Brigade

On February 2, 1968, a foggy, misty day with clouds hanging so low that the helicopters were forced to fly at tree-top level, the First Air Cavalry Division's Second Battalion, 12th Cavalry launched an air-assault just outside PK-17, an Army of the Republic of Vietnam (ARVN) outpost located along Highway 1 about 10 miles northwest of Hue.

Winding southeast the next morning, the battalion stopped when lead elements standing inside a wooded area spotted armed enemy soldiers milling about lazily on the other side of a broad rice paddy, at the edge of a picturesque hamlet called Thon La Chu.

During the next few hours, ground soldiers in the 2/12th slogged their way across the paddy, penetrated the wood line and were soon in a savage firefight with nearly 1,000 North Vietnamese Army (NVA) soldiers.

The First Air Cavalry Division had just met its first ground resistance in the Battle of Hue.

Early in 1968, Hue, the famous old city from which Vietnam's emperors once ruled their country, had been occupied by a mammoth North Vietnamese force during the first days of the Tet offensive.

The First Air Cavalry had arrived just in time to play a role in Tet battles that would rage in Vietnam's I Corps. Just 10 days earlier, the First and Third Brigades both had moved north, the First Brigade from Binh Dinh Province in II Corps and the Third Brigade from the Que Son Valley south of Da Nang. Both now would be based at Camp Evans, some 15 miles northwest of Hue. As the Tet attacks began, the First Brigade found itself battling to keep an NVA regiment out of Quang Tri City. So when troops were needed at Hue, the Third Brigade was called upon to move across miles of unknown territory against an estimated 12,000 soldiers in and around Hue. The enemy numbers would not be known for sure until the battle for the city and its surrounding territories had been completed.

During the Vietnam War, the U.S. military had designated four tactical battle zones: I Corps, South Vietnam's northernmost region; II Corps, the country's Central Highlands region; III Corps, the more densely populated, fertile region between Saigon and the Central Highlands, and IV Corps, the country's marshy Mekong Delta southernmost region.

In late January of 1968, the First Air Cavalry Division had moved its headquarters to Camp Evans. On the last day of January, the North Vietnamese and the Viet Cong (VC) launched their Tet offensive, with both Saigon and Hue key strategic targets.

I would spend most of February with two units of the Third Brigade, the 2/12th and the 5/7th, as they fought toward Hue in an attempt to help relieve the siege there.

As the soldiers of the First Air Cavalry began their first days of fighting, no one in the Third Brigade could have guessed how utterly different the Hue campaign would be from everything they had seen before. Most firefights in Vietnam lasted no more than a day, and almost all were marked by an overwhelming superiority of American firepower. The rifleman on the ground almost always poured out many more bullets than his adversary, and he could call on infinitely more support fire. But this pattern would be disrupted in the Battle of Hue.

The Third Brigade had just completed four months of grueling fighting against the Second NVA Division in the Que Son Valley 25 miles south of Da Nang. During January, soldiers in the brigade met and hurled back a persistent NVA attack on its bases near Que Son, killing more than 1,000 enemy soldiers. Several people had called the Que Son campaign the most bitter fighting the First Air Cavalry had seen in the preceding year. But during the murderous firefights of February, as the brigade pushed its way toward Hue, many soldiers would carry nostalgic memories of Que Son, and call the Hue campaign a nightmare only because they lacked a stronger word.

When the first enemy soldiers were spotted at Thon La Chu, Second of the 12th leaders called for help from First Air Cavalry artillery units. But artillery support would not arrive until later in the day. Ultimately, two Chinook helicopters flew through heavy clouds and mortar rounds at PK-17 to land two 105mm howitzers for Charlie Battery, First Battalion, 77th Artillery. Once Charlie Battery began pumping shells at the NVA, even enemy-launched mortar rounds that crunched into the camp 14 times during the first day couldn't stop the cannons.

Bad weather had kept much of the First Air Cavalry's helicopter fleet on the ground, but pilots in two Aerial Rocket Artillery (ARA) helicopters braved the dense fog to spew 2.75-inch rockets at NVA positions. The rockets would help clear out some of the enemy before Alpha Company of the

2/12th launched its assault across the open paddy toward Thon La Chu. However, in the fog, one of the aerial rockets hit a tree line too close to First Cav positions, killing one soldier and wounding three others.

Still, lead elements of Alpha Company set out across the rice paddy, penetrated the wood line and scrambled into trenches abandoned by the NVA guards. NVA reinforcements, poised in solid bunkers, opened fire on 2/12th soldiers still working their way across the paddy.

By the time the battalion completed its assault, nine First Cav soldiers had been killed, cut down by the withering enemy fire. Another 48 soldiers had been wounded.

The NVA soldiers had been well-armed, and they had poured out heavy fire from every available weapon, including heavy machine guns and mortars. The U.S. troops, more accustomed to fighting NVA and VC soldiers who took careful shots, held their fire and conserved their ammunition, found the initial enemy fire devastating.

"We tried to put out lots of fire," said Sergeant Chris Jensen III, "but whenever we poured out the bullets, they poured them right back at us. I've been here since April [1967] and I couldn't believe a firefight could be this bad. They said there was probably an NVA battalion in there. Well, if they said the whole North Vietnamese Army was in there, I'd believe it."

"In the Que Son [firefights]," said Captain Robert L. Helvey, Alpha Company commander, "we fought the Second NVA Division in several knock-down, drag-out fights. So we knew what we were getting into. We reacted the way we should have reacted, but we were outnumbered and outgunned."

Helvey was an incredible leader. He and Sergeant First Class Sherman Anglin teamed to make their company one of the most effective in all of Vietnam. I spent several days observing them and listening to their thoughts on disrupting enemy activity. I also observed the incredible loyalty the troops felt for both of them. Here were two battle-hardened veterans, and you could see how much the soldiers they led respected them.

Throughout the two-day battle, snipers from the 2/12th took out 31 NVA soldiers, but the First Air Cavalry's most battle-hardened battalion couldn't push back the entrenched enemy. As the battle dragged into its second day, the soldiers, despite being low on food, water and sleep, still fought.

On the evening of February 4, following the second day of intense fighting, smoke grenades were popped to form a screen and the entire battalion began a daring night march to high ground behind the enemy.

Private First Class Hector L. Commacho, a fearless point man who always seemed to have a smile on his face, led the way through a light mist, along sticky rice paddies that held ankle-deep water.

"It was dark," Commacho told me, "but I trust myself. The hardest part was finding some place where everyone could go, and making sure everyone could keep up."

At 6 a.m. the next day, Commacho and the rest of his battalion, understandably exhausted, climbed onto a hill overlooking the river valley that surrounded Thon La Chu.

By now brigade commanders realized they were facing large NVA forces and perhaps important NVA headquarters in two neighboring hamlets—Thon La Chu, where the 2/12th had attacked, and Thon Que Chu, just a few miles to the northwest. They decided they needed to uproot enemy forces from both hamlets, despite thick ground fog and cold, rainy weather that would hamper them throughout the battle.

The First Cav's Fifth Battalion, Seventh Cavalry air-assaulted near PK-17, and by February 11 had moved to the enemy's northern flank. Radar-controlled bombers and naval artillery pounded the NVA positions each day. The 5/7th secured Thon Que Chu two days later, then began pushing southeast toward Thon La Chu and closer to the 2/12th—so the two battalions could squeeze any enemy units between them.

At the same time, Alpha Company of the 2/12th, which had circled south below the hamlet of Thon Bon Tri, swept northwest. The battalion moved through Thon Bon Tri, just south of Thon La Chu, its lead elements spotting and taking out enemy snipers along the way, and ultimately making contact with the enemy's southern flank.

That night, Captain Helvey set the stage for one of the most dramatic episodes of the battle when he asked for volunteers to scout behind enemy lines.

With First Lieutenant Michael Ackerman and 12 other men, Helvey moved through the darkness across a clearing between the 2/12th perimeter and the NVA, until the volunteers reached a graveyard near the middle of the field. From a deserted cement house in the graveyard, Helvey scanned the area with a Starlight scope, a viewer that intensifies images at night by using reflected light from the moon, stars or any other source of light.

Helvey's men fired M-79 rounds into the tree line just outside Thon La Chu. There was no return fire. The men had made their way to a tree line behind enemy lines. When there was still no enemy fire, they moved farther into the enemy camp.

"They found two treelines," Helvey said, "which meant we could attack, get inside the first treeline and still have another to penetrate. The men found the second treeline on their second trip, and that's when we were spotted."

First, an NVA soldier walked right up to Specialist Four Michael Oberg. Oberg was not a tall man and the enemy soldier, perhaps believing they were in the same army, started talking to him in Vietnamese. Oberg shot him dead.

Another man, Specialist Four David Dentinger, stepped on a moving object and glanced down to see an AK-47 with an enemy at the other end frantically pulling on it. Dentinger pulled away, his M-16 blazing at the NVA soldier.

As the patrol withdrew past the building Helvey had used for cover when he peered through his Starlight scope, an enemy recoilless rifle round slammed into the structure. But the round had hit the building too late. Every one of Helvey's volunteers had made it back unhurt, their mission accomplished.

Based on the night patrol's findings, a planned 2/12th attack was put on hold until the following week. Instead of immediately attacking Thon La Chu, the 2/12th once again would sweep south. Helvey's men had discovered 57mm recoilless rifles, B-40 rocket launchers, and machine guns in well-positioned trenches and bunkers.

"To attack would have been suicide," said First Lieutenant Tony Kalbli, Alpha Company's executive officer. "In that case alone, the 14 volunteers saved the battalion from almost complete destruction."

On February 20, a resupplied 2/12th prepared to launch another assault on Thon La Chu. Four companies from the 2/12th attacked from the southeast while three companies from the 5/7th attacked the village from the north.

"Once we started to attack," said Lieutenant Colonel James B. Vaught, a battalion commander, "everything went alright. Charlie Company to our right smacked into an NVA company moving north to bolster defenses against our main attack. Our men were chewing them up pretty well.

"They spotted several dead NVA floating down the river. But then we started taking almost four casualties a minute and started to withdraw."

As darkness fell, the two battalions pulled back, and Air Force bombers roared in to dump 16 tons of bombs and five tons of napalm on Thon La Chu.

On February 21, the remaining Third Brigade units, freed from base defense at Camp Evans and road security tasks by the arrival of two Second Brigade battalions from II Corps, returned to the hamlet in the early morning darkness and resumed their assault. The 5/7th and the 1/7th on its right both attacked southeast while the 2/12th, still south of the enemy, attacked northwest.

Enemy resistance lasted all day. Harassed by enemy riflemen, lead elements of the 5/7th slowly pushed into the tree line at the northwest corner of Thon La Chu. Three NVA snipers in a concrete bunker, supported by mortar fire, had two platoons pinned down in a shallow trench. Private First Class

Albert Rocha worked laboriously along the trench line, stopping once when a sniper's bullet ripped through the handguard of his rifle. He finally crawled atop the snipers' bunker where he was joined by First Lieutenant Frederick Krupa. While Rocha poured bullets into the hole, Krupa worked a satchel charge into the bunker and set it off.

"The snipers were trying to push out the charge," Rocha said, "but the lieutenant held it right there. It went off in their faces. I was almost ready to get up and move out when one of the snipers came up and gave me a big smile. He smiled at me for half a second before I emptied my magazine into him."

From that point, the 5/7th moved swiftly through the hamlet to the east, and the 1/7th swept south. That night, a 1/7th soldier spotted an enemy soldier in a bunker. Grabbing a .38-caliber pistol and a flashlight, he went into the hole, and returned a few moments later with the enemy soldier.

"This soldier told us that the NVA guarding Thon La Chu had rarely gotten out of their bunkers," First Lieutenant Lesley L. DeNamur said. "Food, water, and ammunition were brought to their holes. He also said that almost 1,000 NVA had been in the hamlet before being pushed out." That was the force that repelled the 2/12th, and later the 5/7th.

On February 22, the brigade finished sweeping through Thon La Chu.

Chasing the enemy from this hamlet was a major turning point for the First Air Cavalry in the Battle of Hue. Besides disrupting a regimental headquarters, which had been defended by the NVA's Fifth Infantry Regiment, it severed a major NVA and Viet Cong resupply and reinforcement route along Highway 1. Now as the Third Brigade fanned out northwest, west, and southwest of Hue, the enemy began to feel more cornered.

"He couldn't stand in Hue without resupply and avenues of escape," said Lieutenant Colonel Richard S. Sweet, the 2/12th commander. "Now he had to bring his troops out to deal with us. POWs told us their medevacs and chow routes were all screwed up, and now he had to pull out earlier than planned."

At the same time, U.S. troops, who had been physically and mentally drained after their initial murderous firefights, were in better shape. Supply convoys were rolling down Highway 1 from Quang Tri to Camp Evans. C-130s were making parachute drops of supplies into Camp Evans while Chinook and Huey helicopters brought supplies to the battalions in the field. Soldiers finally were receiving supplies again, getting hot breakfasts and suppers, and were sleeping well. Considering what they had been through, morale was astonishingly high.

A 101st Airborne Division battalion, working under the Third Brigade's operational control, was finding out more about the enemy it was fighting.

In a tiny hamlet three kilometers west of Hue, the GIs found the bodies of 15 women and children. "They had all been shot at close range," said Lieutenant Colonel Zane Finkelstein, division staff judge advocate, who investigated what he called an atrocity. "Some of the children had their skulls crushed by rifle butts. They had been herded into trenches and killed." The brigade never found out why the women and children had been killed.

On February 22, the final push to Hue began. The 2/12th again moved at night, getting almost three kilometers southwest of Hue when NVA soldiers opened up with automatic weapons, rockets, recoilless rifles, and mortars. During the next two days, the 2/12th, joined by the Second Battalion, 501st Airborne of the 101st Airborne Division on its right along the Song Huong River, was in almost constant contact with NVA units.

Bravo Company, 5/7th, air-assaulted into Hue the same day to link up with Armored Personnel Carriers of Bravo Troop, Third Squadron, Fifth Armored Cavalry.

Meanwhile, the main 5/7th force was pinned down a kilometer from Hue.

"Our lead squad was right up on the NVA when the snipers hit us," said Captain Michael S. Davison Jr. of Charlie Company. "The NVA had that place honeycombed with bunkers, had recoilless rifles, mortars, AK-47s and machine guns, what I'd call a well-defended roadblock."

When the first shots rang out, Specialist Four William Phifer slowly crawled through a graveyard to the right of his company and reached an enemy bunker. He tossed two grenades.

"Apparently they didn't take effect," Captain John W. Taylor said following the fight, "because Phifer climbed back onto the bunker and pitched in another grenade while he fired into the hole with his pistol. I saw his grenade hit an NVA grenade coming out, and both fell into the hole and blew, lifting Phifer about two feet off the ground. He was just shaken up, but the four NVA inside were dead."

That night, artillery pounded the positions. The following day, the 5/7th moved past the enemy to rejoin its Bravo Company and the APCs that had struggled west along the northwest wall of the city. The 5/7th took out five NVA soldiers at a river crossing just before reaching a fork in Highway 1 at the edge of Hue. The northwest wall of Hue had been secured. While the 2/12th infantry pushed through an enemy force, killing five and capturing two NVA soldiers who tried to slip past their lines, the 1/7th farther north had run into a mortar barrage about one kilometer from Hue.

"We also started drawing small-arms fire," DeNamur said. "It looked like positions to our right were weaker so we attacked right. ARA pilots overhead said there were plenty of NVA digging. The ARA chewed them up pretty well."

However, the 1/7th had taken some casualties, and with the intense enemy fire, the soldiers had to stay on their bellies in the water-logged rice paddies.

"Nobody could get up," DeNamur said. "Finally we found that blowing up our air mattresses, placing the wounded on them, and crawling along, pulling the mattresses behind us, worked best."

That night, the 1/7th, bedding down in a graveyard, saw large numbers of enemy soldiers filing from Hue.

"We called in artillery where they were walking," said Lieutenant Colonel Joseph Wasiak, commander of the First and the Seventh, "and hit the trails all night. God knows how many we killed."

The next morning, the 1/7th joined the 5/7th, which had moved to the southwest wall of Hue. Once this part of the wall was secured, enemy resistance inside the city collapsed. ARVN and U.S. Marine forces, who had been fighting a bloody battle inside the city for more than three weeks, finally cleared the NVA from the northwest wall, and the northern part of the southwest wall.

For all practical purposes, the Battle of Hue was over.

Soldiers of the First Air Cavalry continued to conduct sweeps outside the city.

On February 25, the 2/12th found a hospital 1.5 kilometers southwest of the city. Bloodstained boats on the Song Sau River indicated that enemy soldiers had been brought from Hue to the hospital. The 2/12th moved almost to the Hue Citadel, completing the barrier that sealed off the Communists from the northwest, west and southwest.

The fighting had been deadly for both sides.

A total of 101 Third Brigade soldiers had been killed and 676 had been wounded in the campaign. But leaders of the U.S. troops considered the Battle of Hue a vital fight. "Had the Third Brigade not gone in when it did," Lieutenant Colonel Alfred E. Spry, brigade S-2 officer during the fight, said two months later, "the three or four regiments waiting outside Hue could have gone into the city to reinforce the enemy there. If that had happened, we might still be fighting for Hue. We kept the enemy from capitalizing on his evacuation from Hue."

In helping wrench the city from Communist control, the Third Brigade killed 404 enemy soldiers, 359 of them NVA. It captured 13 NVA soldiers and two Viet Cong. In addition, pilots of Bravo Troop, First Squadron, Ninth Cavalry, flying in the longest stretch of continuously bad weather they had seen, recorded 156 enemy soldiers killed.

U.S. intelligence sources estimated that 20 enemy battalions had been engaged in fights in and around Hue.

During their drive to help retake the city, soldiers from the First Air Cavalry ended up in battles with soldiers from the Sixth, Ninth, 90th, and 803rd regiments, the Hue City battalion, and even soldiers from the 24th and 29th NVA regiments, thought to be entrenched at faraway Khe Sanh. The 812th NVA Regiment drove south to Hue after the First Brigade of the First Air Cavalry turned back its attack on Quang Tri. It was a well-armed enemy force carrying mortars, recoilless rifles, rocket launchers, machine guns, and plenty of ammunition wherever it went.

But under this massive NVA firepower, the Third Brigade's troops refused to back down.

"These soldiers did things that brought tears to my eyes," one commander from the First Battalion, Seventh Cavalry said. "I've never seen such unselfishness. When you saw what these men did under murderous enemy fire, you know what kind of kids we have fighting over here, and you just don't worry about the United States anymore."

Chapter 2
Midnight escape

During the Tet offensive early in 1968, North Vietnamese Army soldiers overran and secured perimeters in many parts of Hue. Two soldiers attached to the First Air Cavalry Division were caught behind those enemy lines. One of those soldiers escaped; the other did not.

I still remember sitting with other combat reporters and combat photographers in the Public Information Office in our headquarters tent at Camp Evans listening to John Bagwell tell of his harrowing escape from Hue.

Bagwell, a Specialist Four at the time, had traveled to the Armed Forces Vietnam Network (AFVN) station in Hue, along with Specialist Five Steven Stroub. The station was expanding so it could provide both television and radio broadcasts, and the First Air Cavalry wanted to add a radio voice to the permanent staff there. Bagwell and Stroub hoped they could land jobs with the station in Hue, considered plum duty for broadcasters and production people in Vietnam.

I felt a special bond with both Bagwell and Stroub.

Bagwell had been a radio disc jockey in An Khe when I first arrived there. In physical appearance, Bagwell was less than six feet tall, but he always seemed taller because he was ultra-thin. In camp and on the air, he called himself "The Scrawny One."

Stroub hailed from Austin, Minn. He was one of three members of our Public Information Office from Minnesota, the other two being Dan Stoneking, from the Twin Cities, and me, from St. James. Stoneking had been tapped in December to become editor of the *Cavalair,* the First Air Cavalry newspaper, and he spent much of his tour in Tokyo, editing and publishing that paper. Stroub was a husky soldier on a fit frame. His face was dark and his teeth gleamed white when he spoke and when he smiled—and he smiled often.

Bagwell told us how he and Stroub had traveled to Hue and had met with the manager of the AFVN station. Bagwell kept referring to him as "the civilian with the white shirt." Neither Bagwell nor Stroub had done television work, but Bagwell had done lots of broadcasting and both he and Stroub had done plenty of radio production work.

By late January, most of the First Air Cavalry had arrived at Camp Evans northwest of Hue. In the Public Information Office, we were working hard just to get organized. We knew we were missing Bagwell and Stroub, who had spent three days at the AFVN station in Hue. Finally, a PIO captain who was in contact with Bagwell and Stroub said he would be sending a truck to pick them up so they could return to camp. The truck never left Camp Evans. "I just never got around to sending the truck," Bagwell remembered the captain telling him in a call later that day. "We had a lot of stuff that had to get done here—getting organized, filling sandbags, building bunkers—but stay loose and we'll get someone down there to get you."

That night, during the early morning hours of January 31, North Vietnamese Army regulars took control of Hue.

Following his miraculous escape, Bagwell sat on his bunk and told us his story in vivid detail. An hour or so later, when I returned to my tent, I immediately transcribed my notes. Even today, when I reread what I wrote then, complete with quotes, I can almost hear Bagwell's voice as he described a most incredible ordeal.

Early in the morning, the nine men inside the neat white building that housed AFVN studios in Hue had heard shooting and explosions. Quite quickly, they knew something was up.

"I saw somebody run around in back," Stroub had hollered in the darkness. "He had black pajamas on. I know he was VC."

The other eight men in the room glanced at one another, and the civilian with the white shirt finally motioned everyone to a position. Bagwell, who had been lying on a bed, struggled to sit up and he began pulling on his boots. He had finished tying one when a great concussion, a loud blast that rang in his ears long afterward, hurled him forward onto his hands and knees and crushed him to the floor, while the window behind him shattered, raining glass over the bed and across his naked back.

"What was that?" he groaned.

"What did you say?" one of the other men pleaded as he began cowering toward the wall under his bed. "I couldn't hear you. Please speak again. Please."

"Are you OK, John?"

"I … I think so. No blood."

"I can't hear you!" the man screamed. "I can't hear!"

"Quiet," said the civilian with the white shirt, patting the man on the shoulder, trying to reassure him. "That was a satchel charge, and you might as well get used to them. You'll get over it."

"I was looking at it when it went off, John. My eyes hurt."

"Can you see?"

Stroub nodded. "I'll be able to see, I think. Find yourself a position, John. We've gotta stand these guys off."

Bagwell grabbed his shirt, picked up his M-16 rifle and his other boot, and slid along the floor toward the front door. There he pulled on his boot while he peered outside through a hallway window. The morning sun was beginning to break over the horizon. Looking across the trim lawn outside, which fanned out toward a neat hedge, Bagwell was sure he saw enemy soldiers. He glanced toward the AFVN station's pickup truck and saw that the front windshield had been broken out. All four tires were flat.

"They've shot out all the tires on our truck," Bagwell said.

"There goes our escape," Stroub said. He pushed his back against the wall behind him, placed his feet against the end of a bed, and trained his rifle on the door opening. He waited.

Atop the small building, a grenade exploded and another satchel charge followed, tearing into the wood and sending ceiling plaster spraying throughout the house.

The blast left a gaping hole in the roof. Stroub looked at the hole. Then, against the blue morning sky, he spotted a grenade flying through the hole. "Grenade!" Stroub yelled just before it bounced off the floor and exploded; it was followed by a second grenade that Stroub failed to spot. After the second grenade exploded, Stroub wiped his hand and wrist across his chest, leaving a sticky trail of deep red blood.

"I guess I missed the second one," he smiled.

"Yah," Bagwell answered, tears welling in his eyes, "but you got your second Purple Heart."

"Right," Stroub smiled, "but I don't want it."

The neat white building that had attracted Bagwell and Stroub had been turned into a shambles. Only the brick fireplace at one end of the building stood unscathed. The cushioned furniture had been punctured by fragments of grenades and satchel charges; all the wood furniture, torn apart, was scattered about the building; three pictures in the main room had been slashed by shrapnel, and glass from their frames had been strewn across the floor.

Eight men sat at strategic openings on the first floor watching, waiting. The other man still cowered beneath his bed.

Bagwell, filled with anxiety over having to just sit and wait, suddenly spotted movement out of the corner of his eye, and he brought up his rifle.

An enemy soldier, clad in black pajamas, came around a corner of the building, stopped in the doorway and stared blankly. Bagwell fired at the figure once, twice, three and four times. The figure finally reacted, pulling up his rifle and firing once, twice, three times, then disappeared again around the corner.

"I saw one," Bagwell called, his leg beginning to tremble with fear.

"Get him?" Stroub asked, keeping his eye on a huge hole in one wall.

"I don't think so," Bagwell said.

Bagwell started, whirling around terrified, as another NVA soldier scrambled through the back door and charged over the debris of the back hallway. One of the U.S. soldiers pointed his gun and pulled the trigger, but the hammer clicked against a dud round. The civilian with the white shirt, who also had seen the enemy soldier, fired six shots from his .45-caliber pistol. The enemy soldier fell against a wall and slid to the floor. His belly rose and fell as he labored to breathe, loud groans bubbling through the blood covering his mouth.

"Kill him," cried one of the soldiers.

"He's only a kid," said the civilian with the white shirt. "He can't be much more than 13 or 14. We're fighting kids."

The enemy soldier continued to groan. He remained along the wall in the hallway, his face pressed to the wooden floor, his knees drawn up to his stomach.

The man under the bed held his hands over his ears. "Make him stop moaning. Please, someone, make him stop!"

The NVA gave one final gasp as a soldier placed an M-16 against his head, put the weapon on automatic, and pulled the trigger.

"We've got to get out of here," Bagwell said. "They're getting too daring, coming right through the door like that, coming right at us. We've got to make a run for it."

"He's right," Stroub agreed. "We're gonna have to throw out as many grenades as we can, then run out with our rifles on full automatic and turn them on the NVA."

"But we maybe won't make it," the soldier under the bed cried. "I don't wanna die now. I think…."

"Our chance is to get out," Bagwell said. "Eventually they're going to blow out all these walls."

"Everybody keep watch and gather up all the grenades you can," said the civilian in the white shirt. "I'm going to make a run. Whoever wants to can follow me."

The civilian in the white shirt burst through the front doorway out of the house, raced through the yard and across the street to a small hedge, where he fell onto his stomach. Bagwell heard strident gunfire ring out, staccatic like a toy air hammer. He turned around and asked the man behind him: "Are we going?" The man looked back blankly. Finally, without thinking, Bagwell bolted through the door and raced across the yard toward the civilian.

He turned as he ran and fired off 18 shots at five dark figures crouched along the foundation of the AFVN building.

"I know I didn't hit them," he muttered to himself.

Once Bagwell caught up with the civilian, he too dropped onto his belly and looked back toward the AFVN building. "I know they're coming," he said of his comrades. "They've got to be coming." He heard a violent explosion near the building, followed by a large puff of charcoal smoke that billowed from the house as one wall toppled inward. He couldn't see Stroub. "He'll get out," Bagwell said to himself. "He's got to."

"You've gotta do something for me," the civilian in the white shirt was saying, jarring Bagwell back to reality. The civilian had turned to him and now Bagwell saw a patch of blood seeping through the civilian's pants and a thick patch of red spreading outward near the elbow of his white shirt.

"Make me a tourniquet. Do something," the civilian said.

Bagwell's thin face strained, his eyes darting anxiously toward the AFVN building every few moments while he unbuckled his belt, pulled it from his jungle pants and carefully tightened it around the civilian's arm.

"How about your leg?" Bagwell asked.

"I think it's alright."

"We've got to get out of here," Bagwell said. "Those VC will be coming after us any minute. Where's the best place to go?"

"The MACV compound is in that direction," the civilian said. "That would probably be the safest."

They moved deliberately from house to house, using coconut trees, hedges and walls for cover, until they came to a street crossing.

"Which way do we go?" Bagwell whispered, glancing about at the deserted street, pock-marked by artillery and mortars, the houses splintered and crushed, brick beaten to powder, an occasional body lying in the dust. The trees were bare.

The civilian pointed southward. "MACV is that way. Somehow we've got to get across the street."

"Look at all the VC along the street," Bagwell said, pointing at some NVA soldiers he had spotted. "Maybe the other way would be better."

The civilian shook his head.

They sneaked along a brick wall that ran nearly to the edge of the street.

"Ready?" asked the civilian.

Bagwell nodded.

They broke from behind the wall and dashed for the opposite side of the street. As gunfire broke out, with bullets whining and echoing up and down the street, Bagwell took a dive into a hedgerow and crawled terrified toward a nearby stone wall. Once behind the wall, he pressed his head against the stones and gasped for breath.

"We made it," he whispered. He turned back. The civilian was gone. Bagwell slowly made his way back to the street, which was now vacant except for a dead Vietnamese soldier lying near the next corner. Then Bagwell spotted the civilian in the white shirt, sprawled across the street atop what appeared to be a puddle of blood.

"He's not moving," Bagwell thought to himself. "It's no use going out after him, no use for all of us to die." Bagwell felt tears returning to his eyes, but he choked back a cough and began crawling along the stone wall, continuing to crawl until he could no longer see the street. Then he got up again and ran. A loud crack rang out, then another, and he felt something hot hit his toe. A bullet, he thought, but it didn't slow him.

In the distance, Bagwell spotted a much larger building. It has to be a church, he thought to himself. He made his way toward the brick building and soon he was scrambling up the front steps and bursting through one of the front doors.

A Vietnamese man in priest vestments stared at Bagwell as the soldier braced himself against a wall to catch his breath.

Finally, Bagwell was able to speak. "I need your help," he said, grabbing onto the priest. Some Vietnamese refugees standing inside the entryway of the large Catholic church watched as the priest drew the youngster farther into the building.

"Try to remain calm," the priest said.

"There are NVA and VC all over the place," Bagwell whispered. "They'll kill me if you don't help me. I've already seen them shoot one of my friends. They've maybe killed the others, too."

"You must speak more slowly, son," the priest smiled. "I cannot understand English as well as you can speak it. But we will try to help you. See the Vietnamese here? They have all been driven from their homes, wounded, or have gotten sick during the fighting."

Bagwell followed the priest through the church, past another group of refugees, this group much larger, and up the church's narrow stairway that led to the second floor.

"You limp," the priest smiled. "You've been wounded."

"It's not bad," Bagwell said. "It doesn't hurt."

"Take off your boot," the priest instructed. "I'll bandage it up for you." Bagwell pulled off his boot and the priest rinsed the minor wound, put on some gauze, then wrapped a bandage around the toe. "I used just a small bandage," he said, "because I must save most of the bandages for the refugees, the ones who are badly hurt." Bagwell nodded.

"Give me your weapon," said the priest, "and I'll hide it for you so if NVA soldiers come in, they won't know you are a soldier; they won't hurt you."

The priest returned soon with a thick, wide roll of white gauze. He cut off a long band and began wrapping it carefully around Bagwell's face, covering his ears and most of his hair.

"That'll keep them from recognizing you as an American," said the priest. "The refugees will say nothing. Just keep this on and don't say anything. Don't say one word."

Bagwell sat silently among a group of refugees on the second floor of the church. He sat there, and said nothing, for 15 hours. At midnight, the priest came and told him he would have to leave.

"We know the enemy will return any moment, and it's dark now," he explained. "It would be best for you to escape now."

Meticulously, the priest gave Bagwell directions, telling him where he should go and what he should watch for. Bagwell had been in South Vietnam for 10 months, yet as a radio broadcaster, he was certainly no expert in clandestine maneuvers.

"You crawl along the hedge row outside the front door," said the priest. "When you reach the gate, turn along the road to your left and walk until you see a large rice paddy. When you reach the far edge of it, get down along one of the dikes and crawl. When you are across, you will see an American outpost. Wave your hands to them.

"Stay very close to the ground. And be very quiet."

Shortly after midnight, Bagwell, praying all the way, crawled along the hedge until he got to the gate, carefully opened it and, looking up and down the street, stepped through. He shut the gate again, noiselessly. He tiptoed to the other side, then dropped into a trench. He crawled along the road, staying low in the trench, until he reached the spacious rice paddy. He pulled himself up a dirt mound and let himself down on the other side into the wet, sticky mud lining one of the narrow dikes. He started sloshing across the mud on his hands and knees, but stopped when he heard rubber sandals slapping against the wet pavement nearby.

He crouched there, only his face above the viscous liquid, until two men dressed in black pajamas hurried past, disappearing into a row of trees lining the rice paddy. After waiting a few moments, Bagwell began crawling again.

When he reached the other side, mud covered his chest, his pants, his face and hands, even the white shirt the priest had given him to wave when he reached the other side of the paddy. He fell asleep that way—filthy, exhausted.

The following morning, U.S. soldiers found Bagwell there, still motionless against the barbed-wire perimeter of the U.S. military outpost. When they tried to wake him, Bagwell was groggy; at first they thought he was dead, but after a thorough shaking, Bagwell blinked his eyes and looked up.

Bagwell couldn't remember much until nearly a week later when, lying in a hospital bed, he looked up at a U.S. soldier and asked about Stroub.

Those of us who had been listening to Bagwell's story were asking the same question. What about Stroub, we wanted to know.

"Stroub is dead," Bagwell said. I will never forget Bagwell uttering those three words. They hit us like a hard punch to the stomach. The soldier in the hospital had told Bagwell that U.S. Marines on patrol had found Stroub's body lying along a street near the AFVN building.

"At least he tried to get away," Bagwell had responded. "He wouldn't want to give up."

We found out later that six men who had been at the AFVN station had been taken prisoner. Five of them, including the wounded civilian in the white shirt, would spend about five years in captivity before being released. The sixth, Stroub, was summarily executed by gunshot on the street shortly after his capture. His execution was witnessed by Sergeant First Class Harry Ettmueller, one of the other captives. The date was Monday, February 5, 1968. Stroub was 20 years old.

Two other men assigned to the AFVN station also died that day: Thomas Franklin Young, a U.S. Marine sergeant, and Courtney Niles, also a civilian, serving with NBC International. Both were gunned down as they tried to evade enemy soldiers near the AFVN station.

We sat quietly around Bagwell. He still looked exhausted.

"What are you going to do now?" we asked him.

"Go home," he said. "Just go home. I've got about 25 days left here. Then I can go home and think about how lucky I am, and think about how great it is to be alive."

Those of us sitting there just nodded. Slowly, we started to filter out.

Bagwell put his hands behind his head and leaned back on his cot. Then he scratched a mosquito bite on the knuckle of his left hand and buried his head into his pillow. There was a small garden just outside the headquarters tent, and we could smell the aroma of flowers—flowers, green grass and a couple of palm trees, all dancing in the winds of another monsoon season.

Five minutes later, Bagwell was asleep.

Chapter 3
Recapturing a city

The Tet offensive of 1968 led to the end of U.S. involvement in Vietnam hostilities. No serious scholar even questions that anymore.

When we think about the end, most of us recall the images of U.S. helicopters straining to lift off rooftops in Saigon. Scores of South Vietnamese soldiers and civilians desperately tried to reach the helicopter skids and rope ladders as the UH-1 Hueys hovered above them, carrying off the last U.S. troops.

The Battle of Hue played a major part in the changing sentiment back in the United States. Military analysts today agree that the battles on the field cost the North Vietnamese Army and the Viet Cong dearly. But the psychological effect that lingered long after North Vietnamese Army soldiers had fled back over the DMZ proved far greater than any of their leaders could have imagined.

Even though the United States boasts incredible military might, the U.S. people as a whole have little patience with armed conflict on foreign soil. The North Vietnamese and the Viet Cong, by invading cities up and down South Vietnam early in 1968, succeeded in altering the course of the Vietnam War far beyond any battlefield victories. The widespread enemy attacks stunned broad segments of the U.S. populace and further fueled ever-intensifying anti-war protests.

The growing anti-war sentiment at home ultimately led to President Lyndon Johnson announcing, "I shall not seek, nor will I accept, the nomination of my party for another term as your president," and it led to Richard Nixon running for president on a platform of ending the war and bringing the troops home.

The longest and bloodiest battle of the Tet offensive took place in Hue, the most venerated city in South Vietnam. Located along Highway 1 about seven miles west of the coast and about 50 miles south of the DMZ, Hue was the capital of Thua Thien Province and South Vietnam's third largest city, with a wartime population of 140,000, about half of its population today.

Hue stood along a primary land supply route for allied troops, and it served as a major disembarkation point for supplies brought inland upriver from the South China Sea at Da Nang. Despite its strategic importance, however, the city had been respected by both sides during the war and had remained remarkably free of fighting. Sporadic mortar and rocket attacks occurred in the area, but Hue itself had remained relatively peaceful and secure.

Even today, many Vietnamese people esteem Hue as a religious refuge. Many consider the former imperial capital their most important historical and cultural center. Hue served as the political, cultural and religious capital of a unified Vietnam between 1802 and 1945, when the Nguyen emperors ruled the country.

Hue, in effect, is two cities divided by the Perfume River—better known by the Vietnamese as the Song Huong. The river flows through the city from the southwest to the northeast on its way to the South China Sea.

During Tet, when NVA and VC forces moved into the city, the most important landmark was the Citadel, constructed to protect the Imperial Palace. Considered the Old City, the Citadel stood on the north banks of the Song Huong. The fortress contained block after block of row houses, intricate stone buildings, pagodas, parks, beautiful gardens, villas, quaint shops, and Tay Loc Airfield.

Water surrounded the Citadel on all four sides. In 1968, a zigzagging moat protected the picturesque fortress, encircling roughly 75 percent of the interior city. The moat, some 90 feet wide and about 12 feet deep, was reinforced by two massive stone walls.

Four outer walls standing up to 20 meters high and measuring up to 75 meters thick formed a near perfect square, with each of the walls some 2,500 meters long. Three of the outer walls were straight, while the fourth curved slightly to follow the contour of the Song Huong. The walls, honeycombed with bunkers and tunnels constructed by the Japanese when they occupied Hue during World War II, created an almost impregnable defense.

The walls featured 10 gates, all of which provided entry into the fortress.

Within the Citadel, the Imperial Palace compound formed another walled city. The palace stood at the south end of the compound, a square boasting thick walls that measured roughly 600 meters to a side. Emperors held court in the Imperial Palace until 1883, when the French returned to take control of Vietnam. The Citadel also contained the Nine Holy Cannons that once defended the palace, the Imperial Enclosure where the emperor carried out his official business, the Palace of Supreme Harmony and the Hall of the Mandarins.

In 1968, two-thirds of the city's residents lived north of the river, on the same side as the Citadel.

The other third of the city, called the New City, stood on the south bank of the river. This southern third of Hue contained the hospital, the provincial prison, the Catholic Cathedral and many of the city's modern structures, including government administrative buildings, Hue University, the city's high school, and the newer residential districts. Also on the south bank, beyond the former French quarter now known as Khu Pho Moi, was the Dan Nam Giao or the Altar of Heaven. During Hue's first imperial years, this was considered the most important religious site in the country. Today there isn't much to see beyond a series of three raised terraces.

Two bridges—a railroad bridge on the west and the Nguyen Hoang Bridge, over which Highway 1 passed, on the east—connected the two sections of the city. Another bridge, the An Cuu, spanned the Phu Cam Canal closer to the MACV (Military Assistance Command, Vietnam) compound in South Hue.

Post-war Hue in 1993 received official recognition as a UNESCO (United Nations Educational, Scientific and Cultural Organization) World Heritage Site. The city today also is home to many other historic monuments and sites, including eight Royal Tombs outside Hue that contain the remains of the Nguyen emperors.

When the First Air Cavalry redeployed its Third Brigade from Bong Son to Camp Evans, the truck caravan carrying most of us to our new headquarters wound its way up Highway 1 through Hue. We marveled at the incredible beauty of this city. I remember thinking how green it was, and I remember being struck by the beautiful Song Huong. During our trip north, we were told how Hue was known throughout the country for its cultural tradition, for its Vietnamese-city atmosphere, for the sophistication of its cuisine, and for the beauty of its women. We also were told that it rained often here, an observation certainly borne out during the Battle of Hue.

Of course, our trip through occurred before the Tet offensive, before the fighting within the city damaged many of its landmarks and destroyed much of its beauty.

When the NVA and VC soldiers launched their attack, one key objective was to "liberate" the citizens of Hue to help sweep the Communist insurgents into power.

An estimated 12,000 enemy soldiers would take temporary control of the city. NVA and VC units advanced with coordinated attacks on some carefully selected key installations: Tay Loc Airfield and the First Army of the

Republic of Vietnam (ARVN) Division headquarters in the Citadel, and the MACV compound in the New City.

When the attacks began during the early morning hours of January 31, ARVN troops were startled by flares going off above them. Two battalions from the NVA Sixth Regiment had launched an assault against the western wall of the Citadel.

The NVA battalions planned to penetrate one or more of the 10 gates in the Citadel wall, allowing them to take control of the Imperial Palace. North Vietnamese Army documents recovered after the month-long battle showed that the 800th and the 802nd Battalions of the NVA pushed through the Western Gate, then drove north. At that gate, a four-man North Vietnamese sapper team, disguised as South Vietnamese Army troops, had killed the guards. The sappers then opened the gate, allowing the Sixth Regiment to lead the invasion into the Citadel.

At Tay Loc Airfield, perimeter guards fought off elements of the NVA 800th Battalion. The NVA battle account claimed that the South Vietnamese "offered no strong resistance." Yet the account went on to say that "heavy ARVN fire enveloped the entire airfield. By dawn, our troops were still unable to advance."

At the Citadel, NVA and VC soldiers slowly gained control. By 8 a.m., lead elements of the enemy force raised the Viet Cong red-and-blue flag with its gold star over the Citadel flag tower. Their flag would fly there for 26 days.

Inside the city, the campaign to wrest control back from the NVA and the VC fell largely to ARVN forces and to the U.S. Marines. The Marines found themselves in heavy house-to-house fighting for more than three weeks. Most U.S. soldiers in Vietnam were not trained in urban combat, and such close-quarters combat was foreign to most of them, so they had to hone their skills as they fought through the streets.

Complicating the campaign was the religious and cultural reputation of Hue. Allied soldiers were ordered not to bomb or shell the city for fear of destroying its many historic structures and historic sites. But within days, as the U.S. soldiers became bogged down, that order would be rescinded.

During the first day of the battle, ARVN soldiers found themselves in the middle of the most intense fighting. Many of those units inside the city were forced to retreat under the North Vietnamese onslaught.

Early on the first day, Lieutenant Colonel Phan Huu Chi, commander of the ARVN Seventh Armored Cavalry Squadron, made a daring drive to push through enemy lines. However, Chi and his column of tanks could not break the stranglehold. Chi called for reinforcements, then launched another attack behind three tanks. The squadron was able to cross the An Cuu Bridge over the Phu Cam Canal. As they neared Central Police Headquarters in southern Hue, Chi hoped he could reach the ARVN soldiers defending the facility. But before the tank column was able to break through, an NVA B-40 rocket scored a direct hit upon Chi's tank. The lieutenant colonel was killed instantly, and the stunned South Vietnamese armored column pulled back.

Another South Vietnamese unit, the First Battalion of the Third ARVN Regiment, also found itself in retreat. Captain Phan Ngoc Luong, commander of the battalion, pulled his soldiers back to a coastal outpost at Ba Long. The unit arrived there with only three clips of rifle ammunition per man, with each clip holding just eight bullets. The following day, Captain Luong's battalion returned to the Citadel in motorized junks, but still could not break through the NVA perimeter.

As the fighting continued on January 31, the First Battalion of the First Marines moved into Hue city from the south. When the Marines reached the southern suburbs, they came under a hail of fire from NVA and VC soldiers. In one outlying area, a Marine convoy had to stop a number of times so its lead elements could move through houses on both sides of the street to clear out snipers. Shortly after 3 p.m., the lead elements reached the MACV compound and were able to reinforce ARVN soldiers there.

Even though the NVA soldiers had pulled back from the MACV compound, they remained close enough to harass the Marines and the ARVN troops, taking potshots at the allies from virtually every building.

By 8 p.m., the Marines, despite the sporadic sniping, had established a defensive perimeter around the MACV compound. They would use the compound as their base for several days.

Early on February 1, Lieutenant General Robert E. Cushman Jr., III MAF (Marine Amphibious Force) commander, had contacted Major General John J. Tolson, commander of the First Air Cavalry. Cushman told the general he should prepare to send troops from his Third Brigade into enemy strongholds west of Hue.

Tolson drew up a plan calling for the insertion of two battalions of the Third Brigade, the 2/12th and the 5/7th, into those strongholds. On his official stationery, Tolson's handwritten scrawl detailed orders to his commanders: "Mission—1) Seal off city on west and north with right flank based on Song Huong. 2) Destroy enemy forces attempting to either reinforce or escape from Hue Citadel."

Attacking from the northwest, the two battalions would attempt to cut off the enemy supply line into Hue—and block any retreat out of Hue. On February 2, First Air Cavalry soldiers began their push toward the city.

Inside Hue, heavy street fighting continued. Because it was the heavy monsoon season, it was virtually impossible to bring in air support to help the

Marines. The NVA and VC forces continued to snipe, hiding inside buildings or in small foxholes. They also had constructed makeshift machine-gun bunkers and at night, under the cover of darkness, they planted explosive booby traps.

When the order to limit air bombardment was rescinded, Air Force bombs and Naval artillery support began to take their toll, and most areas that had been captured by NVA and VC soldiers were retaken by U.S Marine and ARVN forces.

Within days, as the allied drive to retake control of Hue gained momentum, only the Citadel and the Imperial Palace remained under control of the North Vietnamese. U.S. Navy pilots flying A-4 Skyhawks began dropping bombs and napalm into the Citadel. After three weeks of fighting, U.S. Marine lead forces finally flushed NVA and VC soldiers from the Citadel, and the Marines raised a U.S. flag on the site. However, U.S. commanders ordered them to take down the flag. Under South Vietnamese law, no U.S. flag was to be flown there without an accompanying South Vietnamese flag. Some U.S. Marines objected, even threatening to shoot a few U.S. Army officers who had told them to take down the flag. But finally sanity prevailed, and the Marines lowered the flag themselves under the supervision of their superior officer.

On February 24, the U.S. Marines and ARVN troops secured the Imperial Palace in the Citadel, and the elite Black Panther Company of the First South Vietnamese Division ripped down the Viet Cong flag, which had flown since the battle began.

A few days later, the NVA soldiers withdrew from the city completely.

On March 2, the Battle of Hue was officially declared over. It had been a costly battle for both sides. In 26 days of combat, ARVN units had lost 384 killed and more than 1,800 wounded, plus 30 soldiers missing in action. U.S. Marine units suffered 147 dead and 857 wounded. The First Cav's Third Brigade had suffered 101 dead and 676 wounded.

Casualty estimates for the NVA and the VC vary, but there's no doubt North Vietnamese soldiers paid dearly for their invasion. South Vietnamese leaders reported killing nearly 3,000 NVA and VC soldiers during the battle. U.S. troops reported killing some 1,500 enemy within the city of Hue and another 3,000 enemy in strongholds around the city.

The casualties extended well beyond the soldiers fighting the battles. There were widespread reports of Hue citizens killed by NVA and VC soldiers throughout the city. After the enemy had been driven out, ARVN and U.S. troops unearthed a number of shallow mass graves inside the city and on its outskirts. In those graves, the soldiers found some 2,800 civilians who had been killed by NVA and VC soldiers.

In a later report, Paul Vogel, an American English professor at Hue University, classified these civilian executions into two categories: 1) planned killings of government officials and their families, political and civil servants and collaborators with Americans; 2) random killings of civilians who ran from questioning, citizens who spoke harshly about the occupation and citizens who "displayed a bad attitude" toward the occupiers.

Don Oberdorfer, a researcher and an author who worked with Vogel, said that in Phu Cam, a solidly Catholic area of Hue, "virtually every able-bodied man over the age of 15 who took refuge in the Catholic church was taken away and killed." That Catholic church was the same one where Specialist Four John Bagwell had been given refuge by a Catholic priest, and it showed how close he came to being captured—or worse. A VC commander, known only as Ho Ty, who helped with the advance planning for the "general uprising" to support the NVA and VC invasions, said the Communist party "was particularly anxious to get those people at Phu Cam.... The Catholics were considered particular enemies of ours."

NVA and VC soldiers proved to be incredibly fierce fighters during Tet. But throughout South Vietnam, the allied forces ultimately prevailed, pounding the Communists, delivering devastating losses, and driving them back out of the cities. In retrospect, the Tet offensive would be assessed as a major military defeat for NVA and VC forces.

But in the eyes of the American public, the Tet offensive had been totally shocking. The Battle of Hue was part of the beginning of the end. The American public had become disillusioned with sending off its young men to fight in the jungles and the deltas of Vietnam. During the next five years of the Vietnam War, U.S. involvement slowly but steadily decreased. In 1973, the last U.S. troops left Vietnam, and we watched the final Huey helicopters struggling to lift off those rooftops in Saigon, leaving behind those hoards of Vietnamese who had attempted and failed to get on board. In two short years, the North Vietnamese would take control of the country. For those of us who had left the United States to spend a year helping the South Vietnamese people, it was a surprise ending most of us had not foreseen.

Part Two: An Khe

(July 16, 1967–December 8, 1967)

o o o o o o o o o o o o o o o o o o o o o o o o o o o o o o o o o o

"A division's history helps inspire the *esprit de corps* that makes military personnel feel as if they are part of something larger than themselves. It instills pride. Its effect is palpable in many ways. The Army certainly subscribes to this belief. General Creighton Abrams, a commander during the Vietnam War, said the First Air Cavalry Division's 'big yellow patch does something to an individual that makes him a better soldier, a better team member, and a better American than he otherwise would have been.'"

Troy Vettese
History News Network

Chapter 4
The First Air Cavalry Division

Soldiers assigned to the First Air Cavalry Division in Vietnam usually linked up with the division at An Khe. They would be sent to their units from there.

Today An Khe (the Vietnamese now call it An Tuc) is a sleepy little Vietnamese village, and there are few reminders that the First Air Cavalry Division operated here. But in July of 1968, the division's base camp sprawled across several acres of Binh Dinh Province in the Viet Cong-infested Central Highlands. Called Camp Radcliff, it served as base for a division that boasted the largest concentration of soldiers and weapons in Southeast Asia since 1954, the year the French had left Indo-China.

I had been assigned to Letterman General Hospital in San Francisco in late 1966 following basic training at Fort Lewis, Wash. My wife Kay and I had lived across the bay in Oakland for nine months before my orders came for Vietnam. After a leave to our family farm near St. James, Minn., where I had spent my first 18 years, both of us returned to Oakland. Kay planned to continue her job as an X-ray technologist at an orthopaedic surgeon's office in Oakland. But when she found out she was pregnant with our first child, she decided to return to the Midwest, where she would split her time with our parents, in St. James and in New Richmond, Wis.

Those soldiers in my group destined for Vietnam rode a C-141 Military Air Transport Jet out of Travis Air Force Base, located some 50 miles northeast of San Francisco. The date was July 16, 1967, a Sunday, and the time was 11 p.m. I don't remember much about the flight except that it was one long trip. We were not very comfortable, clinging to canvas seats and riding backwards, facing the rear of the plane. U.S. Air Force enlisted personnel served us sandwiches and sodas during the flight. Other than that, we just sat, talked to our neighbors and used the bathroom.

The flight to Vietnam lasted about 27 hours with one stop for refueling in Guam. The jet landed in Pleiku, where we retrieved duffle bags packed with our belongings and spent the night. The next day, we climbed aboard a cargo plane for a flight to An Khe. In my first letter home, postmarked July 21, 1967, I wrote, "I arrived here with the First Cavalry yesterday—we're stationed about 30 miles east of Pleiku—and we've just been assigned to the Public Information Office."

Most soldiers flying into Camp Radcliff first noticed the huge gold-and-black patch painted on the side of Hon Cong Mountain, the dominant geographical feature at First Cav headquarters. It was a replica of the First Air Cavalry Division emblem all of us would wear on the upper left sleeve of our uniforms. The patch, designed on a field-of-gold Norman shield, featured a black diagonal stripe and a black horse's head. First Cav soldiers referred to their patch as the "Horse Blanket," and for most of us, it was a huge source of pride. General Creighton Abrams, one-time commander of all U.S. forces in Vietnam, once said, "The big yellow patch does something to an individual that makes him a better soldier, a better team member, and a better American than he otherwise would have been." Most of us would keep and revere that patch long after we had left Vietnam.

Gene A. Deegan, a U.S. Marine officer and a boyhood neighbor, once told my father that he considered the First Air Cavalry the best division in Vietnam—and I don't think he was just flattering my dad. Deegan, who took a bullet in his stomach during a firefight in Vietnam, had participated in some actions with the First Cav during his time as a captain with the Second Battalion, First Marines. A few years older than I, he had grown up on the farm right next to ours. He retired from the Marines in 1991 at the rank of major general.

The First Cavalry Division (Airmobile), nicknamed "The First Team," certainly had earned a reputation as the most mobile combat unit in Vietnam.

The division utilized five primary kinds of helicopters to achieve this incredible mobility. The OH-6A and OH-13S Light Observation Helicopters featured Plexiglas bubble cockpits in which two passengers could sit, but they often would be flown by one pilot. The Hueys, the UH-1 series helicopters, were the workhorses of the division. "They carry up to 10 passengers and are used mainly for air-assaults," I wrote. "The First Cav also utilizes the Hueys as rocket ships armed with miniguns and 2.75-inch rockets. Then there are the two cargo helicopters: the Chinook or CH-47 and the Flying Crane or CH-54. The Chinook has two huge overhead rotors (the other types, including the Flying Crane, all have one large overhead rotor plus a smaller vertical stabilization rotor in back to keep the chopper from spinning around). The Chinook can carry upwards of 60 to 70 men, plus equipment, and it's pretty fast. The Flying Crane resembles a large mosquito and can lift nearly any weight. The Flying Crane is used to recover downed aircraft and move heavy equipment and housing materials."

The AH-1G Cobra, a much faster and much more maneuverable attack helicopter, would not arrive in the division until late 1967, and it would exist only in limited numbers during my tour. I first mentioned the gunship in early October: "We're waiting for the new Cobras, a vicious-looking helicopter that is capable of diving toward the ground, just like a fighter-jet, while firing off rockets and cannons. Don't quote me, but I've been told it will dive at 170 mph."

When the Cobra gunship made its appearance, it carried 76 air-to-ground rockets, a 40mm grenade launcher, and a 20mm cannon capable of firing semi-armor piercing bullets at a rate of 650 rounds per minute.

Most of my notes about helicopters focused on the Hueys that were in primary use by the First Cav during 1967 and 1968.

"Riding in the Hueys is strange," I wrote. "In airplanes and jets, a wall separates you from the outside. In a helicopter, there's no wall. We sit right along the edges. You can look over the edge and see the ground flying by, and when the pilots bank, I'm nearly convinced I'll slide right out. But no one does. The centrifugal force holds us in. The helicopters are very safe and even on the smaller ones, if the engine stops, the pilots can use the air rushing past the rotor to turn the rotor backwards and bring the helicopter safely to the ground. The air shooting past the blades of a stalled rotor will turn it sort of like a windmill and pilots can use this to land."

Early on, I rode along on some night-time missions with First Cav pilots. They showed me how to peer at our surroundings through a Starlight scope, a nighttime viewing device.

"In Phan Thiet," I wrote, "I went out with these guys who search for VC at night. We had our lights turned off so no one could see us. They look out through Starlight scopes. You can see very well in the dark. It's just like looking under chlorinated water—pretty romantic for a serious job. I went out twice, an hour at a time, and had a good time."

At Camp Radcliff, the First Cav utilized a huge helipad that we called "The Golf Course." Acres of rolling terrain had been cleared of scrub brush to serve as this helipad, where the First Cav maintained its fleet of more than 400 helicopters, five times the number allocated to any other division in Vietnam.

Camp Radcliff had been named for Major Donald G. Radcliff, a pilot killed on August 18, 1965, while supporting a U.S. Marine operation in southern Quang Tin Province. The executive officer of the First Cav's First Squadron, Ninth Cavalry, Radcliff was flying a UH-1B helicopter gunship while hovering over Marines assaulting into a landing zone. His ship came under intense small-arms fire from Viet Cong troops at the edge of the landing zone, and Radcliff died at the controls of his helicopter.

The first commander of the division's 16,000 men had been Major General Harry William Osborn Kinnard. When the division first arrived at An Khe, Brigadier General John M. Wright, the division's assistant commander, grabbed a machete and began carving out a large landing area. He showed his team of soldiers how to cut out the scrub without disturbing the grass, in order to minimize clouds of dust whipped up by helicopters rotating in and out.

When I arrived at "The Golf Course" in July, the red, dusty soil struck me. For a boy from Minnesota, where we plant crops in soil that's jet black, it was quite a change. However, almost within days, the monsoon season began and that red clay turned to sticky red mud. In one of my first letters home to my wife, I wrote, "It just poured down last evening—the monsoon season has started—and I walked around most of the night in mud ankle deep. I just went out to shower and I sank into the mud several inches. Then one of my sandals came loose. Finally I just carried them and walked barefoot. When I got to the showers—about 150 feet from where we sleep—I really needed a shower. Especially my feet. They have a couple barrels of water on the shower roof and heaters in the barrels. The water is usually too hot or too cold. But at least it's clean and wet, and we appreciate that." I also wrote: "I expected jungle, but it's really more like Minnesota—rolling hills, regular trees and warm summer weather." That would change quickly, though, when I traveled farther north. There would be jungles and elephant grass, and the heat in those jungles could be stifling; the dirt would rise up and coat our bodies, especially during the non-monsoon months when the soil turned to dust.

In some of my early writings, I talked about being responsible for filling that shower water barrel and keeping the fire going beneath it during CQ (Charge of Quarters). We pulled CQ duty every few days, which meant we took care of the water barrel, the latrine barrel and a few other select duties during evening hours. "Night before last," I wrote on August 29, "I was on CQ and had to start the gas burner that heats our shower water. A few minutes later, I went out to check it and the fire had gone out—so I lit a match and dropped it into the burner and it went WHOOM! I saw flames climbing from deep inside coming toward me and just as the flame passed me, I threw my head back. So I didn't get burned except the front of my hair and some of the hair on my arms."

We spent our first few days at Camp Radcliff going through three and a half days of intensive orientation at the 15th Administration Station. We received the standard U.S. Army issue items we would carry with us for the next 12 months: fatigues, T-shirts, jungle combat boots, a combat helmet, a flak vest, a backpack containing a rain poncho and a poncho liner, a mess kit with a canteen cup and a metal fork-spoon combination, and, of course, our M-16 rifles. Each of us also received a small plastic bottle filled with mosquito repellent; most of us would secure that plastic bottle under the elastic camouflage band on our combat helmets.

During our field orientation, we learned how to use our rain poncho to make a pup tent. In the field, we slept inside those little tents. We would dig a fox hole at the foot of our pup tent so in case of enemy attack we could slide out feet-first right into the fox hole. It rained almost constantly during our field orientation, and sleeping inside our pup tents, we felt like drowned rats.

For most of us, the combat boots lasted a long time. Other than rubber sandals we bought from Vietnamese merchants in An Khe, I don't remember wearing anything else. And I don't remember ever requesting or receiving a replacement pair of combat boots. By 1967, jungle combat boots had been redesigned so they contained microscopic drainage holes in the soles. That helped our feet to dry out much faster after we had been wading in a river or walking through a rice paddy.

The rubber sandals we wore were made by the locals out of discarded vehicle tires. When I returned home one year later, my mother chased me out of the house when I wore those sandals. The banishment was well-deserved—my sandals had been making rubber markings all over the linoleum floor in her kitchen.

I would write later about some of our Army issue items. In an August 24 letter home, I noted that we were well-equipped, but went on to say that on most days "I don't even wear underwear. We go out with the infantry a lot and walk. First of all, they don't want any white to show; secondly, you get a rash from shorts, even boxers, so I've conformed. My first day in the field, I went out for just one day and got a rash or irritation. The grunts in the field told me that the underwear is what caused it."

I don't recall much about our orientation sessions, except for a junior officer who showed us a short film that provided graphic images of some frightening diseases we could contract if we paid for sex in Vietnam. For those of us who were married, there was good reason to remain celibate during our tour. But beyond that, the message in the film was clear: if you ended up with the wrong woman, you might find appendages beginning to fall off of your body.

I would soon discover another reason Army commanders worried about our extracurricular activities: Vietnam's economy was a bit upside down. To buy a can of Coke in An Khe, which many of us did, you had to fork over a dollar in Vietnamese money; to buy a girl for a couple of hours, you had to fork over just four dollars.

In our discussions about health, we were told about one other major concern at Camp Radcliff—rats.

"Rats were a big problem when this unit first got here," said First Lieutenant George A. Matuza, the officer in charge at the 20th Preventative Medicine Detachment. "The men would set out 50 to 60 traps and catch up to 20 rats overnight. But last month we had 800 traps around the base and caught only six rats."

Eliminating rats was important because they carried bubonic plague, typhus, amebic dysentery, rabies and even malaria.

The rats needed to be killed before the plague fleas would develop and cause trouble. "Traps and poison are our principal rat-control measures," Matuza said. "We also spray areas that have high rat populations. If spray gets on the rat's coat, it will kill plague fleas."

Soldiers bitten by rats had to undergo rabies shots. Until the 1970s, rabies vaccinations were painful and frightening procedures that consisted of between 16 and 21 shots received in the abdomen. A couple of weeks later, I watched as a doctor inserted his needle just under the skin of a soldier's stomach and injected the vaccine close to his navel. It didn't appear to be that painful, but then I was not the one receiving the injection. Some of the soldiers I spoke with said they had been given the shots in their arms, but they said they found those shots extremely painful.

"I got most of my shots in my arms," one soldier said, "and I had sore arms all the time. They're the worst shots I've ever had."

Today the rabies vaccine is given in the arm muscle, much like a flu or tetanus shot, but new techniques have made the injections much less painful.

Lots of First Cav soldiers offered "rat stories." I spoke with one man who told me about sleeping in his bunk in one of our large Camp Radcliff barracks buildings. The soldier woke up in the middle of the night, surrounded by darkness, to feel a creature nibbling on one of his toes. The next morning, he went to have the bite checked, and the doctor told him he had been bitten by a rat.

Each month, about 10 soldiers would show up at the 616th Medical Company at Camp Radcliff after being bitten by rats, dogs, monkeys, mongooses or other possible rabid animals.

Since there's no cure for rabies, anyone bitten needed to undergo the series of shots.

"Out of the 10, we treat about four," said Specialist Six Dayton L. Larose, a clinical specialist at 616th Med. "The other six will receive treatment at their own units. But they must get the shots. We give them no choice."

For many of the soldiers, the anti-rabies regimen could be worse than the bite: one injection in the stomach every day for 14 days running, then a 15th injection one week later and a final injection the week after that. The shots would be given in the stomach all around the soldier's navel primarily because that area, being large, best tolerated the pain—at least 16 shots, and if a soldier missed any of those shots, the procedure would have to begin all over again.

James Joyce (that really was his name), who served with the First Cav in Vietnam, also described being bitten by a rat. In his book, "Pucker Factor 10: Memoir of a U.S. Army Helicopter Pilot in Vietnam," Joyce told of bunking down in Camp Radcliff barracks a few days before Christmas. Joyce stirred in the middle of the night after feeling a sharp pain at the tip of his ring finger.

"In the morning when I awoke, I immediately remembered the incident and started hoping it had been a bad dream. 'Please make it a dream,' I thought (make that prayed) as I lifted my arm. It was not a dream. Dried blood covered my hand and part of my forearm. I couldn't believe it. The place was strewn with open cans and boxes of every kind of sweet food you could name, and a rat decided to chew on me instead. That's a mean rat.

"I vacillated for perhaps half an hour before deciding to turn myself in as a rat-bite victim. We all knew the medical procedure for rabies prevention—16 extremely painful shots in the stomach. But we also knew that to die of rabies was about as bad as dying got. When my head was fully cleared (how much vodka did I drink?) I walked over to the medic's tent and told our flight surgeon what happened. He examined my finger and said, 'Yep, that's a rat bite.' He said the skin would grow back over it, however, and he didn't think there'd be a scar. 'He must have just gotten started on you,' he said and told me I was lucky I woke up. Yesterday he had seen a soldier who was missing most of his upper lip. He'd gotten drunk, too, but he passed out with peanut butter on his lips. The doctor said there must have been three or four rats working on him before he woke up screaming."

We also learned about malaria. Our fears of contracting such an illness led to almost all of us taking malaria tablets and sleeping on canvas cots or air mattresses surrounded by mosquito netting. We would tuck the netting under us to keep the mosquitoes, and the rats if need be, off of us.

"We maintain two light traps in the camp," Matuza said. "They're sort of pointless in a way because our findings prove that less than one percent of all malaria cases have been caught in a base camp. Eventually, we hope to take mosquito surveys into the field and determine where spraying would be economical and worthwhile. In base camps, we're mainly concerned with mosquitoes laying eggs in artificial containers—barrels not overturned and puddles in tire tracks and other depressions—that collect water and become mosquito breeding areas, spawning mosquito larvae and mosquitoes."

In our final orientation session, Lieutenant Colonel Gene Brown warned us about the dangers posed by helicopters. His message was especially relevant for soldiers serving in a division featuring some 400 helicopters constantly on the move.

"Safety is something that must never be forgotten. If it is, then the effectiveness of the airmobile concept will also be forgotten," said Brown, the First Cav's safety officer.

The First Cav always had been proud of its safety record, but during the past month, a number of careless accidents had solidified the role safety plays in a helicopter unit.

Ranking high among the accidents were soldiers walking into the blades of rear helicopter rotors. This kind of accident should never occur, Brown said, and with a little foresight and an awareness of surroundings, soldiers should stay safe.

Brown said soldiers should never approach helicopters from the rear. With the UH-1 Huey, especially, at least a few soldiers had walked into the vertical stabilizer blades and had been seriously injured or killed. Always approach a helicopter from the front, he said.

When leaving a helicopter, Brown said, never go to high ground around the aircraft. Always stay on level ground. Also, never approach the ships from high ground.

The most important advice, he said, was to be ever vigilant, to always know where the aircraft was at all times. It was excellent advice that would serve us well during our tour.

At Camp Radcliff, I had moved into barracks located close to a building that housed The First Air Cavalry Division's Public Information Office. It made sense for me to be attached to PIO. My service designation was information specialist. I had just graduated from the University of Minnesota with a Bachelor of Arts Degree in journalism. I had worked for a few months as a reporter at the *St. Paul Dispatch*, the afternoon daily in Minnesota's capital city. During my nine months in San Francisco, I had worked in PIO at Letterman General Hospital on the Presidio. The Presidio, originally a Spanish Fort sited by Juan Bautista de Anza on March 28, 1776, was transferred to the National Park Service in 1994. Letterman General Hospital, which stood on that site, was demolished in 2001.

During my first few weeks in Vietnam, I performed a variety of jobs. I conducted some interviews and wrote some stories of my own. I edited a number of articles sent in to us from reporters in the field. I helped select photographs we would publish in the *Cavalair* as well as in other publications such as *Stars and Stripes* and the *Army Reporter*. I also spent time working with our radio people, helping them with production work and spending at least some time behind the microphone.

Early on, I learned the value of hanging around any First Cav Tactical Operations Center (TOC), where commanders planned and directed major troop movements. PIO reporters usually were welcome to attend briefings there. I found this habit especially helpful after the division had moved to Camp Evans—and during the Battle of Hue and the siege at Khe Sanh. In a letter dated April 6, 1968, I wrote from LZ Stud near Khe Sanh, "Right now I'm sitting at TOC getting the war story for this evening, and I'll continue writing [this letter] until they get the information I need." These First Cav reports from the field provided us with invaluable information about the enemy numbers and the enemy units our troops were fighting.

At Camp Radcliff, I enjoyed evenings the most. That's when those of us in the unit could visit "The Bar," a nearby tent draped on a large, wooden frame where the top PIO sergeants served up drinks for us. We could buy beer and we could buy mixed drinks. Early in October, I had written, "We had a big party at our little club tonight. We grilled steaks and listened to deafening music, like rock 'n' roll at home." But such festive occasions were rare. Most of the time, we were content just to belly up to the bar and sip on a can of Coke and pop open a can of crisp Cheetos. I can still remember downing a whole can of those in a single evening.

Some men in our base camps also occupied their free time by tending to pets. Our PIO office at Camp Radcliff adopted a dog we named Myrtle. In October of 1967, I wrote about an event that could precipitate puppies: "Today our epileptic dog, Mrytle, came into heat, and she and a male got stuck together. It's the first time I've ever seen that happen. I'd read all about the male bulb swelling up and shrinking only with climax. If you scare him, he will not release and the bulb remains. So one of our men poured cold water over them to get them apart. He was dragging her all over our office. Then, a few minutes later, the same male and another female.... You guessed it. They got together and...." The gestation period for dogs is about nine weeks, so an event I referenced later, in the spring of 1968 from Camp Evans, certainly came from another coupling. I had written to my father asking how many of his Hereford cows had delivered calves, then added: "The PIO dog had seven pups. I guess it's just the season."

At Bong Son, one PIO trooper kept a very friendly but exotic mongoose to ward off rodents and reptiles. The mongoose loved to run along atop the ropes that held up the mosquito netting inside our sleeping tent. I called the mongoose Rikki-Tikki.

Within a month after arriving in country, I would be shuttling between An Khe and Bong Son, where the First Cav's Third Brigade had moved. During my days at An Khe, I would be introduced to a couple other diversions for soldiers in the First Cav: latrine duty and kitchen police (KP).

Latrine duty meant tending to large steel barrels that had been cut in half at their midsection, placed under our outdoor bathrooms, then half filled with human waste. If you had latrine duty, you had to pull out the half-filled barrel, then replace it with one that had been fire-treated. That's how we dealt with the excrement: we would pour fuel oil into the barrels, light it on fire, and let it burn itself out.

It was not a glamorous job, but it was memorable. In fact, poems were written about the process. Bruce Weigl, who has been referred to as the poetic voice of Vietnam, wrote a full poem entitled "Burning Shit at An Khe." You can find the entire poem on the Internet, but some of his verse includes the memorable lines:

Into that pit
I had to climb down
With a rake and matches; eventually,
You had to do something
Because it just kept piling up
And it wasn't our country, it wasn't
Our air thick with the sick smoke
So another soldier and I
Lifted the shelter off its blocks
To expose the home-made toilets:
Fifty-five gallon drums cut in half
With crude wood seats that splintered.
We soaked the piles in fuel oil
And lit the stuff
And tried to keep the fire burning.

My first day on KP came on Monday, September 4, 1967. I know the date because I wrote about it, saying it was the first time I had served on KP since basic training at Fort Lewis, Wash. I guessed that my last KP duty had been on about Aug. 25 of 1966.

On that Monday, September 4, I worked KP with two other soldiers from the Public Information Office: Herb Denton and Don Graham. I hadn't met either one, and I didn't know them from Adam.

We spent a pleasant day talking together as we peeled potatoes, filling huge containers for the noon meal and the evening meal. I learned that both were graduates of Harvard University, and both had worked at *The Harvard Crimson*, the campus newspaper. Denton grew up in Little Rock, Ark., and graduated from Harvard in 1965. After Vietnam, he would return to *The Washington Post* as a writer, then an editor. Other blacks on staff there would point to Denton as an incredible mentor for them, one who helped them grow and become successful in their jobs. Graham grew up in Washington, D.C., and he graduated from Harvard in 1966. I wouldn't realize until a few days later, when Sergeant Dan Stoneking told me, that Graham was heir apparent to *The Washington Post* empire.

Journalists tend to consider themselves "above the fray," somewhat removed from the mainstream, if you will. In Vietnam, that meant spending little time on KP, on latrine duty, or on guard duty. During my entire 12-month tour, I remember being on KP only a few times in An Khe, being on latrine duty only a couple of times, and serving on guard duty only one time—in Bong Son. We also were never big on decorum—spit-polishing our boots to an inspection shine, for example. I mean, what would have been the point? And when we traveled with soldiers in the field, we were never encouraged to salute. In fact, some officers discouraged it. They believed that if North Vietnamese or Viet Cong soldiers saw the salutes, the U.S. officers might become more highly prized targets. Ignoring salutes in the field, or anywhere else for that matter, was just fine with me.

In October, I wrote about the national elections in Vietnam and about some threats we were hearing at Camp Radcliff. On Oct. 21, 1967, the South Vietnam National Assembly had approved the election of Nguyen Van Thieu as president of the country, and it was feared that enemy soldiers would attack us to make a statement against Thieu. We would be restricted to base.

"An Khe will soon be off-limits again, during the National Assembly elections," I wrote. "We heard intelligence reports saying that a 10-man Viet Cong assassination team came into An Khe last week and is hiding there. Other reports indicate all except the last barbed wire strands around our Camp Radcliff perimeter have been cut in strategic spots. Around the camp, several strands of barbed wire, rolled barbed wire with inch-long barbs, and a 30-foot watchtower about every 100 yards, forms our perimeter. The watchtowers stand on tall, stocky poles, and they are heavily sandbagged. Perimeter guards work in shifts: three men to a tower, each watching for two hours twice a night. Four hours each.

"Our most strategic spot is a tall mountain—Hon Cong Mountain—just outside An Khe. It has a helipad, large weapons, and a wealth of radar equipment and spotlights. They say the radar can pick up and pinpoint the origin of a mortar or artillery round before it strikes its target. This might be fable.

"Hon Cong Mountain once was outside our perimeter barriers. I can't quite conceive that. It was attacked before they extended the perimeter. That I can imagine. At the summit of the mountain, they have a huge First Cav patch along the mountainside. It's an easy way to tell directions."

Looking back now at Camp Radcliff and realizing how safe it really was, I'd have to say those alarming intelligence reports were more than just a little overblown.

Chapter 5
Those daring young men

In Francis Ford Coppola's movie "Apocalypse Now," Robert Duvall as Lieutenant Colonel Bill Kilgore leads his helicopter squadron in an assault on a Vietnamese village. We see Kilgore's fleet of helicopters coming up from the horizon in the distance. We've already been introduced to this squadron so we know it's the First Air Cavalry Division's First of the Ninth.

As Kilgore's squadron nears the village, a village portrayed in the film as a Viet Cong stronghold, we hear Richard Wagner's grandiose "Ride of The Valkyries" being played over loudspeakers attached to Kilgore's helicopter gunship. Wagner's symphony is intended to terrify the enemy soldiers. Kilgore pushes to expedite the assault on the village because he has seen that the surf is up in the South China Sea and he wants to hop on his surfboard, which he always carries with him. We can see the gold-and-black First Cav patch on the surfboard during a close-up. When Kilgore lands his gunship and orders the landing zone secured, he utters his most quoted line from the film: "I love the smell of napalm in the morning!"

Some Hollywood producers and directors have called the extravagant depiction of the First Squadron, Ninth Cavalry the finest and most spectacular helicopter attack sequence ever filmed.

I understand that some First Cav veterans became incensed when they first saw this sequence because they considered it so overdone. But I didn't have that reaction. I always took pride in the exploits of the First and the Ninth, and Duvall's character, though certainly exaggerated, epitomized much of the bravado I saw in those daring young men.

Pilots of the 1/9th spearheaded the arrival of the First Air Cavalry Division in Vietnam. The helicopter-rich squadron rode in to support the First Cav's foot soldiers in the first major engagement of the war, the November 1965 battle in the Ia Drang Valley. Instead of riding in on horses, this cavalry rode in on helicopters. It had never been done before, and it would change the face of warfare forever.

The 1/9th became a very sophisticated operation in Vietnam. The squadron was organized into four troops, Alpha, Bravo, Charlie and Delta, company-sized elements each including a White, a Red, and a Blue platoon. The Whites featured scout ships, OH-6A and OH-13S Light Observation Helicopters with Plexiglas bubble cockpits. The Reds featured gunships armed with miniguns and 2.75-inch rockets. The Blues, also heavily armed, carried the rifle platoons, the airmobile infantrymen. It was a powerful combination that could bring swift and devastating firepower to bear on enemy soldiers.

Alpha, Bravo and Charlie troops were heliborne. Delta Troop, which specialized in ground reconnaissance, included scout Jeeps, gun Jeeps and three-quarter-ton trucks. Although Delta Troop's primary responsibility was road reconnaissance, all of its equipment could be dropped in and lifted out by helicopters as well.

Pilots from a Red platoon gave me my first helicopter ride after I reached Camp Radcliff, securing me into a Huey aerial rocket ship armed with miniguns and 2.75-inch rockets. Both of the door-gunners were sitting on thick plates of steel. If I wanted to be similarly protected, one of them said, I could take off my helmet and sit on that. What I remember most on that flight was the incredible tight turns the pilots made as they fired off their rockets in the direction of suspected Viet Cong positions. For someone who sometimes developed airsickness on airplane flights, it was a bold experiment. However, I don't recall ever becoming airsick when riding in a helicopter.

In the field, it was most often the Blue platoons we would watch as they swooped into battle with riflemen standing on the helicopter skids. When those skids were a few feet off the ground, the riflemen, joining the helicopter door-gunners in firing at any suspected enemy, would leap off and begin securing their perimeters.

In a typical 1/9th operation, scout pilots from the White platoon buzzed in on reconnaissance to flush enemy soldiers from their positions. When they spotted NVA or VC soldiers, the scout pilots called in rocket ships from the Red platoon to unleash additional firepower at the enemy. The Reds also helped clear out the landing zones for the Blues.

In Vietnam, of course, there were no guarantees that any operation would be typical, so 1/9th pilots sometimes had to improvise. Even the White scouts often performed tasks well beyond their reconnaissance roles.

During one mission in late 1967, two pilots in OH-13 scout helicopters were flying a reconnaissance mission near LZ Baldy as aerial rocket ships nearby blasted away to help clear a landing zone. Soldiers from the First Battalion, 35th Infantry were poised to ride into the cleared landing zone for a cordon-and-search operation to flush Viet Cong from the tiny hamlet of Tra Kieu Nam.

As the rocket ships continued to prepare the LZ, Warrant Officer Phillip Flanagan and Warrant Officer George Francioni spotted enemy soldiers. Flanagan saw five uniformed North Vietnamese Army soldiers running from the area. All were carrying weapons. Francioni dove in with his scout ship and took out all five soldiers, blasting them with his M-60 machine gun and his M-79 grenade launcher.

Suddenly more enemy soldiers appeared, a platoon-sized group racing toward a stream bed east of Tra Kieu Nam. Flanagan called for aerial rocket artillery and Huey gunships. Then he and Francioni cut down five more enemy soldiers that had broken away from the main group.

The scouts then directed a barrage of gunfire in the direction of the platoon-sized element. Finally Flanagan and Francioni had to break off the attack because they had used up all their ammunition.

That's when Major George D. Burrow, commander of Bravo Troop of the 1/9th, arrived on the scene with another gunship. Burrow and his co-pilot steered their craft toward the enemy platoon. They gunned down 10 of the soldiers trying to escape along the creek bed.

A couple of squads from the 1/35th had air-assaulted into the hot LZ, but they were told to hunker down in nearby rice paddies while the gunships continued their assault. Those gunships pumped 7,000 rounds toward the enemy soldiers. "On several occasions, one NVA would shoot at us and we would uncover five or six more in the bushes," said Warrant Officer Larry Kreps, one of the pilots.

Private First Class Mike Simpson, a door-gunner on Kreps' gunship, trained his M-60 machine gun on the enemy soldiers as the gunship passed over their positions. He took out one North Vietnamese Army soldier who fired several shots at the gunships with his AK-47 rifle. Major Burrow said later that Simpson had been credited with 38 of the kills. "His accuracy was the best I've seen since I've been here," the major said.

Whenever enemy snipers were able to bring down U.S. helicopters in Vietnam, they celebrated. They also reveled in being able to hit pilots or door-gunners. I can remember sitting near a helicopter landing pad at Camp Evans, waiting for a ride into the field, when a scout pilot landed his OH-6A craft. He had radioed back to the base that an NVA bullet had ripped through his leg. Members of the ground crew helped him climb out of his craft, and a medic pulled off his boot. To me, the boot looked full of blood. I could see inside the small cockpit, and I could see streaks of blood everywhere. The pilot ultimately recovered just fine. The medic said later that many pilots who bled that much would fall unconscious and their crafts would crash.

Scouts, Hueys, Chinooks and Flying Cranes all made for attractive targets, especially in battle areas heavily infested with enemy soldiers. During the Battle of Hue, for example, the First Cav saw more than 100 helicopters go down, most carrying two pilots and two door-gunners.

In one incident during that campaign, Warrant Officer One Thomas Maehrlein, flying a gunship with Bravo Troop of the 1/9th, rescued a pilot and a door-gunner from a helicopter that had been shot down. Maehrlein was flying east of Hue when he heard that another helicopter from Bravo Troop had been grounded by heavy fog in a Viet Cong area. Four helicopters from Bravo diverted to hunt for the lost ship and all began receiving heavy automatic weapons fire.

"We made our first pass along the ground just east of Hue with one gunship," Maehrlein told me following the rescue, "and as soon as we got close to the ground, we began picking up such heavy enemy fire that I had to pull out right away." Maehrlein said he could see only about a quarter of a mile in front of him, and he estimated the cloud ceiling at about 200 feet.

"On the second run, we picked up another gunship, but as we got down to the ground again, we received more heavy fire and one of the pilots in Blazer Two, one of the gunships, was hit in the leg and we had to escort him back to camp for treatment."

After getting Blazer Two back to base, Maehrlein returned to the rescue operation. Accompanied by another gunship, Maehrlein took his chopper into a dive to get below the clouds, and he quickly spotted black smoke rising in the distance. With the other gunship hovering above him, Maehrlein flew in toward the downed helicopter.

"We saw no one near the ship, but then as we jumped over a clump of trees bordering a flat, sandy field, we dropped onto about 50 Viet Cong in black pajamas and carrying weapons. They were in two groups of about 25 men, and when they saw us, they scattered.

"We went for the front group and flew by as my door-gunners cut loose with M-60s. That's when we saw two Americans with the front group break in another direction, hold up their hands and drop to the ground. It's just lucky we didn't shoot them."

Maehrlein made a tight circle and landed about 150 meters from a grove of trees where the Viet Cong had disappeared. First Lieutenant William Babcock, a pilot from the downed ship, and one of his door-gunners crawled on board to complete the rescue.

Later, I would talk with Babcock about the rescue. Babcock, a blocky man who was an experienced pilot, said that when enemy gunfire brought down his ship, he kept in mind what he had been told about becoming a prisoner of war: the best time to escape is early on, preferably right after being captured, when the enemy might be somewhat disorganized.

"We had received heavy fire all around the Hue area," Babcock said. "Suddenly our ship started to shudder, to tremble, and I couldn't keep enough power to stay in the air so I had to let her down and we spiraled to the ground. The area in which we landed looked real good—there were some farmers plowing, and some cows, but then the farmers left and the cows went away, and we started getting intense fire from behind a hedgerow. It was a miracle no one was hit.

"In a few minutes we were surrounded by a good-sized force and there was nothing we could do. They took us out of the chopper and set satchel charges to it.

"I'd say there were about 30 or 40 VC in the group," Babcock said. "These guys were all VC and they were well-equipped, all carrying an AK-47 or larger. They started walking us across the field, away from the chopper and that's when the Bravo ship swooped down and the VC scattered."

Back in camp, Babcock sat back in his chair and wiped his forehead.

Even though the Viet Cong had "full gear and plenty of weapons, when that chopper came in on them, it was so sudden that they simply panicked and ran. It's good to be with Bravo. They'll come after you no matter what."

Even to this day, when my thoughts return to Vietnam, one of my strongest memories is of the staccatic pounding of those rapidly spinning helicopter rotors that accompanied the roar of the UH-1 Huey engines. For most of us, the sound of those helicopters in the distance was most welcome—usually it meant supplies or hot food would arrive soon. For those of us working in PIO, it also meant an opportunity to return to our base to write our stories, develop our film and print our pictures. To this day, I love the sound of helicopter blades beating against the air to generate lift.

Without question, the pilots of the 1/9th were daring. Most of them also possessed good judgment. I still remember one vivid example. Richard Conrad, a most talented First Cav photographer, and I were waiting at a landing zone inside Camp Evans. When a Huey pilot landed his craft, we asked to hitch a ride when he returned to an infantry unit. He refused. The landing zone out there was too hot, he said, and he had drawn heavy fire from enemy soldiers as he lifted off. That was during the Battle of Hue, and the 2/12th was under siege from North Vietnamese soldiers. Conrad and I should thank our lucky stars that the pilot used solid judgment and declined to drop us into a hot LZ.

The pilot's boss, Major Burrow, would have agreed with that call. The major had told me that when he flew during the Battle of Hue, his ship had drawn incredible enemy fire.

"The moment we reached this area," Burrow said after one sortie, "we started receiving heavy small-arms fire, AK-47 and .30-caliber machine guns, from every bush, every tree. I'd say a minimum of 1,000 rounds were fired at my chopper alone. This is the hottest area I've been in and that includes the Que Son Valley."

The First Squadron, Ninth Cavalry dated from 1957 at Fort Rucker, Ala. The original unit, a single platoon of infantry, gunships and recon helicopters, was prophetically called "The Cavalry of the Future." One of the champions of the new concept was John J. Tolson III, then commandant of Fort Rucker's Aviation School. By the time many of us joined the First Cav's Public Information Office in Vietnam, Tolson had assumed command of the entire division.

Throughout 1963 and 1964, the airmobile concept would be tested in a series of war games that culminated in the largest post-World War II maneuvers ever conducted in the United States. The resulting successes were phenomenal. Major General Kinnard's troops called themselves "Sky Soldiers." Later, many soldiers in the First Cav would change that term, preferring "Skytroopers."

A few weeks ago, I found one veteran's comments in an Internet chat room. It was not signed, but it certainly reflected the pride many of us felt when we served with the First Air Cavalry Division.

"I don't know what they do in this day and age," the veteran wrote, "but back in Vietnam, I was in the First Air Cavalry. They moved all their troops and supplies to forward areas by helicopter. If a hot spot erupted, they could get you there real fast. If something went wrong, they could evacuate you real fast also. The First Air Cavalry was the best unit to fight in Vietnam."

Chapter 6
Staring death in the face

Early in my time at An Khe, I met Captain Oscar L. O'Connor, commander of Delta Company of the Second Battalion, Seventh Cavalry.

I had gone into the field on one of my first assignments with the First Air Cavalry PIO, and I linked up with O'Connor's unit. On my first night with Delta Company, a few of O'Connor's men sat down with me to dine on C-rations and briefed me on an act of incredible courage by their commander.

When I returned to An Khe a few days later, I wrote the story and turned it in to our editors. Sergeant Dan Stoneking, who at that time vetted and improved many of my reports, tweaked it a bit and wrote a new first paragraph for me.

"Captain Oscar L. O'Connor," my story now began, "wasn't just inches from death, he was right on top of it."

Stoneking later asked me, "Did you like the new lead I put on your story?"

"Absolutely," I responded. "It's probably the best first paragraph *I've* ever written."

I first met Captain O'Connor in late August of 1967 near Phan Thiet, a small village along the South China Sea, just east of Saigon.

The incident O'Connor's men related to me began with their captain leading a platoon through the Le Hong Forest, 12 miles northeast of Phan Thiet, when one of his soldiers picked up a tin can that had been driven into the ground.

When the soldier picked up the tin can, out tumbled a grenade.

"I hollered, 'Grenade!'" O'Connor said later. "Everyone scattered.

"We had found a number of bunkers, caches, metal cans sticking in the ground, and this was the clincher."

A nearby South Vietnamese Army outpost had been receiving enemy fire most of the previous night. O'Connor began organizing a few small scouting and ambush squads to conduct reconnaissance, in case some Viet Cong soldiers remained in the area. The captain was getting the first scouting party together when his radio operator brushed against a small bush and knocked a tin can off of a top branch. The tin can bounced off the ground; a grenade flipped out and rolled toward a group of First Cav soldiers.

That grenade exploded, but no soldiers were hit by the shrapnel.

"We were still a bit jittery from that first grenade going off," O'Connor said. "Now I saw this second one, lying there with its pin pulled."

O'Connor threw himself on top of the grenade while the men around him scrambled for cover. O'Connor pressed himself against the grenade and held it firmly beneath him.

Everyone waited.

Nothing happened.

When his radioman began moving back toward him, O'Connor waved him off, hollering at him to stay away from the grenade. The RTO got back down.

O'Connor felt the grenade against his lower chest. He began laboriously inching his hand under his side toward the grenade. He forced his hand between the ground and his shirt until he felt the grenade against his fingers. His men watched anxiously as he moved his fingers around the grenade, grasped it and squeezed.

Calling to his troops to stay down, O'Connor drew himself up and hurled the grenade hard toward a nearby foxhole.

"About one second after I let go of it," O'Connor said, "the grenade exploded. I tried to scramble away as soon as I threw it, but a fragment caught me in the left foot."

"He looked awfully weak for awhile," one of O'Connor's men said afterwards, still trying to absorb the fact that his captain really had fallen on a grenade and had been able to walk away from it.

"I guess I was just concerned about the men," O'Connor said. "At the time, it all happened so fast that I really didn't realize what I was doing. All I can figure out is that the grenade handle didn't pop all the way out, and my weight kept it down.

"I'm still a bit nervous about the grenade," he said. "I must have shook for four hours afterwards. But we all have our lives, and that's what really counts."

Chapter 7
A visit to Saigon

U.S. soldiers in Vietnam who ended up stationed in Saigon could thank their lucky stars. It was relatively safe duty in one of the most exotic and most vibrant cities in the world. For the rest of us, we could only hope for an occasional visit to the South Vietnamese capital.

Today much has changed. It has been renamed Ho Chi Minh City. Its population has grown to some 10 million people. The downtown has become much more affluent and far more cosmopolitan. Shops today include Cartier, Gucci, Louis Viutton, Prada and even Starbucks.

In many ways, however, the Ho Chi Minh City of today still resembles the Saigon of the Vietnam War. It's a sprawling community of some 2,000 square kilometers. Its downtown still teems with activity. Many areas contain markets and shops where residents and visitors pick through fresh fruits, vegetables, and fish and meat offerings. The streets continue to spill over with vehicles of all kinds, with people on bikes and motor scooters darting in and out of heavy traffic.

Today I tell people that if they want to see what Saigon looked like during my year in Vietnam, they need only watch "Good Morning, Vietnam," the movie starring actor Robin Williams as disc jockey Adrian Cronauer. In the movie, several scenes show the frenzied traffic in Saigon, where it seemed almost suicidal to venture into the roadways. Pedestrians who attempted to cross streets virtually took their lives into their own hands. I don't remember noticing many traffic signs or signal lights, although I know they were there, and only the locals seemed to understand the rules of the road.

"Good Morning, Vietnam" also provides a glimpse of the tropical beauty of Saigon during that time, as well as the colorful, sometimes garish architecture and the historic sites that dotted the city. And it shows us a bevy of beautiful young Vietnamese girls in their traditional ao dai, most often bright white, the country's national dress for females. In some of the first scenes of the movie, we see Robin Williams as Cronauer pursuing a couple of Vietnamese girls wearing those wispy white dresses.

Cronauer, by the way, was a real person, a very popular disc jockey broadcasting in 1965 for the Armed Forces Vietnam Network out of Saigon. The First Air Cav had a famous disc jockey, too, John Bagwell, who enjoyed similar popularity broadcasting out of An Khe. Cronauer always has said the portrayal of him by Williams was not entirely on target. "If I were half as funny as Robin Williams, I'd be out in Hollywood going na-noo, na-noo and making a million dollars," said Cronauer, who worked with the actor on the film. "Once people get to know me, they realize very quickly that I'm not Robin Williams, and it doesn't seem to bother them after that."

My first mention of Saigon came in a letter home on September 9 when I wrote that Specialist Four Robert Kirk, my first roommate in An Khe, "will be going to Saigon Sunday. We have a weekly courier run so I hope to make the trip once." I didn't mention it until later, but Kirk managed to finagle a number of Rest and Recreation (R&R) trips for himself. As I recall, during his tour in Vietnam, he somehow made it to Bangkok, Hong Kong and Tokyo—as well as taking occasional courier trips to Saigon. I knew Kirk was much brighter than most of us, but it was still quite a coup for an enlisted man.

My chance to visit Saigon came a couple of weeks later, and I was able to stay in the city for two days.

"Saigon is much different than I expected," I wrote. "People there appear much more content than I expected. They live day to day, like the rest of us, contented and free, and busy—just like people in any world capital. The city is beautiful, sprawling, filled with people—busy people—and it was worth seeing.

"They drive like crazy here, and it's funny there aren't more accidents. They have traffic lights, and they drive a variety of cars, everything from Cadillacs to Volkswagens. Some of the larger streets have gigantic boulevards—four one-way streets with three green lawn-like strips running between them. Normally, scooters travel in the outside lanes with cars in the middle lanes, but the drivers often mix it up. On a normal street, usually one-way, cars end up packed close together, and the cyclists dart through any opening. When the light changes, a solid mass surges forward. I've never seen so many scooters on main streets."

I had flown from An Khe into Tan Son Nhut Air Base outside of the city, and I decided to take a taxi to get into town. I rode in taxis twice, and both times I felt very uneasy. The first taxi driver took me into the city, but the ride seemed very long. I began to wonder if he was hauling me into some unsafe areas where enemy soldiers would take me prisoner. I think most of us had heard such stories, and we shared those fears.

The taxi driver provided quite a tour, however. As we bumped along, he pointed out several landmarks, and I was able to drink in the capital's sights and sounds and smells—a fascinating sensory experience in South Vietnam's largest city.

Cars, other taxis, buses, motorbikes and mopeds were all around us; three-wheeled cyclos came out of nowhere; drivers sounded their horns constantly. Above the streets, thick telephone and utility wires sagged between wooden power poles. Brick and stucco buildings, many with rickety balconies jutting out, stood alongside the roadways; clothes lines on many of those balconies held freshly laundered garments whipping in the breezes. Small sales stands set up along nearly every street and alley offered a variety of items for sale: cigarettes, sodas, beer, fresh fruit, fresh fish, stews, soups and rice—always rice.

Along many of the streets, I saw elderly women in long, dark dresses and yellow conical straw hats, bending forward under sturdy wooden poles atop their shoulders, bearing unbelievably weighty burdens, carrying goods to market or back home again.

One of my most vivid memories from the markets was seeing so many of these older women chewing beetle nuts, a particularly nasty habit. Some Americans compared it to chewing snuff, and I was told that the beetle nut, a red nut grown throughout Vietnam, possessed addictive qualities much like tobacco. Chewing beetle nuts extended well beyond the capital, of course, and I witnessed the habit in most of the hamlets we visited. Many men chewed the red nuts as well. It blackened the teeth of those who developed the habit—if they still had teeth—and it's amazing we didn't have to provide more dental care.

The taxi driver dropped me off at a hotel that had been recommended to me. When I tried to check in, however, the desk clerk said no rooms were available. I walked outside to begin searching for another hotel. Another taxi driver along the street said he knew of a cheap hotel. "I no bow'shit," he said to me. So I hopped into his cab. This driver, too, took me on a wild, meandering and extended ride. When he dropped me off at the second hotel, I swear it was just a couple of blocks from my first destination. The hotel he had suggested also was full so I started to walk away. From behind, the taxi driver tapped me on the shoulder and demanded his money. After the ride around the city, I felt totally ripped off, but I wasn't about to irritate the driver. I paid him a couple of bucks, and he drove away.

"At first, I thought taxicabs were Saigon's major business," I wrote later. "But then I discovered that whenever I turned down a ride offered by a driver, he would invariably offer a 'Number One Girl.' These pimps plus girls beckoning soldiers from windows along the street makes prostitution the most popular trade—we have made it that way. Girls accost you in restaurants and bars, too; but in the hotel where I stayed, I ate in a roof restaurant and no girls were in sight. Guys here warned me that if approached, I should just say, 'I have a girl friend,' and they would leave me alone. By the way, I ate lobster—an oriental recipe of some sort, but it was good. Very good." I also remember eating marvelous bowlfuls of ice cream. Our ice cream at Camp Radcliff, whenever we might get it, was not very good at all. So eating rich ice cream in Saigon was a wonderful treat.

After my second taxi experience, I walked for a couple of blocks and found myself in front of the Astor Hotel. The man at the front desk said he did have a room available. For all of these years, I have saved a piece of stationery from the hotel, which lists the address as "70, Tu Do St., Saigon." The rate was the equivalent of 25 U.S. dollars for each night, paid by the U.S. Army. The room was not huge, but it was very nice and very clean. It struck me how much tile was in this room—all of the floors, and seemingly everywhere in the bathroom. I also remember being impressed with the bathtub, where I would be able to soak in privacy, something I would not enjoy again for several months. Three steaming hot baths in two days felt very good.

While walking along the streets during my second day in the city, I recall seeing four young Vietnamese girls leaning out of a second-floor window and beckoning to me. They were trying to make a little extra money, but I was on my way to see Notre Dame Cathedral. Prostitutes and a Cathedral—quite a contrast.

"It's a beautiful old church," I wrote, "with two tall spires on each side of the front, resembling French Gothic. A statue of Mary, the Madonna of Peace, carved out of huge white marble, stood on a green mall in the front of the church. The mall's name was John F. Kennedy Square." That name would change, of course, after Saigon and South Vietnam fell to the North Vietnamese.

At the end of my visit, I had decided to catch a bus for the ride back to Tan Son Nhut Air Base. Before boarding that bus, however, I wanted to track down Sergeant Fred Fernelius, who had worked with me at Letterman General Hospital. I had heard he worked near Tan Son Nhut, and I was determined to find him. "I tried to find him twice, but he has moved to a new part of Saigon," I wrote. "Just before I caught the bus to the airport, I saw him outside the U.S.O. cafeteria—I wanted to get a final taste of food (two straight mornings I ate pancakes—the best I've had [An Khe pancakes made with powdered milk are bad news]). It didn't seem funny to see him or anything—just a casual meeting on the corner of the block. He looked fine and the same as ever."

Sergeant Fernelius and I had been writers for *The Foghorn,* the little hospital news magazine published by the U.S. Army at the Presidio. My most vivid memory of Fernelius is his coverage of fencing matches at the Presidio. He and I would write reports of those matches for *The Foghorn.* Until then, I had known nothing about fencing, but I learned to describe actions the swordsmen and swordswomen made with their epees—epee, a word I use to this day because it appears often in crossword puzzles.

M. Gloria Hetherington, a civilian, edited *The Foghorn.* She was a dear woman, she taught us a lot, and both of us were devastated a few years later when she died way too young after being struck down by a particularly aggressive form of cancer. *The Foghorn* ceased publication soon thereafter.

As my helicopter lifted off the pad, I didn't realize this would be my only trip to Saigon. Nor did I realize that just a few months later, during the Tet offensive, Tan Son Nhut Air Base would come under intense attack from the Viet Cong and North Vietnamese Army regulars.

Saigon, the capital of South Vietnam, and Hue, the provincial capital, were obvious targets. Many of Saigon's most historic sites would lay in ruins long after the fighting had ended, mirroring similar devastation in Hue.

Many historians believe the frustration of the Tet offensive led to events such as the My Lai massacre, where a U.S. Army company swept through a Vietnamese village, killing innocent men, women, children and anything else standing in their way. Americans also would see Vietnam's national police chief, Brigadier General Nguyen Ngoc Loan, execute a Viet Cong officer on the streets of Saigon with a pistol shot to the head, an event captured by Associated Press photographer Eddie Adams in a photograph that later would win a Pulitzer Prize.

In vivid television footage and newspaper photos, Americans would watch Communist soldiers overrunning the U.S. Embassy compound in Saigon, and they would see images of U.S. Marines struggling to rescue their wounded and bloodied comrades during the intense fighting inside Hue.

Regarded as particularly significant was news anchor Walter Cronkite's most famous broadcast on February 27, 1968, when he said the war was "mired in stalemate" and that the "only rational way out then will be to negotiate, not as victors, but as honorable people.…" Cronkite's shift into the opposition camp—followed in short order by the editors and opinion-makers at *Time* and *Life* magazines—made it far more fashionable for U.S. journalists to oppose the war.

On April 29, 1975, the United States withdrew completely from Saigon, leaving the old non-Communist capital to ultimately fall to North Vietnamese troops.

"For the first time in modern history," Robert Elegant wrote in the *Los Angeles Times,* "the outcome of a war was determined not on the battlefield but on the printed page and, above all, on the television screen."

Chapter 8
Small treasures for the troops

Whether in base camp or in the field, soldiers loved mail call. Letters from home meant so much to all of us in Vietnam. We also enjoyed our care packages from home. Even cookies or cupcakes that had crumbled by the time they reached us would be shared with fellow soldiers and wolfed down in a matter of moments—good to the last crumb.

On one occasion, early in December, I received a bonus.

"We got ditty bags today," I wrote. "These are bags people all over the United States pack up. Mine was bright red and contained pens, combs, a book by James Fennimore Cooper, soap, a soap dish, envelopes and a notebook I can use here. My biggest surprise came when I had almost reached the bottom of the ditty bag. I pulled out an empty boot polish tin. Across the front of it, my young benefactor, a fifth-grade boy, had Scotch-taped a note: 'Put your bullet in here.' I thought that was cute and some of the guys here laughed. One of our writers, Herb Denton, said he felt like writing a story on letters from home.

"These fifth-graders were from a small town in Ohio, and they contributed our ditty bags through the Red Cross. Mine also contained two washcloths and I really needed them. But the combs I didn't need—I have hardly combed my hair since I left home."

On occasion not everything in our care packages arrived in good order. After one mailing, I wrote to my parents to thank them for sending food. "However, the sausage spoiled—it had mold of some sort on it—and I didn't dare eat it or feed it to anyone else so I threw it away. But the cupcakes were delicious, and they kept very well. One of the guys here said you could send all the cupcakes like that you wanted and he wouldn't mind a bit."

Any cookies and cupcakes we received from home were nicely complemented by the tasty products turned out by a most popular bakery at Camp Radcliff. As I told the bakers there, bread and donuts in Vietnam were worth their weight in gold.

We considered the bakery at Camp Radcliff one of the First Air Cavalry Division's most productive units. Each day its bakers turned out some 3,200 loaves of bread—all the bread eaten at Camp Radcliff—and 5,000 donuts, enough so each unit mess hall would be able to offer donuts once a week.

During my time at An Khe, I would complain, at least on occasion, about the ice cream, the milk and the pancakes. All of them tasted sterile. But I never complained about the fresh bread or the fresh donuts.

"We think we make the best bread over here," said Staff Sergeant Charles R. Villars, the bakery platoon leader. "This plant is the pride of Lieutenant Colonel William Hunzeker [the 34th Supply and Service commanding officer]."

Bread for the soldiers took about five and a half hours to bake: 30 to 45 minutes for mixing and pouring into large tubs to moisten, two hours to ferment or rise, half an hour for makeup, an hour for what was called the proofing period, and 65 to 70 minutes for baking. Bakers produced 6,000 pounds of fresh bread daily, 4,000 for local distribution, and 2,000 for distribution to Quin Nhon.

After baking, the bread was placed in a cooling room, where it would be dumped out of the pans and cooled for five hours before being bagged and shipped out.

The Camp Radcliff bakery became noted for a variety of tasty breads—white bread, wheat bread, raisin bread and French bread. "If we could get rye flour," Villars said, "we would be making rye bread."

But the most popular product coming out of the bakery was the donuts.

In one month, October of 1967, 500 glazed donuts, hand-baked using Villars' personal recipe, were airlifted to Landing Zone Laramie. Villars explained: "We figured men back at An Khe are getting donuts all the time, while the men who deserved them the most, those up front, didn't get any at all. We planned the trip for several weeks, distributed the donuts with Kool-Aid, and it was a great success."

The Camp Radcliff Bakery also served as a great example of Vietnamese-American cooperation.

"Fourteen of our 27 workers are Vietnamese," said Sergeant Fredrick Sewall. "They're fast, efficient, and they take great pride in their work.

"They've received a big push recently when we promoted some of them. They now realize they can advance in position and pay so they do a good job. They come to work regularly. Two of them have risen from cleanup men to baker's apprentice to second-baker."

Sewall said he expected to see one of the Vietnamese someday make the top grade of baker. In November of 1967, one of the Vietnamese workers was close, a second baker nicknamed "Throw-Away." Throw-Away worked on a donut machine, a small tub with an inner cylinder that turned slowly, churning out more than 400 dozen donuts each day.

Throw-Away made excellent donuts, Sewall said. In fact, Throw-Away would laugh outrageously at any American baker who, trying to duplicate his mastery, would end up with flat or deformed donuts.

"It took Throw-Away about three months to become real good," Sewall said, "and now he's got real prestige. He's the typical Vietnamese worker here: he has lots of fun, he realizes he can better himself, and he works hard."

Chapter 9
Great stores of rice

During the Vietnam War, rice loomed large. Then, as now, rice was the country's most significant crop. But all too often, the stores of rice ended up in the hands of Viet Cong or North Vietnamese Army soldiers.

One of the primary directives for the First Cav was to slow the flow of rice to enemy soldiers. Military intelligence officers estimated that nearly 90 percent of enemy rice requirements were being met by South Vietnamese farmers. Viet Cong recruits, often young local villagers, were able to pressure rice-producing farmers to deliver the needed foodstuffs.

When U.S. soldiers found large amounts of rice, stockpiled for obvious consumption by enemy soldiers, they would confiscate the crop.

At the same time, U.S. soldiers tried to avoid disturbing crops produced by Vietnamese farmers who were making their livelihood by growing rice. These farmers used flooded acres, usually rectangles, to grow their rice and other semiaquatic crops. Some of the farmers grew rice in dry fields, but by the time of the Vietnam War, flooded paddies had become the dominant form of production.

Infantry soldiers found these flooded fields formidable obstacles. The irrigation forced them to plow their way through ankle-deep—and sometimes knee-deep—water and mud. The troops had to be extra careful if they walked along the edges of the fields because enemy soldiers often targeted these edges to plant booby traps—they knew many U.S. soldiers would rather skirt the fields along the berms than slog their way through the paddies.

As soldiers moved across the fields, Vietnamese farmers—women as well as men—and their children often would be working. Dressed in rolled-up black tops and trousers, and usually wearing conical straw hats to shade their faces, they remained stooped over, focused on their work, as we passed. They certainly knew we were there, but usually, they just went about their business.

I had never seen rice farming before. It was a fascinating new experience. I was especially intrigued watching the Vietnamese farm boys driving their domesticated water buffalo along the fields. Most of the boys wore short pants to keep them out of the water, and they carried slender bamboo reeds to control their animals.

Farmers considered water buffalo an essential part of rice farming. They used them to till the fields, and they utilized their manure for fertilizer. Most of the farmers also raised ducks. During harvests, the ducks, which ate insects in the rice paddies, dined on scattered rice grains not brought in by the harvesters. The manure from ducks also provided rich fertilizer. Many farmers fattened and sold their ducks at local markets for extra income.

The water buffalo grazed on the natural grass lands—or they would be fed rice straw and other crop residues. Some farmers provided their animals with small shelters constructed out of wood and bamboo sticks and with palm leaves arranged to make a roof. Many farmers kept their animals tethered in their gardens or their fields by controlling them with nose grips attached to lead ropes.

I made my first notes about water buffalo during a trip with a First Cav unit into "Happy Valley," a lush area near An Khe.

"It's a good agricultural country," I wrote. "We saw a farmer and his two sons turning up soil in a rice paddy. The sons were disking. They have two water buffalo pulling a wide piece of wood; along the wood, there are sharp wooden spikes forced through. The sons stand on the disk and whip the water buffalo along. The farmer came behind with his two water buffalo pulling a one-bottom wooden plow. It worked pretty well.

"As we walked around a village to find ourselves a night location, we saw some farmers planting vegetables—corn or something similar. Two men drove along on their plows and their wives walked behind digging out seeds from their apron pockets and dropping them into the furrows. The men rode; the women walked."

It was in Happy Valley where I first saw a First Cav infantry unit discover rice that had been set aside for enemy soldiers.

The First Cav soldiers, from Charlie Company, Second Battalion, 12th Cavalry, ran across three well-stocked rock caverns, later found to be part of the Third NVA Division Headquarters.

The caverns, measuring 10 feet high, 9 feet wide and 20 feet long, contained ammunition for M-1 and 7.02mm rifles, woven baskets, several medicine bottles and about 60 pounds of rice.

Charlie Company soldiers found eight bunk beds, constructed out of sticks in one large cavern that measured 10 feet by 12 feet, and they found a cooking area nearby with various eating utensils and cooking pots and pans.

The soldiers also discovered 10 pages of documents, including a letter from a Viet Cong who wrote that he was in a rest area camp and that VC soldiers were low on both food and clothing.

The 60 pounds of rice was a modest find, as I would discover when First Cav soldiers unearthed rice stores of far greater tonnage. Just a few weeks later, Alpha Company of the First Battalion, Seventh Cavalry uncovered a 4,500-pound rice cache in a hamlet four kilometers west of Landing Zone Baldy.

"We knew it was something unusual," said Captain Thomas Richardson, the company commander, "because the rice was all ready to cook. Unlike the rice the villagers store in their houses, it was already threshed."

Second Lieutenant Robert Leupold of the company's Second Platoon said such finds definitely interfered with enemy activities. "Yesterday we passed through a village where people told us that VC came down every night, spent the night in the village, and got food. But when we came, they ran into the hills. See that high hill we left yesterday afternoon? I looked up there with my binoculars this morning, and I could see four military-age men trying to police up leftover rice. You know Charlie's hungry when you see that."

Alpha Company soldiers also found a series of well-built and strongly fortified tunnels, some up to 30 feet deep. A nearby railroad had been ransacked for steel rails and ties to fortify the tunnels.

Specialist Five Weidon Maness and his squad blew up the tunnels with dynamite. One of the blasts set off an incredible second explosion, and Maness guessed that enemy soldiers had been storing TNT of their own in the tunnels.

Alpha Company set off more explosions, imploding all of the enemy tunnels. Then the foot soldiers marched off again, making their way back to LZ Baldy. Many of them would be pulling security in the rain that night, knowing full well that they would be leaving camp again in the morning, visiting more hamlets in search of more tunnels and more rice.

Most rice farmers in Vietnam planted and harvested two or more crops each year. Under normal conditions in South Vietnam, harvested rice would be dried in the sun for two days before storing. The husk or the skin would be left on the grain, allowing it to be preserved for up to two years.

The 4,500-pound find was far more typical of the rice stores the First Cav uncovered. When foot soldiers discovered rice stores of this magnitude, they would destroy the rice or they would secure it so it could be redirected to feed hungry villagers.

During much of the year in Vietnam, the Red River Delta in the North, the Mekong Delta in the South, and almost the entire coastal strip up and down the country served as prime areas for rice growing. From the air, we could admire the patchwork of brilliant green rice paddies.

The richest rice region in Vietnam today is still the Mekong Delta, which sprawls across the southernmost region of the country. Formed by sediment deposited by the Mekong River, more than half of the Mekong Delta is under cultivation. The farmers call the Delta Vietnam's Bread Basket, and it produces enough rice to feed the entire country—with a sizeable amount left over.

On occasion, First Cav soldiers discovered NVA and VC soldiers growing and harvesting their own rice crops. That happened in the An Lao Valley during Operation Pershing, when First Cav patrols discouraged enemy soldiers from visiting the local farmers, their traditional source of food. The NVA and VC forces had been forced to remain in the mountainous regions of the An Lao Valley.

Those enemy soldiers set up relatively secluded acres where they could till the soil themselves. When First Cav soldiers stumbled upon such fields, they called in reconnaissance helicopters. Once the enemy plots had been mapped, helicopter crews from the First Cav's 184th Chemical Platoon would conduct daily flights to spray defoliants to kill the crops.

Early in 1968, after the First Cav Division had moved north to Camp Evans, the infantry began turning up even greater stores of rice that had been hidden for NVA and VC troops. Many of those large stashes were buried in graveyards.

In one operation, Alpha Company of the Second Battalion, Seventh Cavalry found a stockpile of rice in a graveyard near Cai Mon, a hamlet some 20 miles northwest of Hue. The hamlet chief had approached Lieutenant James Peters, the company commander, and, through an interpreter, disclosed the location of the rice. A platoon from Alpha Company followed the chief's directions to four caches of rice containing 10 tons. Other people from the village began approaching the interpreter to disclose other rice caches. Before the day was over, many additional stores of rice had been located.

Alpha Company made arrangements for the rice to be hauled to Huong Dien, the district capital, where it was distributed to refugees.

In another operation, the First Cav's Second Battalion, Fifth Cavalry also found stocks of rice in a cemetery. Soldiers from the 2/5th were making their way through what appeared to be a typical graveyard when lead elements noticed that many freshly dug graves had no headstone markers. In addition, they noticed that piles of straw had been placed on top of the dirt mounds.

Sergeant Dennis Rockwell stopped beside one of the mounds. "It doesn't look like the others," he said to a couple of soldiers nearby. Rockwell brushed the straw aside and began digging at the fresh dirt. After shoveling away about a foot of soil, Rockwell hit a piece of plastic atop a mat woven of straw. Beneath that mat, Rockwell discovered nine 100-pound bags of rice. At the bottom of the hole, Rockwell found several hundred pounds of additional rice piled loose.

Soldiers from the 2/5th went on to search a nearby village and discovered a surplus of grain stored beneath the huts as well as several packages of plastic like that used to cover the buried stockpiles. Soldiers interrupted one of the villagers weaving a mat similar to the mats covering the rice in the graveyard.

The First Cav bagged up the loose rice and airlifted it to Hai Lang where it was placed in storage for use by the South Vietnamese government.

There certainly were times when U.S. soldiers worked their way through the rice paddies and caused damage to the crops. I always hoped we were keeping such damage to a minimum as we made our way through the blades of rice.

In response to such concerns, the First Cav organized special efforts to help Vietnamese farmers raise their crops in a safer setting.

One positive effort occurred near Camp Evans. Focusing on the rice-growing areas around the camp, U.S. troops worked to protect these rice farmers as they harvested their crops. The farmers would harvest and store what they needed for themselves and their families, and then they would earmark their surplus for sale. They hauled this surplus rice to nearby warehouses in Phong Dien, three miles north of Camp Evans. There the rice would be stored or sold to the South Vietnamese government.

"We have two primary missions during the harvest," said Lieutenant Colonel Thomas W. Stockton, commander of the First Cav's Fifth Battalion, Seventh Cavalry. "One is to demonstrate to the local population that they can enjoy the fruits of their own labor, that they won't lose their harvest if they support South Vietnam's government. The other mission is to prevent the NVA and VC from getting access to the rice grown by these villagers."

To protect the farmers' crops, soldiers from the 5/7th patrolled the area and secured the roads to Phong Dien by day. They also set up ambushes at night to take out enemy infiltrators. The 5/7th had been called into the operation when the American district advisor said he didn't have enough people to provide protection during the rice harvest. The First Cav operation generated a ton of goodwill.

During the first day of the harvest, farmers gathered the rice and stored it in their homes to dry. On the second day, they removed the heads from the surplus rice they planned to bring to Phong Dien. During the third day, they cleaned the grain by holding a basketful head high and allowing the wind to blow away the chaff and lighter seeds while the good rice flowed into a basket on the ground. Then they hauled their surplus crop to Phong Dien.

"After the third day," said Stockman, surveying the rice paddies surrounding us as far as the eye could see, "all these operations are going on simultaneously, and it's important we keep the enemy away. The enemy needs rice to survive.

"You can see what a job we have by looking at the rice fields in the area. Everything that's yellow is rice ready to harvest."

Part Three: Bong Son

(July 30, 1967–January 27, 1968)

o o o o o o o o o o o o o o o o o o o o o o o o o o o o o o o o o o o

"The Cav changed its theater of operations. Its new mission is in Central Vietnam: the borders of the Bong Son plain, the length of the coast to the north of Qui Nhon. This region is one of the most densely populated in Vietnam with almost 500,000 inhabitants. It is a vast rice granary that already had been a Vietminh sanctuary at the time of war against the French."

Jacques-François de Chaunac
The American Cavalry in Vietnam: "First Cav."

Chapter 10
My first taste of Bong Son

Bong Son lies deep within Vietnam's Central Highlands, about six miles from the South China Sea and some 260 miles northeast of Saigon. It is a picturesque village, surrounded on four sides by tall, sylvan mountains tangled with dense shrubbery. Villagers scurry along the dusty streets and into the marketplace, supporting sturdy poles on their shoulders, balancing woven baskets heavily laden with coconuts, bananas, wood for fuel, oranges and apples, Army C-rations, and cans of Coca Cola.

During the dry season, warm sunshine beats down on tiny thatched huts and small stores, numerous copses of palm trees, and swimmers cooling off in the shallow and wide Song Lai Giang River in the An Lao Valley. Most U.S. soldiers referred to it as the Bong Son River.

When the monsoons arrive, as they do about the same time every year, water deluges the village, seeping into the thatched huts through their thin roofs and mud-packed walls. Market activity slows or stops altogether. The rains turn the ruddy dust along roads, paths and between the tiny homes, into thick orange mud.

Most First Cav soldiers liked being stationed near Bong Son. Most of the time, we were allowed to go into the village to shop, to purchase cans of soda, to frequent the shoeshine boys, to get haircuts or to sample some genuine Vietnamese food.

I vividly remember my first haircut there. When the barber finished my trim, he pulled out a thin metal rod, about the size of a Number 2 pencil, inserted it into my ears and whirled it so the little blades on it could cut out any hair there. Other than being caught in a firefight, I don't remember ever feeling more uneasy. One quick thrust and the barber could have performed brain surgery.

Soldiers certainly made friends in An Khe. Some of the youngsters there had helped me begin to learn to speak Vietnamese. One of our photographers had taken a photo of me walking in An Khe village with two Vietnamese boys flanking me, each clasping one of my hands.

But there was something special about Bong Son. Even though the village had been labeled as "Viet Cong infested," the people were friendly to U.S. soldiers.

A shoeshine boy there became my best little friend. We called him Ty. I have photos of him standing on a Bong Son village street wearing my Army helmet.

Ty even invited us into his home. I can remember large, warm raindrops splashing off of us as we left our Jeep on the road into town and ducked into the house. Ty held the sackcloth door aside to beckon three of us inside.

Glancing around the room, I marveled at its simplicity—hard-packed mud walls internally reinforced with bamboo strips woven like a large, sturdy basket; three hammock beds hanging from rickety wooden supports; a crude, homemade wooden table in front of a Vietnamese woman, where she and two children sat chipping the white meat out of coconuts; a tiny stack of wood formed into cabinet shelves, with a kerosene lamp balanced precariously on the top. It was a very basic shelter, but all of us realized Ty's family called this home.

Early in December, I expressed a concern for Ty. "Today in downtown Bong Son, I saw one of the shoeshine boys—Vic. But there's no sign of Ty, my favorite one, so I hope nothing has happened to him. It's bad to live in a place like this, especially for those poor kids. If they feel like running in the woods, like we did as kids, they have to be careful. Someone might shoot them. So I sure hope he's alright."

But on January 5, I recorded an update. "Yesterday in Bong Son, I saw my old shoeshine boy again—Ty. He has graduated from shining shoes to selling taffy in the marketplace. He gave me a piece of it, and it was really great. We talked for a little while. He's really a wonderful kid. I was afraid someone might have kidnapped or killed him because over here you don't know, so it was good to see he was well."

A number of us also became very close friends with the family that operated a popular eating place on one corner of downtown Bong Son. I remember talking with the man who owned the shop, and with his daughter, a beautiful teen who always seemed to be helping her dad.

I ate my first Vietnamese food in Bong Son. When I had arrived in Vietnam, one older veteran had told me, "Never eat Vietnamese food." That may have been good advice, generally, but I always found the food in Bong Son very good.

"Specialist Four Dave Frank, a photographer friend of mine, found this restaurant in downtown Bong Son," I wrote. "He ate there once with

Vietnamese soldiers after an assignment. It has no signs or anything, but it has excellent food. We've eaten there twice. The first time, the cook made fried rice—we pour seaweed soup over it and it's great—covered with beef rectangles about the size of two sugar cubes stuck end to end, a ham-and-egg omelet and beer.

"Each time, the cook asked us what we wanted. The first time, he brought us the meal after we just nodded our heads to everything he said. He realized, I'm sure, that we were pretty much at sea.

"The second meal, Dave met an old Vietnamese friend of his (who paid for the meal, by the way) and he ordered for us. We got fried rice with beef rectangles once again and two gigantic shrimp. It was delicious. The shrimp still had a hard shell, and we're supposed to dig the meat out of the shell, which is nearly impossible with chopsticks. The others gave up so I just popped the shrimp into my mouth and ate them, shells and all. By the second meal, I was catching on to chopsticks pretty well. Except toward the end, I fumbled around a bit, probably because we had downed two beers, and Vietnamese beer is very strong."

The First Cav soldiers stationed here in Binh Dinh Province could view the countryside, with its palm trees and its very green grass and think that, in a different time, this could be a tropical paradise.

Even from our base camp, we could see beyond the barbed wire fences on our perimeter to the tall green grain in the flat rice paddies, the lush jungle just beyond and the steep hills in the distance. Those hills proved formidable for foot soldiers.

"Elephant grass grows upwards of 12 feet to 15 feet on those hills, and we had to chop our way through," I wrote after traveling with one infantry unit. "The stalks are thick and the leaves from the middle up are razor sharp. I cut myself about five times on each hand and wrist when I fell over a rock or slipped on stalks lying across our trail.

"The hills—out here, they call them mountains—are steep. We would walk (stumble, run, take your pick) down one and drag ourselves up the next (walk up three steps, slide back two)."

In the Bong Son valley, I remember looking at the rice-rich countryside and thinking what a bountiful farming area to support this Vietnamese village.

"The vegetation and terrain here seems much like Da Nang," I wrote early in October of 1967. "We've increased the area we patrol, moving our forward point from Bong Son to Chu Lai, which is a beautiful city on the coast, and we'll probably be covering an even greater area before we rotate.

"Farmers here, like at Da Nang, primarily raise rice, with some corn alongside their huts and a few chickens running around. They have poor soil, though, a sticky hard red clay, not suited for much of anything except rice.

"The farmers irrigate a lot with a long rope and a bucket in the middle. One Vietnamese stands at each end of the rope, and they swing it much like a jump rope. The bucket picks up water from a stream and dumps it or throws it into an irrigation ditch as the bucket swings back and forth.

"They also raise pigs, but I've rarely seen a cow—just a few scattered ones being driven by little boys."

Chapter 11
Forced landings

I had shuttled between Bong Son and An Khe a number of times before being able to move to Bong Son permanently.

My first mention of those trips came in a letter dated Saturday, July 29, 1967, sent to my sister, in which I wrote, "Tomorrow I'll be going for a couple months of work in Bong Son in the Central Highlands. The First Cavalry is carrying on most of its activity on the Bong Son Plains so chances are I'll see more action than I'd like."

But during those two months, I would travel often between Bong Son and An Khe. On one of those trips, late in August, I had climbed aboard a two-engine C-123 cargo plane rather than a helicopter. During the flight from Landing Zone English outside of Bong Son, we drew enemy gunfire, and the bullets knocked out one of our engines. Our pilots decided to make an emergency landing at Phu Cat Air Base at Qui Nhon, which was close and which had a much longer landing strip. With one dead engine, the pilots brought the plane in at a 45-degree angle. They set it down on one wheel, slowly eased the other wheel safely to the ground, then rolled us to a stop. It was the only time during my tour that I feared crashing after getting airborne.

Certainly, there were other close calls for our reporters and photographers. While in Bong Son, I had heard reports that Graham had gone down in a helicopter that had been hit by gunfire and had been forced to crash-land. I was told that he walked away just fine, but I also heard that Major William S. Witters, the commander of our PIO detachment, almost had a heart attack after hearing of the forced landing. That was understandable. He didn't want to see the future publisher of *The Washington Post* come to any harm on his watch.

A few weeks later, Graham would write about another helicopter crash-landing, a story of genuine terror. Heavy enemy machine-gun fire had blasted the helicopter out of the sky. Lieutenant Colonel M.C. Ross, commander of the Second Battalion, 12th Cavalry, was among the passengers in a UH-1 Huey flying about 2,500 feet over a North Vietnamese Army stronghold in Quang Nam Province, about 25 miles southwest of Da Nang.

At least three enemy rounds hit the helicopter, bursting through the Plexiglas canopy of the helicopter, setting the instrument panel on fire and wounding both of the pilots. "One of the pilots slumped over the controls," Graham wrote, "sending the speeding ship into a steep power dive. The helicopter was plunging straight toward the ground when the other pilot, badly wounded, fought to tear the Huey out of the dive."

Even during the dive, Ross had sent out a "May Day" message and relayed their position. The craft dropped into a mushy rice paddy miles from the nearest First Cav infantry unit. Another helicopter soon arrived and everyone from the downed helicopter was rescued and flown away from the crash site within about 15 minutes.

"There were Charlies thick in the valley," Ross said. Ross also gave full credit to the wounded pilots. "They are outstanding pilots. After all, we walked away."

While splitting time between An Khe and Bong Son, I always voiced a preference for Bong Son. I felt a special affinity for this village, and I honestly believed First Cav soldiers could wield a positive influence on the people here.

There were times when we fell short, of course.

On August 6, 1967, I wrote about the orange soil around the village. "It probably contains lots of iron that wouldn't grow corn but sure is great for pineapples and coconuts. I drank some coconut milk last week, and it sure tastes sweet. I get sick of it. One of the soldiers here knew how to chop off the end of it, poke a hole through the meat and the milk comes out. It's clear, like water, but very sweet. They're green on the outside, but the meat or nut part tastes just like you gave us at home—sort of like pecans.

"A little Vietnamese boy climbed up the tree—fantastic climbing when the trunk is so narrow and slippery—and threw the coconuts down to us. We found out later we should have paid him 50 piasters (50 cents) for the nuts. That's the price they get on the market.

"What usually happens, one troop commander told us, is that a member of the South Vietnamese Army orders the boy into the tree 'or else these American soldiers are going to shoot you.' He climbs into the tree, detaches the coconuts, then throws them down. We enjoy the treat, but after we leave, the little boy hates Americans. So see what a funny war we have—we have to be so careful how we act."

I contributed to this dilemma in my own way a few weeks later while at Bong Son.

On one of my first stays at the First Cav's base camp there, a group of us were driving into town in a U.S. Army Jeep. The children in the village—they reminded me of waifs from a Charles Dickens novel—often followed us. We would carry small pieces of wrapped hard candy, Lifesavers and Hershey bars, and we would fling that candy into the street as we drove, then watch the youngsters scramble for it.

On this trip, I remember wondering if the youngsters would race out for the candy even if they knew they would be in the path of our Jeep. Without a thought, I took a fistful of candy pieces and threw them out in front of our Jeep. The kids raced into the street.

Thankfully, the sergeant driving our vehicle had been paying attention and he hit his brakes before we slammed into a child. I don't recall the sergeant saying anything to me—I'm not even sure he knew I was the one who had thrown the candy—but I have thought since that if we had hit a youngster, we would have faced some kind of military inquiry. What a stupid, stupid move on my part, and it didn't ever happen again.

Most of us found Bong Son to be a most beautiful little village. That's how I described it in a letter dated August 3. "And the people are so friendly," I wrote, "especially the youngsters. 'Hey, boy,' one of them called to me, 'what's your name? Hawson? Lawsom? Lawson? Larson?' And they're cute, too. One kid who couldn't have been over 6 ran up, 'Hey, you got cigarettes?' He's been Americanized."

Chapter 12
Health care for villagers

Many U.S. soldiers worked diligently to establish positive relationships with the Vietnamese people and felt extremely satisfied when they could help the villagers.

One of my favorite stories focused on a girl we called Mary, who had been adopted by the First Cav's 545th MP Company.

Mary was a Montagnard girl of about 10 (no one knew her real name or her age for sure) who had been wounded in the An Lao Valley. The Montagnards were mountain people, aboriginal tribes, who lived in the hills and mountains of central and northern Vietnam. There were several different tribes in the highlands, speaking different dialects, following different customs and practicing different traditions. Some Montagnards lived in mountain hamlets near Bong Son, and I always considered them friendly to us. Most of their men were savage fighters, and they often were at odds with NVA and VC forces.

After she had been wounded in her leg, Mary had been taken to the 545th MP Company, then sent on to a hospital. There the doctors amputated what remained of Mary's left foot and gave her a prosthetic boot to wear. She returned to the MP company, where First Lieutenant Arthur Jack made arrangements for her to be placed in an orphanage.

"Nobody knows much about her," the lieutenant said. "Her parents are dead and her home was probably destroyed. She doesn't speak Vietnamese, and she won't speak Montagnard."

I watched Mary run around the tent where she was staying in the MP area. She was chasing the MP's puppy, Tiger. She stopped where we were standing and asked in Pidgin English to ride in one of the MP Jeeps.

"The Jeep is her best entertainment," said Danny Rose, the platoon sergeant. "She also likes movies—and chow."

Mary gaily flashed an enthusiastic smile as she was allowed to climb into the Jeep. "Go there? Go there?" Questions and directions poured from her effusive personal happiness.

"We made her an honorary MP captain when she came back to us," said Noble Candline, civilian head of the orphanage. "She is very partial to MPs."

"When she first got out of the hospital," Candline continued, "she wanted to be carried everywhere. But we refused to carry her and she learned to walk."

Now she seemed to have forgotten about her handicap.

When she stopped next to a chaplain's tent on the base, Mary asked if she could go "click, click" with a camera. She took it, and, looking for a subject, spotted the U.S. flag flying near a tent. "Number One," she pointed, and she clicked off two pictures.

In late August, I saw another Montagnard girl being helped, and I had taken photographs of a medic treating her.

"She was a sack of bones," I wrote of the little girl, "so they gave her vitamins, wormers and a malaria formula. A few of the children in this village had bellies swelled to twice normal size because of worms or malnutrition."

Preventative medicine specialists often accompanied medics into the villages to check for flies and mosquitoes and to make insect population estimates to gauge the effectiveness of their spraying program.

"The Montagnards throw their left-over food outside their doors," I wrote, "and you can see little bright yellow kernels of corn and white rice lying in muddy puddles. With the monsoons, every depression around the village collects water and becomes a breeding area for flies and mosquitoes. One of the men had shown me before we went into the village what mosquito larvae look like, but we couldn't find any in the water."

I also described the people: "The children are naked, the women barebreasted, and the men wear loincloths, just a thin strip around their waists.

"Montagnard huts stand on poles about six feet high so water during monsoons doesn't bother them," I wrote. "The huts are crude, but strangely solid. Two huts were packed with people when we were there—a funeral service, I believe, because several of the women were wailing."

A few months later, I would write about additional medical efforts to help Vietnamese near Bong Son.

Villagers and members of the First Air Cavalry Division's Team 14, 41st Civil Affairs Company had cooperated to build a small dispensary just outside the main gate of Landing Zone Two Bits.

Captain John Taylor of the Division's G-5 section had suggested the dispensary to First Lieutenant W. M. Stewart of the 14th Civil Affairs Team.

Stewart and his men began making plans for the building, and they received much local help.

"One Bong Son man, who owns the land where the dispensary stands, said we could build there," Stewart said, "and he donated the land to us. We decided to use wood from ammo boxes to construct the sides [of the building], so we brought a load of ammo boxes and shipping crates to the building site. All the Vietnamese gathered around and began helping us tear down the boxes. We had one man organize four Vietnamese workers from here for us, and they helped us put up the siding."

Once the sides were up, constructed with ammo boxes, villagers used boards from the shipping crates to shape the roof. They covered it with roofing tar paper. The entire project took two weeks.

"This dispensary is intended for the Vietnamese around Two Bits," Stewart said. "Most of the people who come here are around [age] 20 or 30, and of course we always have the kids hanging around outside."

"So far we've had a case of acute pneumonia, some bad burns, and a typhoid fever case," said Specialist Four David Solum, a medic with the 14th Civil Affairs Team. "If we get something we can't handle, we'll send them to Bong Son hospital."

The dispensary was kept open six days a week.

First Air Cavalry soldiers also helped construct two little churches at Bong Son. Both chapels hosted weekly Protestant and Catholic services.

Men from the Second Battalion, Fifth Cavalry built one chapel just outside Landing Zone English.

Soldiers from Colonel Richard M. Winfield's artillery unit constructed the other chapel just outside Landing Zone Two Bits, and they dubbed it the "All-Artillery Chapel."

"Everything in the chapel except the roof and floor is made from ammunition boxes," said Captain Henry C. Hilliard, one of the artillery unit's Protestant chaplains. "The pews, the altar, and the walls are all made from ammo boxes."

Colonel Winfield donated his former officer's mess for use as the chapel when the monsoon season arrived in the Central Highlands.

Soldiers painted the building after it became the chapel. "Red Leg" or red hangings were added to the front of the chapel behind the altar. Red Leg is a symbolic reference to artillery soldiers. The metal roof also was painted red, the traditional artillery color.

"We've named the chapel 'Div Arty Chapel of St. Barbara,' " Hilliard said. "St. Barbara is the patron saint of artillerymen."

I also had written about churches and worship in An Khe.

"Today I overslept and missed Mass, but an afternoon assignment made up for it," I wrote on Nov. 5. "I went to a tiny church in downtown An Khe where one of our men gave a sermon to a Vietnamese congregation. An interpreter translated the sermon—quite good; a good experience.

"The outside of the church is light orange. The inside is white. It's made completely of concrete except for two huge beams that ran above our heads below the roof and a few tiny wood slats beneath the roofing, all for support. The roof outside was red tile.

"A fire-engine-red cross hung on the front wall of the church and another red cross stood on the small altar.

"Three missionaries came, one an older man with snowy hair who could speak Vietnamese fluently. From his conversation, I'd guess he's been here four or five years, and he plans to stay at least one more year. His wife, also with white hair, was with him. Both seemed very enthusiastic and really tore into some Vietnamese hymns. They have no piano or organ in the church, but the Vietnamese here really sing with gusto—very loud, but pretty good.

"The little kids' choir sang a song. They sounded just like American kids—loud and off-key—and when they finished, they had quite a time filing back to their pews. They had a teacher pointing and trying to get them to go in the right direction.

"During services, the men and boys sit on the left side of the aisle, women and girls to the right, much like some of our Colonists. Kids wiggled and whispered, and mothers screamed so I didn't hear much of the sermon, but it was fun—and something to talk about."

Chapter 13
The Third Brigade under fire

The Third Brigade at Bong Son found itself in plenty of combat action. I still considered myself a green soldier, still "newly in-country," and I certainly was unprepared for some of my early, intense experiences.

"We went into this village a few miles north of here and swept through," I wrote on August 2. "We saw five Viet Cong killed and 10 suspects taken. One family of six was evacuated to a new area. The worst part, though, was seeing these guys dead and dying. Even though you realize they're supposed to be enemy, it seems a waste. I'm sure most of them are decent human beings, too—they just have a different point of view."

Growing up on a farm in Southern Minnesota, I had helped pull calves from Hereford cows during birthing seasons, I had seen animals die from diseases or from eating poisonous plants, and I had seen pigs stuck and bled before they were butchered so we could have hams, ribs and pork chops. But nothing had prepared me to see soldiers killed.

"I felt very faint after watching this for a while, and I had to sit down and swallow some water," I wrote. "I talked with one infantryman, and he said he's been here seven months and he still isn't used to it."

Nor was I prepared to see U.S. soldiers who had been killed. I remember the first time that happened to me. The soldier, still in his fatigues and his combat boots had been placed face up on a large, flat boulder. His helmet had been removed and we could see his ashen face, which no one had bothered to cover. He looked husky, a man built to play football or rugby, and I remember how weak I felt seeing a dead First Cav soldier on this battlefield.

A few weeks later, I found myself walking across another battlefield in central South Vietnam with soldiers from the First Cav's First Battalion, 12th Cavalry.

Rays of the setting sun flashed through the trees as we made our way over the war-torn field. It was a small piece of land where enemy soldiers had been forced to stand and fight in what would become known as the Battle of Tam Quan.

Smoke still rising from broken and charred tree trunks and fallen palm leaves burned our nostrils as we walked. Coconut trees lay strewn across the field, their trunks frayed by shrapnel. Split and cracked coconuts had been scattered about by the huge bomb explosions. An occasional piece of frayed black clothing rolled along over the soft dirt.

Two dead steers lay beside a huge crater where a 750-pound bomb had exploded upon impact. A sow wandered aimlessly through the debris, followed by eight little pigs.

The battle had begun when a First Cav observation helicopter drew fire from North Vietnamese Army snipers. A six-man squad from the 1/12th assaulted in to probe the area, near the village of My An, four miles north of Bong Son. Squad members spotted a sniper in a tree and moved in to flank him. Suddenly, a volley of gunfire burst out at them from in front and from their right flank. The gunfire hit four of the squad members, killing two of them and wounding two others. Two other squad members, who could have pulled back but chose to stay with the wounded, were not hit.

The rest of the company tried to rescue the ambushed squad, but withering NVA gunfire drove them back. Armored Personnel Carriers (APCs) of the First Cav's First Battalion, 50th Infantry joined the battalion to attack the NVA positions.

"We had the feeling we were just going to go in there and pull them out by their shirts," one soldier said.

NVA automatic weapons opened up again, forcing American units back, leaving behind one platoon that had tried to rescue the six ambushed men. Only when U.S. Air Force jets roared in firing their cannons and dropping 750-pound bombs did the enemy firepower die down.

"It was frustrating," said Private First Class Eddie Hardee, a forward artillery observer. "Our artillery was right on target, and the NVA just kept firing. But when those jets dropped bombs for two hours, they literally blew this area away. Every five to eight seconds, you could hear bombs going off."

When the APCs and the First of the 12th troopers assaulted again, they met no resistance.

"These men were mad," Hardee said. "A battle like this hurts, but the morale stayed high."

In the wake of the Battle of Tam Quan, First Cav soldiers found the bodies of more than 400 NVA soldiers.

Lieutenant Colonel Daniel French, First of the 12th commander, who had taken control of one company during the battle after it had lost its commanding officer, talked with the men.

"A detainee told us who we were fighting," French said. "You were fighting the Seventh and Eighth NVA battalions, the 22nd Regimental Headquarters, the 132nd Signal Company and the 135th Recoilless Rifle Company. That's 900 people. Some of the bravery exhibited with fire coming from all sides was unbelievable. You came through like champs."

"A tour in Vietnam," one soldier said after the battle, "consists of extended periods of boredom punctuated by flashes of sheer terror."

The following morning, that soldier's company would climb aboard Chinook helicopters, half going to LZ Laramie and half to LZ English, for a rest, a regrouping and, he hoped, some well-deserved boredom.

Early in October of 1967, soldiers from the Third Brigade began Operation Wallowa in the Que Son Valley. The campaign, which would continue into January of 1968, began when the Third Brigade moved north 125 miles from the An Lao Valley to LZ Baldy, known to the Fifth Marines as Hill 63.

Arriving October 4, the Third Brigade made the move in just two days and began maneuvers almost immediately. The First Cav had supply lines back in order so rapidly that hot meals were being airlifted to troops in the field within the week.

Chinooks and Flying Cranes carried several loads of helicopter jet fuel into LZ Baldy and LZ Ross. The Eighth Engineer Battalion expanded the helicopter landing area and began constructing a runway at LZ Baldy so C-7 Caribou cargo planes could begin bringing in more supplies. Within the month, the Third Brigade was carrying on its business as usual.

The smooth move 125 miles north would prove an incredible contrast to the Third Brigade's next move four months later to Camp Evans, when heavy monsoons and acute supply shortages would plague the First Cav for nearly three weeks.

Aided by a break in the monsoon season during Operation Wallowa, Third Brigade troops met North Vietnamese forces in three major ground battles, all in the eastern section of the brigade's area of operations. In each battle, NVA soldiers took heavy casualties—75 killed in one battle, and more than 100 in each of the other two.

The greatest successes in the Que Son Valley were scored from the air where the pilots and gunners of Bravo Troop, First Squadron, Ninth Cavalry cut down 503 NVA and 412 Viet Cong for 915 confirmed kills. They also took 305 detainees and confiscated 37 weapons.

Major George D. Burrow, Bravo Troop commander, led the way. On November 9, his gunship took out 41 enemy soldiers, even though his ship was low on hydraulic fluid, which forced him to use his miniguns sparingly.

Bravo Troop grabbed the offensive immediately in October, killing more than 350 enemy soldiers during the first month of the operation. Even an attack on the headquarters of the 227th Assault Helicopter Battalion, a small sliver of land near Chu Lai nicknamed "Gilligan's Island," an attack that destroyed four helicopters and damaged seven others, didn't halt the Third Brigade's air activity.

The pilots of the 1/9th continued their successes throughout Operation Wallowa.

One of the stories they loved to tell dated from December. Late in the morning, gunships and scout ships were flying reconnaissance for the Third Brigade in the Que Son Valley. There had been some contact with enemy soldiers, and 1/9th pilots had recorded nine enemy kills. Major Burrow had invited a new warrant officer to join him for a flight to observe the recon activity.

A few kilometers from a fire base, Burrow and his passenger spotted four khaki-clad North Vietnamese Army soldiers trying to flee. The commander's ship opened fire on the soldiers, cutting them down, then began recon fire. More NVA soldiers jumped out of their hiding places and 13 more enemy soldiers fell to the ground. At that point, soldiers from the Blue Platoon of the 1/9th were air-assaulted into the area. When they examined the enemy soldiers who had been killed, the infantrymen discovered that nine of the enemy soldiers had been armed with pistols. They also found a number of maps and North Vietnamese documents in backpacks still secured to the bodies of the dead soldiers.

The information was ferried back to the headquarters of the 1/9th, where brigade leaders discovered that the gunships had slain the commander of the Third Regiment, Second NVA Division; the political officer of the division (a full colonel); the division intelligence officer; the operations officer, and members of the political staff, supply section and signal element.

Captured documents revealed a battle plan, fully detailed with maps and operations orders, for an attack on First Cav bases in the area. By securing these documents, the 1/9th provided a critical early warning for the Third Brigade, and the U.S. soldiers were able to solidly beat back the attacks when they came at two landing zones, Ross and Leslie, almost a month later.

Charles A. Krohn described the same incident in his book "The Lost Battalion." Krohn, then a captain and intelligence officer for the 2/12th, sent his Vietnamese interpreter to help translate the documents. Krohn wrote that "the trophies of the kill—the maps, the plans, the documents, and the highly prized pistols—changed the course of history, at least as far as the 2/12th Cav is concerned."

Krohn also detailed the attack that ultimately took place, the attack planned in the captured documents.

"The long-awaited attack on [LZ] Ross was launched precisely at 1:30 a.m. on January 3," he wrote. "We were rewarded for our preparedness: we killed 242 NVA soldiers with only one friendly KIA and 63 WIA (wounded in action). The best part was that the NVA weren't able to penetrate our perimeter fence. Not one sapper made it through. Bodies by the score lay in front of our wire, dozens dangling from the strands they could touch but not cross."

The NVA's unsuccessful attempts to overrun Landing Zones Ross and Leslie represented the heaviest action for the Third Brigade during Operation Wallowa. Before the attack, U.S. troops had spotted enemy soldiers outside the LZs early in the morning. Thirty minutes later, both LZs were under heavy attack, with enemy troops concentrated on the southwest side of each.

At LZ Ross, perimeter guards spotted about 100 NVA soldiers approaching from the west while NVA artillerymen walked 82mm mortar rounds across their line of advance. After the NVA soldiers retreated from Ross, carrying many dead and wounded with them, First Cav troops discovered 143 bodies of enemy soldiers around the perimeter.

At LZ Leslie, an unknown number of 82mm mortar and 122mm rocket rounds crunched into the camp throughout the night. The incoming rounds became more sporadic as dawn approached. At one point, guards at LZ Leslie reported sniper fire inside their perimeter, but ultimately, the enemy soldiers were beaten back, leaving 38 dead behind.

"It was our finest hour," Krohn wrote, "and I was not even there, having taken a few days' leave to rest in Japan. The only thing I remember now of the R&R is waking up with a terrific headache on the floor of a Kyoto hotel and watching the snow fall. When I got back, I was told that the attack—conducted by three NVA battalions—had developed precisely as I had predicted: first they fired hundreds of mortars and several dozen 122mm rockets, all carried by hand from North Vietnam. Recoilless rifles were also used to support the attack. By 5:30 a.m., the enemy had broken contact and withdrawn. It was a brave attack, certainly risky, but a complete failure. The prevailing wisdom was that it probably would have succeeded if we hadn't been prepared."

Chapter 14
The medic in the field

The field medic in Vietnam performed one of the war's most challenging and most important jobs. It was also one of the most dangerous.

The medic walked where the foot soldiers walked, he carried a larger pack than anyone except the radio operator, and when a battle broke out, it was his job to go right to the action—to find wounded soldiers and patch them up.

When a six-man squad from the First of the 12th came under ambush in the Battle of Tam Quan, one of the first people on the scene was Specialist Four Joseph W. O'Keefe, a field medic. Several more soldiers had been wounded when they moved in to rescue members of the ambushed squad.

While bullets whined overhead, Doc O'Keefe made his rounds.

"The NVA really had us outflanked," said O'Keefe, who had been in the field several months with Charlie Company. "I couldn't get to the six ambushed men, but we had quite a few others wounded, and that kept me busy."

Three men walking behind a First Battalion, 50th Infantry (Mechanized) track also had been hit by an NVA sniper, and another medic ran to help them.

"They were really pouring out the bullets," O'Keefe said, "but I was finally able to get to the men and drag them behind a track. I got them patched up alright and got them inside the track and we called in a medevac."

As he moved across the battlefield, O'Keefe spotted another U.S. soldier who had been wounded. "He had a belly wound and I patched him up as well as I could. The guy started to go. He probably had internal bleeding, but after I gave him a shot of albumin, he came back."

A medevac ship was called in to carry the man out, but both he and O'Keefe were too close to the front lines. "When that medevac chopper came in," said Private First Class Eddie Hardee, the forward artillery observer, "those NVA really opened up. They were trying to knock it out of the sky."

One of the gunners on the medevac ship kicked out a stretcher, and O'Keefe called three other men to help him. They placed the wounded soldier on the stretcher and, with enemy bullets kicking up dirt all around them, they carried the man some 100 meters to a medevac ship that had just landed.

Once he helped get the soldier aboard the medevac, O'Keefe hurried back to the battlefield.

"When they saw doc," Hardee said, "they opened up again. He finally made it to three wounded men and pulled them into a trench. He tried to bandage them, but each time he would reach up to apply a patch, the NVA would catch sight of his first-aid pack and fire at him. Finally Doc just said 'to hell with the NVA,' and he patched up the men."

When the 50th Infantry tracks began receiving some recoilless rifle fire, knocking out one of them, killing one man and wounding three others, they pulled back for artillery, ARA, and jet strikes. O'Keefe pulled back with them.

Jets pounded the area with 750-pound bombs for two solid hours. The tracks and the 1/12th foot soldiers assaulted again. This time they met no resistance.

O'Keefe turned to help the wounded men aboard the medevac ships. The next morning, Charlie Company had two more men wounded by sniper fire. O'Keefe was there again to patch them up.

"He lives a charmed life," one of O'Keefe's fellow soldiers said. Hardee agreed. "He did a tremendous job. He was running all over the field, helping our wounded men and really leaving himself out in the open. And when those NVA saw his medical supplies, they would open up on him."

"These men were great," O'Keefe said. "Once they saw their own men getting hit, there was no stopping them. Of the six men ambushed, two were killed and two were wounded. The other two, not hit, could have escaped, but they chose to stay with the wounded men."

I felt special admiration for the field medics. Letterman General Hospital on the Presidio in San Francisco, my previous assignment, had been named after Dr. Jonathan Letterman, head of Medical Services for the Army of the Potomac during the Civil War. Dr. Letterman, known as the Father of Modern Battlefield Medicine, in 1862 came up with a plan to use wagons pulled by teams of horses to pick up wounded soldiers on the battlefield and bring them to field hospitals for initial treatment. Field medics in Vietnam used a similar though certainly far more sophisticated plan to place wounded soldiers on medevac helicopters to be flown to base hospitals.

Dr. Letterman also designed the three-tier treatment and evacuation system that medics still use today: 1) First-aid stations in the field; 2) field hospitals, MASH (Mobile Army Surgical Hospital) units, providing emergency surgery and treatment; 3) larger hospitals away from the battlefield, such as Letterman General Hospital, where many wounded soldiers from Vietnam were brought for treatment.

In Vietnam, the medic's job was to treat wounded soldiers and evacuate those who needed additional care. In some cases, medics would hop aboard the medevac helicopters to continue treating soldiers while transporting them to field hospitals. During the Vietnam War, the survival rate exceeded 90 percent for soldiers who could be evacuated within the first hour after being wounded; obviously, incredible strides had been made since the Civil War and Dr. Letterman's original evacuation plan.

Most Army medics came out of Fort Sam Houston, Texas, where they received 10 weeks of intense training. During this Advanced Individual Training, the aspiring medics learned how to treat gunshot wounds, head wounds, shock, burns, broken bones, dislocations, seizures and venereal disease. They also learned how to give inoculations, draw blood, give CPR and perform tracheotomies. Their training included techniques for approaching and treating the wounded on the battlefield, instruction in properly moving and carrying patients—and for lifting patients into the helicopters. The medics also needed to know about suturing and amputating. It was a broad but in-depth spectrum of medical training that brought instant respect in the field.

In addition to carrying large backpacks containing the tools of their trade, medics in Vietnam carried M-16s, the first time medics in battle had been armed by the military.

One of the medics assigned to a First Cav field hospital was Michael Herrera, with the 15th Medical Battalion. Herrera was in his second tour. He had spent one year as a foot soldier with the 101st Airborne Division, and he had spent five months as a medic with the First Cav.

"My job with the 15th Med," Herrera said, "is to hold routine sick call from morning until noon and take care of mass casualties whenever they come in from the field on medevacs. The medics and technicians at 15th Med welcomed me with open arms, and we work as a team assisting each other in minor surgery removing bullets or shrapnel. We pull routine sick call and perform most minor surgery in a Quonset hut. Connected to it is a heavily sandbagged and fortified bunker where we take care of casualties coming in from the field.

"The motto of the U.S. Army medic is 'To conserve the fighting strength,' meaning we take care of soldiers in order to send them back out into the field again as quickly as possible to fight again. But we also take care of enemy POWs and civilians who get wounded or get caught in the crossfire."

Herrera and his fellow medics viewed this as "winning the hearts and minds" of the people. They took the role of being "an ambassador in green" very seriously.

On the battlefield, medics always seemed at risk. Many found themselves targets of NVA and VC marksmen when they went to the aid of wounded soldiers. It's one reason the medics in Vietnam no longer wore red crosses on their helmets or on arm bands, which had been the practice on earlier battlefields. Even the flash of a medic removing a bandage from his backpack to apply it to a wounded soldier could draw enemy fire.

Many medics considered their "risk factor" a badge of honor. Many of them took risks well beyond what was expected of them.

Specialist Five Dennis Apana told me one story of daring aerial acrobatics, even though he himself downplayed the event.

Apana, a medic, loved to fly, so he fit right into the First Cav mold.

While working with the Cav's First Battalion, 50th Mechanized Infantry, a man in Apana's unit triggered a booby trap on a nearby mountainside.

"I was in our ambulance track," Apana said, "but the brush on the mountain was so thick we couldn't get up there. Finally a bubble ship came down and picked up one of our litters [a stretcher]. I grabbed onto the skid and pulled myself up, and stood on the skid while the OH-13 pilot flew us to the wounded man."

The observation helicopter carried Apana well up into the sky before lowering him so the wounded soldier could be loaded into the helicopter and medevaced.

"A gunship dropped down to provide cover, and we evacuated the man," Apana said.

Apana found himself in other "on-the-edge" situations following that evacuation, but it was this action that his more cautious buddies remembered most, and they continued to marvel at his "crazy" trip while on the skid of the OH-13. They kidded him for weeks about his ride into the wild blue yonder.

Apana just shrugged it off. "I didn't see any risk in it," he said.

Chapter 15
Psychological operations

Most U.S. soldiers in Vietnam had heard of Hanoi Hannah. In broadcasts from North Vietnam, she would blend sweet talk and coercion in an attempt to convert U.S. and South Vietnamese soldiers to Hanoi's point of view. Ideally, she wanted them to defect.

The U.S. Army offered something comparable with its Psychological Operations (PsyOps) Battalions. The mission for soldiers in these units was to "encourage" North Vietnamese Army regulars and Viet Cong insurgents to defect to the American or the South Vietnamese side.

In PsyOps, specialists prepared propaganda leaflets and loudspeaker broadcasts designed to recruit enemy soldiers.

"During December [of 1967], we dropped 6½ million leaflets," said First Lieutenant Ken Mostella of the Eighth PsyOps Battalion, supporting the First Cav's First Brigade. "We also spent 60 hours in the air broadcasting from helicopters.

"We get leads from the intelligence and operations sections on where they have enemy, suspect enemy or when they have a village aiding the enemy. If one of the First Cav units gets contact with the enemy, we'll saturate the area with leaflets and play tapes over loudspeakers while we fly over the battlefield. We now have a 1,000-watt loudspeaker that we use for propaganda. It can almost kill the VC with sound."

One purpose of the PsyOps program was to promote Viet Cong and NVA defections as what we called Hoi Chanhs. As First Lieutenant Jeffrey Blume of the Eighth PsyOps Battalion explained, "We have to aim toward the enemy who has doubts about his side's cause. We show them how to put the idea into effect that has been in the back of their minds for some months."

Added Mostella, "We have 250-wattt backpack speakers that we can use when the infantry traps enemy soldiers in caves or bunker complexes. We must convince them that it's better to surrender than to die. If they don't believe us, we use force."

Mostella and his men talked with me after they had been called to an area where the First Cav had made contact with an enemy force of unknown size. Mostella and his Vietnamese interpreter loaded their 1,000-watt speaker onto a helicopter and took flight over the battlefield, unleashing a barrage of words toward enemy positions.

"My interpreter warned them to surrender or die," Mostella said. "Then he told them we were going to call in air strikes and air-rocket artillery."

After the air strikes ended, the PsyOps team returned and announced that enemy soldiers could surrender by coming out and throwing down their weapons. The effort resulted in 11 Hoi Chanhs. Mostella said he had 14 Hoi Chanhs helping his PsyOps team convince wives, mothers and fathers to talk to their VC sons and get them to join the South Vietnamese government's side.

"One of my men, only 21 years old, was a Viet Cong for two years. He told us he had been running for two years. He never came out during the daytime. He lived underground and did only what he was told. He had been scared for two years. A guy like this knows what being a VC is like, and when he talks to the wives and the parents, he pours his heart out.

"The only way we're ever going to win is with the people on our side," Mostella said. "They're our link to the VC. If the people get sick of the VC and the NVA, the enemy might as well leave."

One of the best means of opening the eyes of the VC to the allied cause, Mostella said, was through the Medical Civic Action Program.

Sergeant First Class Arthur D. Talbert, assistant S-2 for the First Cav's Second Battalion, Fifth Cavalry, often took his interpreters into a village along with an Armed Propaganda Team for a Medcap.

"When we keep people healthy," Talbert said, "we win their confidence, and after a while, you sometimes find more spectators than patients. When they find out you do what you say you're going to, they'll really help you out.

"The Armed Propaganda Team will tell the people the difference between living under VC control and under the control of the people."

Talbert and other soldiers concerned with PsyOps realized that their program would be more effective if they continued to expand and intensify it.

"The more material PsyOps puts out," Mostella said, "the more enemy soldiers we'll get to defect and come to our side. When we'll be extremely successful is when our areas all become as pacified as Phan Thiet. There teams go into the village not necessarily to help the villagers but to entertain them. I recall they once showed a Mickey Mouse cartoon with the characters speaking in English and the kids went wild. I guess when you're 4 years old, you don't listen to the words anyway."

Vietnamese interpreters were attached to most First Cav units to help interrogate enemy soldiers.

While traveling with the First Battalion, 12th Cavalry, I met Sergeant First Class Bui Thanh Han, who had known nothing but war for his 21 years. Han's primary job was talking with the Vietnamese people and with suspected enemy soldiers to get information the First Cav could use to track enemy movements. After joining the South Vietnamese Army on December 15, 1965, Han, a native of Saigon, spent one month at the Armed Forces Language School in the capital city. He spoke English well, and he read it even better.

"My job is asking people questions," he said, "and there are times when I realize they won't tell me anything."

Han had been speaking with some villagers in An Que in an area where North Vietnamese soldiers had been seen frequently.

"I tried to find out about NVA movement through An Que," he said. "The people told me they saw 100 and some soldiers move through the village. But as far as weapons or anything else we would like to know, they either won't say or they don't know.

"This war is especially bad for the people because they're caught right between the two sides. The NVA hide around a village, then when the Americans come, the NVA move out. Naturally, the people cannot move from the place where they were born so it ends up being a big problem for the villagers, the government and for the American troops."

Han said his dream was to see the war end.

"It's much better now than it was two and a half years ago when I first worked this area with American units," he said. "It's safer for the soldiers and for the people. And right now, I think everyone is waiting for the war to end.

"I find the Vietnamese people think differently in different parts of the country. In a large village, they might be very concerned with the South Vietnamese government, while out here in the country the people aren't too aware of the government in Saigon. They think mostly about their rice. But they all want the war to end."

Enemy soldiers who defected as Hoi Chanhs would be subjected to rigorous but humane interviews. Enemy soldiers who were captured in battle faced much more intense interrogations.

In September of 1967, I had made notes about some of the interrogation techniques described to me by infantry soldiers.

"The Vietnamese regulars do most of the questioning, and they are good at it," I wrote. "They have a way of dropping a man on his back and bending his head way back—then pouring water down his throat. It bypasses his windpipe, going right into his stomach, but the sensation is one of drowning. And, in due course, he must try to take a breath and realizes he cannot get air. So he begins to talk—or he will suffocate.

"Another trick is draping a rag over a prisoner's mouth and saturating it with water. Again, he cannot breathe and gets a drowning sensation." I had watched South Vietnamese soldiers perform such interrogation. It would not be until years later, however, that I would hear of this technique referred to as water-boarding.

I also made notes about prisoners being "transported by and questioned on helicopters. Americans will sometimes get the chopper in the air with four or five enemy soldiers inside with their hands tied behind their backs. They refuse to answer questions. They refuse to talk—or sometimes they just talk back. So, en route to their destination, an American will push out one of the suspects who, in clear sight of the others, twists toward the ground, falling a thousand or more feet, struggling in the air the entire time. The rest of the prisoners often start babbling all at once. It's effective."

It may also have been apocryphal. It's a great description, and I'm sure the foot soldiers enjoyed telling me the story. But I never witnessed it, and in researching for this book, I couldn't find a single reference to definitively confirm that "push-the-prisoner-out-of-the-helicopter" interrogation techniques ever took place in Vietnam.

Chapter 16
Navigating through the monsoons

The monsoon season in Vietnam begins with a weak breeze from the northeast. Gradually it grows into a stiff wind of eight to 10 knots, gusting to 20 knots, and pushing gray clouds and white sheets of rain over the Central Highlands.

During the First Cav's time in Vietnam, the monsoon rains would continue up to 36 hours; yet almost always throughout the seasonal challenge, the division's helicopters would continue to fly.

Usually, only the smaller OH-13 observation helicopters would be seriously limited by the dense fog and heavy rains.

"Once you fly into fog and lose sight of the ground," said Warrant Officer John Edwards, a pilot with the 227th Assault Helicopter Battalion, "you can be in a bank, a stall, or a dive, and never know it.

"It's like walking down the road with your eyes closed, only you're on a floating carpet."

Pilots use the term "vertigo" when they refer to the sensation of losing their bearings. They lose their reference point and cannot maintain their balance. "We tell OH-13 pilots to cut their engines and go into auto-rotation the minute they get stuck in fog, because the observers are most stable in auto-rotation."

In Vietnam, the monsoon season of maximum rainfall runs from September through January for coastal areas and for parts of the Central Highlands facing northeast. These regions receive torrential rain from typhoons that move in from the South China Sea, and the weather usually is cloudy with frequent drizzles.

It's this mixture of torrential rains and fog or low cloud cover that challenged First Cav helicopter pilots around Bong Son. The division's UH-1 Huey helicopters also would experience occasional difficulty during foggy or rainy weather.

"Hueys have an automatic direction finder, an ADF [Automatic Direction Finder] radio," said Warrant Officer Jerry Bonham, a pilot with Alpha Company, 227th Assault Helicopter Battalion. "But we have no radar or instrument capabilities so when we do land in heavy fog, we try to be where ground radar can help us."

"In the case of medevac," Edwards said, "we usually let the medic on the ground decide whether a man needs to be extracted."

Pilots making medevac runs often had to perform incredible feats of daring to avoid enemy gunfire when trying to extract wounded soldiers.

In one incident in the Kim Son Valley, a man needed to be hauled out, but dense fog and rain had made flying virtually impossible. Six artillery tubes from the First Battalion, 77th Artillery, were swung around to fire illumination rounds to lead one helicopter to the landing area with the wounded soldier. The first illumination round went off just above the clouds as the chopper left LZ Uplift, and successive rounds went off just ahead of the helicopter. At the ambush scene, continuous illumination flooded the ground. The artillerymen reversed the entire process for the helicopter's trip back.

"Flying at night is especially dangerous during monsoons," Edwards said, "because you'll be flying along with some reference to the ground and suddenly everything goes black. You've flown into a cloud. This is especially true here where we have night hunters."

"Chinooks are the best instrument-equipped helicopter in the division," said Captain Robert Deppey, the 228th Assault Helicopter Battalion safety officer, "and 75 percent of our pilots are instrument-qualified."

Still, when a cloud hangs over a landing zone, it can be very difficult to land, even with instruments.

"A familiar landing zone is a little problem," Deppey said, "but it's really hard to set down on a strange one. You can't judge your altitude."

Captain George W. Kyle, a pilot with the 478th Aviation Battalion (Flying Cranes), said the monsoon season actually offered some advantages for his helicopters.

"With our seat facing backwards, we can easily coordinate hookups, even in heavy rain, and some rain helps a little bit by keeping down the dust from our backwash.

"All our pilots are second-tour men, all are instrument-qualified, and 25 percent are instrument exempt. Our pilots have flown an average of 3,400 hours each. We only have one problem: water occasionally seeps in and causes electrical shortages. But the monsoon does not limit our flights."

Kyle said he had flown a Crane from Camp Radcliff to Phu Cat a few weeks before to help lift a 30-vehicle convoy across a swollen river that had torn away a supply-route bridge.

"We were in the soup as soon as we left Camp Radcliff," he said. "Clouds were so low and so thick we had to fly on instruments all the way."

The monsoon season would run even longer a few weeks later when the division moved its headquarters to Camp Evans, 15 miles northwest of Hue.

But it wouldn't be just heavy rains and low cloud cover hampering the pilots. An NVA rocket attack scored a direct hit on the Camp Evans ammunition dump and shrapnel from secondary explosions damaged a number of helicopters, rendering them unflyable. The rocket attack also hit a fuel bladder, and the resulting explosion sent smoke and flames high into the Camp Evans sky. The First Cav's usually reliable supply lines would be disrupted, leaving pilots with too little JP4 jet fuel for the helicopters they could fly, artillerymen with too few shells for their tubes, and troops in the field with inadequate supplies of ammunition.

It's the only time during my year in Vietnam that I could remember the helicopter pilots unable to perform their usual acts of daring. The supply disruptions would go on for nearly three weeks, and the resulting shortages in the field would put the First Cav's foot soldiers to the ultimate test.

Part Four: Camp Evans

(January 27, 1968–July 10, 1968)

o o o o o o o o o o o o o o o o o o o o o o o o o o o o o o o o

"We are lifted to Da Nang, then loaded onto C-130s for the trip north. We land at Quang Tri. This place is just south of the DMZ. The rumor is that we are going to do a huge air-assault across the DMZ. This will disrupt their supply lines and stop the flow of people and ammo that we ran into so much in the Que Son. We move from Quang Tri to a place called Camp Evans, our new forward home. It has all of the comforts of all of our other forward homes: Sandbags, concertina wire, an airstrip and a water filtration plant. We never spend much time on the LZs anyway."

Dan Toney, Sergeant
Company A
First Battalion, Seventh Cavalry
First Air Cavalry Division

Chapter 17
The First Cav moves north

In January of 1968, the First Air Cav launched the largest-scale move the division would make during its operation in South Vietnam.

It was just days before my 24th birthday, and I remember thinking, "What a wonderful way to celebrate, bouncing along in the back of a U.S. Army convoy truck!"

In the move, the First Cav pulled up stakes from South Vietnam's Central Highlands and replanted them some 200 miles to the north. The division's new headquarters would be at Camp Evans, just below the DMZ, along Highway 1 midway between Hue and Quang Tri City.

On January 16 in a letter home, I wrote, "The entire First Air Cavalry Division is moving out: LZ Two Bits, where we are now, will be going to Hue, halfway between Da Nang and the DMZ, which means it's right up there. The projected First Cav rear unit headquarters is Da Nang.

"LZ English, just outside Bong Son, will be the farthest south the Cav will be conducting operations. So apparently someone in Saigon believes our arrogance and thinks the First Cav can calm things down a bit up north. Gradually the ARVNs are taking over the DMZ and the Marines are moving south. Anyway we should make news."

Obviously, I was off target with some of my tactical information. But I wasn't alone. We would find out later that the First Cav had been moved to I Corps so abruptly because top military leaders in Saigon had deciphered captured enemy documents indicating that North Vietnam was planning a major ground attack across the DMZ during the Tet holiday. But that explanation never reached most of us.

The First Cav's move began on January 17 when elements of the First Battalion, Fifth Cavalry began flying out of Phu Cat. Five days later, soldiers in the division's Tactical Operations Center were directing activities from two airmobile pods, cooks in the Division Artillery mess hall were serving hot chili con carne with rice and fresh milk, and rows of tents identified in the

Army manuals as "general purpose, medium" were standing on a field of red clay and tombstones located five miles south of Hue, which division leaders had named Landing Zone El Paso.

On January 22, the major caravans began moving toward Camp Evans. On that first day, scout ship and gunship pilots from the First and the Ninth spotted enemy soldiers along the route and recorded 52 North Vietnamese soldier KIAs.

On January 27, First Cav soldiers packed up from LZ El Paso and moved again, 15 miles northwest of Hue, to Camp Evans, which had most recently been a U.S. Marine base. Camp Evans had been named to honor Paul Evans, a U.S. Marine who had been killed near the camp by a mortar round on December 22, 1966.

"We've been busy getting organized so that's why I haven't written for a few days," I said in a letter after we had completed our part of the move. "Two brigades of the First Cav moved near Hue while one brigade stayed near Bong Son—for now. We went through Hue last night, and it really is a beautiful city. Right now we have our office fixed up extra nice and, of course, I have been busy jotting things in my diary.

"We came here by truck convoy. We rode in the back of a deuce-and-a-half, which would be a bad place to be during an attack, but it was excellent for taking pictures. The people are great up here, too, and they're good to work with—we worked hard all day yesterday lining up our office, and it seems real homey."

Even though we had felt vulnerable riding in the bed of that truck, we were at least somewhat reassured when First Cav helicopters began flying back and forth on both sides of us. Our Cav caravan, made up mostly of Army Jeeps and trucks, stretched for miles as it snaked northward. The pilots from the 1/9th protected our flanks for the entire move.

Our caravan took two days to weave its way through Hue and up Highway 1 to Camp Evans. The move for the entire division took about two weeks. In total, the Cav moved two brigades, a division command post and a number of combat support elements to I Corps, South Vietnam's northernmost tactical zone.

Thinking about our Jeep and truck caravan today, I realize how lucky we were to get through Hue. North Vietnamese Army forces had been massing there, hidden within the city in preparation for their Tet offensive. We had no idea they were there in such numbers, and they could have unleashed an attack on us. But they did not, and we ended up safely at Camp Evans.

While our part of the move crawled through the mud along Highway 1, other units arrived by air, and still others came up on the South China Sea. LSTs (Landing Ship, Tank), LCUs (Landing Craft, Utility) and LCMs

(Landing Craft, Mechanized) all participated. The U.S. Navy had been enlisted to help with the moving effort, and the sailors directed all these craft up the South China Sea and the Gulf of Tonkin, and sent supplies down the Song Bo Dieu River.

Air Force C-130 pilots flew 498 sorties carrying troops and supplies out of Landing Zone English at Bong Son and out of Phu Cat Air Force Base, hauling individual loads of more than 25,000 pounds. The C-130s had to land at Quang Tri or at Hue-Phu Bai because our new base camp did not yet have a landing strip long enough for cargo planes. The supplies then had to be trucked overland to Camp Evans.

Additional supplies would be parachuted into our camp from C-130 planes, whose pilots braved the low, heavy clouds of a severe monsoon season.

Tom A. Johnson, in his book, "To the Limit: An Air Cav Huey Pilot in Vietnam," vividly describes those daring air-drop missions.

"For two days, more rain pours down from low clouds," Johnson wrote about his first days at Camp Evans. "Our only rations and ammo are coming in via parachute from C-130 aircraft at the east end of the LZ. Since there is no airfield where this giant aircraft can land in such bad weather, this is the only means of replenishing itself available to the Cav. The sorties by the C-130s are almost continuous during the semi-daylight hours. The Air Force has set up a portable TACAN [Tactical Air Navigation] radio beacon on the east side of Highway 1, which is well away from Camp Evans. Low-flying C-130s descend to 300 feet in the clouds and rain, using the TACAN beacon as a navigation device.

"At the right moment, they unload their cargo on pallets pulled out of the aircraft by parachutes. Sometimes we can't even see the aircraft making its pass; we just see pallets of supplies drifting suddenly out of the bottoms of the low clouds."

Despite the heroic efforts of these Air Force pilots, a number of supply problems plagued the division during and after its move. Many First Cav units found themselves short of jet fuel and short of ammunition. Without JP4 jet fuel, the helicopters could not fly; without ammunition, the foot soldiers could not fight. Both of these shortages would create major problems for the First Cav during the Battle of Hue.

As Johnson wrote: "In II Corps, the Cav depended on supply channels long since developed through Qui Nhon and An Khe. Now the First Cavalry is totally without its own supply chain. The hundreds of supply-laden trucks in convoys from LZ English will take nearly a week to reach our new home."

Charles Krohn also addressed the supply issue in his book, "The Lost Battalion." Krohn's First Cav unit, the 2/12th, had been ordered to move from LZ Ross to Camp Evans without packing ammunition onto trucks "as we usually did. Instead we would be completely resupplied from new division stocks when we reached Camp Evans. 'Don't ask for any more trucks,' [William I.] Scudder [commander of Charlie Company, 2/12th] was told, 'because there aren't any.'"

Despite the order, Krohn wrote, Scudder "intended to take some of our ammunition with us, as we always did, hiding as many boxes as he could in the bed of each truck sent to help us move.

"On January 25, we started the move as planned. While most of us were busy boarding helicopters, Scudder quietly loaded the trucks according to plan, piling tents and supplies over the ammunition. He had to make some compromises, but the ammunition got loaded.

"The next day we all married up at muddy Camp Evans, first the helicopters and then the trucks. We found, much to our surprise, that we had the only ammunition in the camp. There were no fresh stocks. Scudder's judgment was totally vindicated. The irony was that, without the ammunition we had smuggled into Camp Evans on trucks against orders, we could not have later been deployed toward Hue...."

By the time the 2/12th ended up in the middle of the Battle of Hue, Scudder, now a major, had been promoted to executive officer for his battalion. He spent much of his time at Camp Evans, Krohn wrote, "to ensure that the combat elements of the battalion received the support needed to sustain themselves in battle—food, ammunition, replacements, and so forth."

Other officers at the division's support command and the logistical and supply section would describe the First Cav move, in a word, as "hectic." The division's base camp had been at An Khe since September of 1965. The division's forward command had been at Landing Zone Two Bits in Bong Son for about a year. Many First Cav soldiers at those two bases had accumulated tons of possessions, probably figuring they would never move again until they returned to The World. When the announcement came for the move to Camp Evans, the base soldiers were told to break down equipment into "mission-essential" equipment, which would be transported by air, and "nice-to-have" items, which would follow later by land.

Units of the division came from scattered locations. The Cav's Second Battalion, Seventh Cavalry rode north from Phan Thiet at the southern edge of the Central Highlands to join the Second Brigade in Binh Dinh Province. The Cav's Third Brigade came from south of Da Nang, where it had been operating under the Americal Division. The Cav's command post and the First Brigade moved north from Bong Son. Rear support elements moved from An Khe. The Second Brigade, 101st Airborne, under control of the First Cav during Operation Jeb Stuart, moved north from Cu Chi.

When the move had been completed, a reporter for the *Cavalair* interviewed Specialist Four Conrad P. Schefer, a clerk and a driver for the division's civil action section. The move had exhausted him. He leaned back, yawned heavily, and said, "It's so nice just to sleep on the same cot in the same tent in the same place for two straight nights."

During our first days at Camp Evans, we spent most of our time with our shovels. We built bunkers, and we filled sandbags.

"Today we dug a couple more feet in our bunker," I wrote early during our stay at Camp Evans. "We hit some shale or something similar. We managed to dig a couple of feet, but I've got about three blisters on my hands."

Our bunker ended up being quite small and a bit too shallow, but we were able to make it deep enough to carve a couple of hard clay benches on two sides of it. During any attack, we could sit on those dirt benches with plenty of room to stretch out our legs. We lined the sides of the bunker with a couple of rows of sandbags, then we placed a thick plywood board over the top and lined the top with several layers of sandbags.

Our favorite feature was a short tunnel we carved out from the bunker to our combination office and sleeping area. We cut a hole into our wood floor at one corner of our building. If an incoming mortar or rocket attack occurred, we would be able to slide or low-crawl across the floor, drop into the tunnel and scramble into our bunker.

A couple of days later, I wrote, "Things are cooling a little now over here, but Khe Sanh and its 6,000 men are poised for an attack. We hope they ward off anything that comes. The First Cav is supposed to be a quick reaction force in case anything happens. We've got 10 battalions up here now of some 500 to 600 men plus parts of the 101st Airborne and the First Battalion, 50th Infantry (Mechanized) plus our clerks, etc., so we should have close to 8,000 men here."

Little did I know what lay ahead.

Chapter 18
Digging in at Camp Evans

First Air Cav soldiers at Camp Evans spent their first few days putting up tents and frame buildings. We would be venturing back into the field shortly, but first we wanted to make sure we were in good shape with our offices, sleeping quarters, showers and mess halls.

We filled sandbags by the hundreds to place around our tents, to reinforce the lower walls of our wooden-frame buildings and to construct bunkers. Artillery ammo boxes came in handy as well. We ripped them apart and used the lumber to construct floors, build bookcases, provide makeshift desks and set up shelves inside our bunkers.

Among the first buildings completed would be a church and a PX (Post Exchange). Church services would be offered a number of times on Sundays. The PX would be open at least a few hours every day. On occasion, we would even find soda and potato chips there.

In trying to support First Cav infantry units once they returned to the field, we would discover how uncooperative the monsoon season could be. At Camp Evans, we recorded 23 straight days of steady misting interspersed with frequent rain squalls. The water and the mud became two more of our enemies.

Many parts of the roads inside and outside of our camp were washed away and had to be rebuilt. Driving conditions for the Jeeps and the trucks grew worse and worse.

The main runway for the airstrip at Camp Evans would not be completed until late in March. Engineers leveled and packed down the first 1,500 feet of runway, enough to land the C-7A Caribou, during the first days of March. But they would not be able to finish the full runway, measuring 3,100 feet in length, until later in March. In order to land C-130s, the entire runway had to be completed.

"When it's finished," said Captain Ed W. Hendren, Eighth Engineers assistant S-3, project officer for the airstrip, "it will go beyond both borders of the camp. We had to move the fence out to set in bunkers and construct a road at the end of the airfield."

Navy Seabees had begun working on the airfield before the First Cav arrived, when Camp Evans was still secured by U.S. Marines. But rain, constant damp fog cover and mud prevented work on the strip for almost a month.

"You can't grade the soil when it is wet," First Lieutenant Michael J. Burke said, "because the dirt just crumbles up and won't roll. You can't get any compactness, either."

Weather conditions improved enough during the last days of February so Eighth Engineers could begin their work. Within a week, they had finished the Caribou strip.

"We used mobile road scrapers, D-12 cats or graders, and the D-4 bulldozers to build up a base of laterite, a soil-type common to the tropical climates," said Sergeant John T. Holland. "Laterite is a soil mixture of clay and chalk. I believe about 15 percent chalk. Once the soil is solid, we blue-top it, then put on a peneprime surface."

The Eighth Engineers built the strip in sections, beginning from the north. Once they completed the first 1,500 feet, they put down three layers of the peneprime, thinned-out asphalt, to waterproof the runway, prevent water saturation and prevent potholes.

Once they finished the 3,100-foot runway, the Eighth Engineers built a parking apron measuring 200 feet by 750 feet, an apron large enough to handle five C-130s on the ground at once. Before C-130s began landing at Camp Evans, the engineers covered the runway with aluminum matting. They used steel matting for the taxiing, parking and unloading areas.

"The C-130 runway should be finished in less than a month," Hendren told me in February. "It will be the only C-130 pad between Hue-Phu Bai and Quang Tri. The Cav base camp won't be as dependent on road supply as in the past."

With the airstrip completed, it would assure a more consistent stream of supplies into Camp Evans. In addition to better delivery of ammunition and jet fuel, the First Cav would be assured of receiving adequate medical supplies. That would allow the division to resurrect its Medcap program. Such programs had forged incredible friendships with the Vietnamese at both An Khe and Bong Son. Now the program could be continued at Camp Evans.

"Being a medic," Sergeant First Class Jack McCracken said in explaining the Medcap program, "is extremely rewarding, especially if you're in an area where you can see what you're doing for the people." McCracken pointed to Landing Zone Colt, 25 miles south of Da Nang, as a great example of his unit providing medical services for the Vietnamese people. "We could check back with the Vietnamese and see what we'd done for them."

With the entire First Cav now based 15 miles northwest of Hue, McCracken, medical platoon sergeant for the Cav's Fifth Battalion, Seventh Cavalry, had been handicapped. For tactical reasons, being located in a more dangerous area, the 5/7th medics had not been allowed to hold sick call for the Vietnamese. Now the 5/7th was given responsibility for protecting Vietnamese farmers and their crops during rice harvest. The battalion also was charged with securing bridges along Highway 1 north of Camp Evans.

Suddenly, Vietnamese with aches and minor ailments began seeking out the First Cav medics.

"The whole thing started to grow when a couple of little girls came up to Specialist Five Raymond Anstett, our Charlie Company senior aid man," McCracken said.

"One girl, about age 7, had lost her leg in an explosion about a year ago, and the company wanted to donate to buy her an artificial limb. A second girl, about 3 years old, had an abscessed ankle. She had apparently been pierced by a punji stake long ago. Now she needs X-rays and immediate treatment or she may lose the foot."

With medical supplies arriving at Camp Evans on a more regular basis, McCracken and Major Joseph V. Arnold, battalion executive officer, set up a weekly Medcap for the villagers around Phong Dien. In that operation, Arnold said, "We're now treating about 60 people each day."

"Now I go out with a doctor and two other medics," McCrackin said. "We stay out until we treat everyone who comes to us. Right now they just straggle in, but once they get used to our routine and begin to know and depend on us, we should do a brisk business.

"The most common ailment up here is body scars or skin lesions. Some of the youngsters also have ear infections. We wash them up, paint them, and if it's bad enough, we give them an injection of antibiotics plus oral antibiotics to follow up."

Chapter 19
First Cav heroics in I Corps

As we settled into our base at Camp Evans, we made friends with many new soldiers. Every one of them seemed to have a story to tell.

Specialist Four John Casarez, for example, loved to talk about his job as a scout observer. I considered it one of the most dangerous jobs in Vietnam—sitting inside a small bubble cockpit exposed to enemy gunfire.

Casarez flew reconnaissance with the First Squadron, Ninth Cavalry, working to detect and pinpoint enemy positions. Ground troops depended upon him to spot enemy soldiers they could not see from the ground.

Many scout observers with the 1/9th flew as door gunners on the OH-13s, the tiny two-man helicopters that skimmed the treetops and almost begged to be shot at.

"We try to be careful," Casarez said. "Sometimes Charles might get lucky and hit you. But he can't shoot straight.

"When I volunteered for the First Cav, I knew I'd have a good chance of getting in an armored vehicle. Then when I got here, they told me I'd be flying, but I don't mind that. It's just as safe in the air as on the ground."

The 19-year-old scout had arrived in Vietnam in January of 1968. Before being assigned to an OH-13, however, Casarez spent a month with the Blues, the 1/9th's rapid-response ground troops. Casarez recalled his first days with the Blues as "the first time I was really scared."

"Gunships and scouts saw gooks walking around in the mountains southwest of Evans, shot some, then called in the Blues. My squad [about 12 men] went in first, and we started moving up the trail. Every two or three yards, we saw gooks in elephant grass."

The Blues took out seven enemy soldiers. Casarez said one of the enemy soldiers even called out to the squad, "Hey Joe! Hey, Joe!" "One of my buddies just swung around and shot him. That's how close we were."

Even U.S. Marines who had been based at Camp Evans marveled at the First Cav's air mobility. In one assault, Marines from the First Battalion,

Third Regiment, Third Marine Division were carried into a new landing zone on the skids of First Cav choppers. At the time, the Marine unit was under operational control of the Cav's First Brigade.

"That was the damnedest recon-by-fire I've ever seen," Lance Corporal Jimmie A. Dolen, a team leader, told one of our PIO reporters after he had been swept in by a helicopter flying just above the ground, zigzagging in between trees to avoid enemy ground fire.

Before the assault, the Marines had watched as artillery rounds, rockets from gunships and machine-gun bullets from door gunners helped clear the LZ.

"It's kind of nice to have helicopter support from an airmobile unit like the Cav," said Corporal Joseph L. Rocchio, another squad leader.

When First Cav soldiers talked about their experiences, some of the most fascinating stories revealed how close those soldiers came to enemy firepower.

Specialist Four Jim Baines, a rifleman with Bravo Company of the First Battalion, Fifth Cavalry, talked about snaring two small ducks near a river. He planned to roast the ducks for supper.

Shortly thereafter, Baines' company moved out to set up camp in a new location. Determined to keep his ducks, Baines tossed out his C-rations and placed the two live ducks in an empty sandbag, threw the bag over his shoulder, and marched off with his prize.

"We hadn't moved too far when we came under heavy enemy fire," Baines said. "I hit the ground hard. We were pinned down for about 10 minutes. I remember feeling a jerk on my back, but thought nothing of it."

The First Cav soldiers hugged the ground as rocket rounds, mortars and AK-47 gunfire threatened them. When the enemy fire died down, the 1/5th moved out again. That's when Baines felt something wet on his arm. "I could see it was blood," he said. "My back felt all wet, and I thought sure it must be all torn up."

Baines removed the sandbag and discovered one of the ducks was dead and the other one wounded. "Shrapnel from a B-40 rocket had gone through the ducks and my pack without hitting me. I had one KIA and one WIA as a result of the action."

The ducks were so full of shrapnel that Baines decided he couldn't roast them. That night when Bravo Company finally made camp, Baines begged some C-rations off a buddy in order to take the edge off at least some of his hunger.

In some instances, heroic acts in the First Cav would bring combat medals to the soldiers. In other instances, there would be no medals—the soldiers would have to be content with the satisfaction of showing courage under fire.

During one awards ceremony at Camp Evans, two First Cav soldiers received a Soldiers Medal for reaching a downed helicopter and saving two of its passengers. The Soldiers Medal goes to warriors who have saved the lives of others.

Alpha Company of the First Battalion, Seventh Cavalry was working in an area near the Third Brigade base camp when a helicopter made a forced landing nearby. A fire on board had caused ordnance inside to begin going off, and it was difficult for the crew to get away from the ship. Three crew members made it off, but two others remained on board.

Specialist Four Charles Reed and Specialist Four Tony Gonzales moved around the helicopter, trying to avoid the machine-gun bullets and rockets going off inside.

As they reached the first wounded man, he warned them, "Look out! It's gonna blow!"

As they pulled him from the helicopter, it exploded, and all three were knocked to the ground. The second trapped crew member had been thrown out in the explosion, but he remained very close to the ship. Reed and Gonzales returned to the man, pulled him away from the helicopter, and had the two men medevaced in a matter of minutes.

Another First Cav soldier, Corporal James L. Behling of the First Cav's First Battalion, 21st Artillery, also received a medal at Camp Evans, a Silver Star.

Working as a reconnaissance sergeant for Bravo Company, Second Battalion, Seventh Cavalry, Behling was walking with the First Platoon about 10 miles east of Camp Evans when fire rang out from a suspected North Vietnamese Army regimental headquarters.

"A Second Platoon man was hit right away, and I helped him onto a stretcher," Behling said. "Then I joined the forward observer to call in air strikes and aerial rocket artillery.

"Most of my buddies were in the Third Platoon. They were off to our right about 150 meters, drawing heavy fire, so I wanted to get to them."

Behling low-crawled across a graveyard toward the platoon. "The platoon leader said they still had three men lying wounded between us and Charlie."

While sharpshooters from the Third Platoon covered them, Behling and another soldier crawled into the open area three times to laboriously drag back the wounded.

"We got them behind a hedgerow, and some other men brought them to the medevac ship. One of the machine-gunners was keeping the enemy pinned down and we were just catching our breath behind a clump of dirt when I saw this frag grenade come flying against the blue. It hit the machine gun and wiped it out."

The other machine-gunner was helping medevac the three wounded men, so Behling jumped behind the machine gun and while another Cavalryman fed the weapon, he pumped out 1,000 rounds "just to keep the enemy down. That's when I got hit. But I never felt it, never felt it at all until they pulled back. It was a frag wound of some sort.

"I did only what anyone else would have done," Behling said, "only they were too busy at the time."

Behling said he looked forward to getting back to Rockton, Ill., where he would be reunited with his wife, Donna. Before entering the Army, Behling drove truck there for Wolohan Lumber Company, and he suggested he might want to do that again.

"At least it's halfway quiet," he said.

Chapter 20
Walking point with the scouts

The point man in Vietnam performed one of the most crucial jobs for the infantry.

"Your life depends on him," Specialist Four Dennis Herin said. "He's up there in front to protect the men behind him."

Herin walked point for the First Air Cavalary's First Battalion, 12th Cavalry. The point man walked several yards in front of the main column of soldiers. That meant he often had to clear underbrush in the jungles, carving out a path for the soldiers following him. It also meant he would be the most likely person to make first contact with the enemy.

I talked with Herin and some of his fellow soldiers during the First Cav's operations at Dak To, near the Cambodian border.

Herin said he always preferred to walk point, even though it was one of the war's most dangerous jobs. "If someone else is walking point," he said, "it's easy to daydream. I find I'm more observant when I walk point. And I like to trust myself to find the way."

A few weeks later, while working with the First Cav's Second Battalion, 12th Cavalry, I met Hector Commacho, the best point man I observed during my time in Vietnam. His fellow soldiers referred to him as a true scout of Wild West proportions. Charles A. Krohn, in his book "The Lost Battalion," said Commacho for several months served as permanent point man for the 2/12th. As Krohn described it, Commacho "served his company and his country with distinction, defeating several enemy ambushes. So extraordinary was his ability, it is difficult to think of him without reference to the occult.

"Commacho had all the ingredients of a good point: he was young, uncomplicated, and a dead shot. He and men like him cannot be recruited or selected by the Army—any Army—they can only be found on a battlefield after they decide for themselves to step forward."

Krohn, who served as intelligence officer for the 2/12th, told of Commacho walking point during a night march, an incident Commacho would tell me about a few days later. As part of the march, he had to lead his battalion across a river. To facilitate that, he had to find a shallow crossing point. " 'I wouldn't have worried if I'd been alone. I could have made it,' " Commacho told Krohn. " 'But I had to find a place the whole battalion could go. That was my big problem all night. That and I had to make sure everyone could keep up with me.'

"On his first attempt to find a shallow crossing," Krohn wrote, "Commacho ventured into the water about five yards and walked off a drop-off. 'He was out so far we couldn't see him,' said Platoon Sergeant Sherman T. Anglin, from Goleta, Calif. " 'Finally, we heard him splashing toward us and we knew he was swimming back in.'

"Commacho was a fearless one-of-a-kind soldier with natural scouting abilities. He was uniquely qualified to lead Company A and the battalion out of hell. He was the ultimate point man."

While talking with Herin at Dak To, I also met Private First Class James L. Rasmussen, another point man for the 1/12th. He agreed that walking point kept him more alert. "If you walk behind," he said, "you often tend to ease off and that's when you get hit."

In enemy hotbeds, of course, an NVA or VC unit that wanted to ambush an American company, platoon or squad, might decide not to hit the unit's forward element. However, if soldiers in that U.S. company happened to walk up on an enemy encampment, "point can be a bad place to be," Rasmussen said.

Specialist Four Ernest D. Aeilts walked point for the First Cav's Second Battalion, Eighth Cavalry. Aeilts realized how tough his job could be in enemy-infested areas.

His company also was operating near Dak To. Ten air strikes had pounded a hill riddled with a vast North Vietnamese Army tunnel complex that had enabled NVA soldiers to pin down and repel American units trying to capture the hill.

Aeilts cautiously led his company toward the top. When he reached the summit, not a single shot had been fired. His unit had taken the hill.

"We were lucky," Aeilts admitted, a bit relieved. "Point man is a hard job anytime, but when we started up this hill, we knew other platoons had pulled back for air strikes after some of their men had been wounded. And everyone was counting on us to take it."

Point men needed to spot booby traps, detect signs of enemy movement, and sniff out ambushes and snipers. Where there was no trail, they needed to create one, using machetes to cut through dense jungle growth and pushing down 10-foot-high elephant grass. In the heat of Vietnam, with the backpack and ammunition load the U.S. foot soldier carried, it was exhausting work.

"I have an additional problem," Herin said. "People want me to move too fast. Dak To had the thickest brush I had ever seen, and even though I was finding punji stakes and I was trying to break them or knock them down, they still wanted me to move faster."

But Herin had learned his lesson about moving too fast before he ever got to Dak To. In another operation, working along the South China Sea coastline, Herin had led his company up to a hedgerow. He carefully checked the top of the hedge for trip wires. Finding none, he hopped over.

"As soon as I hit the ground on the other side," Herin said, "I saw this 105 [artillery] round. 'Booby trap' flashed through my mind, and I dived right back over. We tossed a grenade on the trap."

Specialist Four George Benton walked point for the First Cav's Second Battalion, Eighth Cavalry. "When we were working in the mountains," he said, "I must have walked up on two or three foxholes. If the enemy had been there, he could have got me every time."

For a new man, one just arriving in Vietnam, walking point must have seemed ominous.

"When you're new," Private First Class Joe J. Rahnis said, "you don't know what to look for because you really haven't seen anything yet." Rahnis, who had been in country for just two months when we talked, already was walking point for the 1/12th.

"But I'm gaining confidence every day," he said. "Most of the guys here take you under their wing; the man behind keeps telling me what to do, what to look for and to take my time. At first, I was afraid of walking point. But I figure men who have been here eight and nine months have taken their turn and it's just not right to keep them walking point."

Infantry commanders in Vietnam tried to rotate their point men to keep them fresh. They also knew that no matter how good the point man might be, his luck could run out.

That happened even with some of the best. It happened with Commacho. Commacho, who loved to walk point, constantly asked for that duty. But, finally, he would take an enemy bullet.

Commacho had helped uproot five enemy snipers nesting in foxholes across a bridge from his battalion. The snipers had been firing at the First Cav soldiers, keeping them from crossing the deep river. Commacho offered to lead a charge of seven Alpha Company volunteers across the bridge. When the squad was about halfway across, the snipers opened fire, sending the U.S. soldiers scrambling off the bridge. Only one man was hit—Commacho.

Commacho endured the pain while his fellow troops attacked the enemy snipers, finally killing four of them. The fifth one crawled away and was never found, but he left behind a trail of blood.

"The foot wound wasn't serious, but he had to be evacuated," Krohn wrote of Commacho. "Before the helicopter arrived to take him away, he had a request: would someone carry him over to the bodies of the five snipers he'd helped kill? My last recollection of Commacho is seeing the smile on his face as two buddies lifted him Indian-style toward the bridge where the bodies were piled."

Chapter 21
Dressing up those C-rations

Napoleon Bonaparte once said, "An Army travels on its stomach."

Food certainly was important to the soldiers in Vietnam. But those serving in the First Air Cavalry Division enjoyed advantages not available to fighting men in previous theaters of operation.

When helicopters dropped into our landing zones, they often brought ammunition, supplies and large chests of hot food.

During the Third Brigade's campaign to help retake Hue, however, the heavy monsoons grounded many of those flights. Some of the brigade commanders complained bitterly that the terrible weather had interfered incredibly with the effectiveness of the foot soldiers.

It also meant we rarely received hot food in the field. We had to rely on C-rations and ingenuity. Nonetheless, with soldiers who were Americans and epicureans at heart, they created tasty meals—even with C-rations.

C-rations in Vietnam could be improved with simple touches. Many soldiers found that cheese melted on top of spaghetti and meat balls or beans and franks, for example, rejuvenated their flavor. One soldier who said he didn't originally like ham and lima beans discovered that if he drained out all the juice, put cheese on top of the beans, then heated it, the cheese would coat the beans and give the meal a much better flavor. In another variation, he crumbled two crackers into a fine powder, then sprinkled them over the top of the melted cheese.

Captain Robert L. Helvey of the First Air Cav's 2/12th discovered a dessert that, at least for him, approached strawberry shortcake.

"You need fruit cocktail and the pound cake," Helvey said. "First you drain the juice from the fruit cocktail and pour it over the pound cake. Then you heat the fruit cocktail, and when it's hot enough, pour some of the fruit over the pound cake."

Another soldier poured canned peaches over the pound cake, and he called that the ultimate dessert treat.

Soldiers who liked their hot chocolate but ran short of the powdered mix found that chocolate tropical bars made a decent substitute. You heated a B-3 unit can filled with water, then added one finely chopped tropical bar to the boiling water. Then you stirred it thoroughly while adding one package of powdered cream and two packages of sugar.

Veterans of the field had known for a long time that one package of cream and a package of sugar enhanced powdered hot chocolate mix.

C-rations combinations produced entirely new and unique meals. *Pacific Stars and Stripes* published a recipe for pizza. After that, nearly every soldier knew how to make it. The original recipe called for a bread C-ration cut into four pieces, a can of cheese and beef spiced with sauce. You put one piece of bread in the bottom of the empty bread can, and another piece in the bottom of an empty B-2 unit can. Then to each can you added some beef spiced with sauce, cheese, the final slices of bread and more beef spiced with sauce. You topped it off with the rest of your cheese. Then you placed the cans in an empty C-ration box and set it on fire, letting the box burn completely to heat the pizza. Many soldiers discovered that heating the meal with a heat tablet proved more effective because it heated the bread more thoroughly.

C-rations in Vietnam came in small cardboard boxes containing plastic spoons, salt and pepper packets, instant coffee, sugar and creamer packets, containers of peanut butter and jam, a piece of gum, matches, small sheets of toilet paper and cigarettes—four smokes to the package. I remember that Winston and Lucky Strike cigarettes seemed to be the most popular, and those of us who didn't smoke could trade our cigarettes for cookies, pieces of chocolate, canned peaches or pound cakes. Also in the cardboard boxes came the olive drab tin cans containing our food. We all carried little P-38 can openers to slice open all those tin containers. Our C-ration choices in the field included ham and eggs, ham and lima beans, spaghetti and meatballs, beans and franks, beef and gravy with potatoes, turkey loaf, boned chicken, chicken and noodles, and spiced beef. Special prizes included canned peaches and pears and those little pound cakes you could use to create special desserts.

For me, the pound cake bathed in fruit cocktail tasted better than any other dessert. Other soldiers, however, labored to create more elaborate treats. Specialist Five Richard Conrad, a First Cav combat photographer who spent many days with me in the field, created a dessert treat he called "Dinky-Poo." "You take one can of peanut butter," he said, "a can of either pineapple or apricot jam, preferably pineapple. Place them both in a B-2 or B-1A unit can and stir them together." Dinky-Poo needed to be eaten as a treat because it was extremely rich. "Still, it's tasty," Conrad said, "and it saves peanut butter when the oil has risen to the top."

Many of us in the field really liked the powdered chocolate. We would dump some of the chocolate into our metal canteen cups and mix it with a little water. You had to do that. If you just dumped the powdered chocolate into water, it would just float and not mix very well. After creating a paste at the bottom of your cup, you could add the rest of the powdered chocolate and more water. If you were lucky enough to have a campfire, you could heat it up and drink it steaming hot.

Some favorite C-rations came from my hometown. Cans containing chicken and turkey meals were packed by the Tony Downs Foods Co., which operated plants in St. James, Madelia and Butterfield. During the middle of March, I wrote, "I'm sitting here eating some boned chicken. The chicken is made in St. James, Minn. It's good, but what they mean by boned chicken, I don't know." At least three C-ration choices, boned chicken, turkey loaf and the chicken and noodles, came from Tony Downs.

C-rations featuring poultry generally tasted pretty good on their own. However, they couldn't hold a candle to some of the innovative and tasty concoctions put together by Platoon Sergeant Sherman T. Anglin, also of the 2/12th.

One misty evening in the field, between firefights as the 2/12th pushed its way toward Hue, Anglin sat down with a huge blackened cooking pot, filled it with water and began cooking over his fire.

First he threw in some onions he had found near a village during the day's maneuvers. After the onions boiled a little, Anglin added spaghetti and meatballs, beans and franks, canned beefsteak, beef with spiced sauce, a packet of salt, and a packet of sugar. He topped his creation by adding cheese from two C-ration tins.

Anglin shared his creation with a few other soldiers from the unit. When the pot had been emptied, Captain Helvey, the company commander, smacked his lips and with a bright smile, gave Anglin a thumbs up.

"It was delicious," he said.

Mike Larson, in full field gear, reads a paperback book as he waits to move out north on a truck caravan traveling from Bong Son in the Central Highlands to Camp Evans in I Corps.

Mike Larson strolls through An Khe flanked by two Vietnamese boys from the village.

Soldiers from the First Air Cavalry wade through a rice paddy as a Vietnamese farm boy in a yellow cone straw hat walks beside a water buffalo.

Vietnamese women sit along the curb of a busy street in Saigon, selling goods in the 1967 capital city marketplace.

Ty, a shoeshine boy in Bong Son, and a great buddy of mine.

Soldiers from the First Air Cavalry wade in a column through one of the many rivers near Bong Son.

Soldiers in the field heat their C-rations and warm their hands over a small fire.

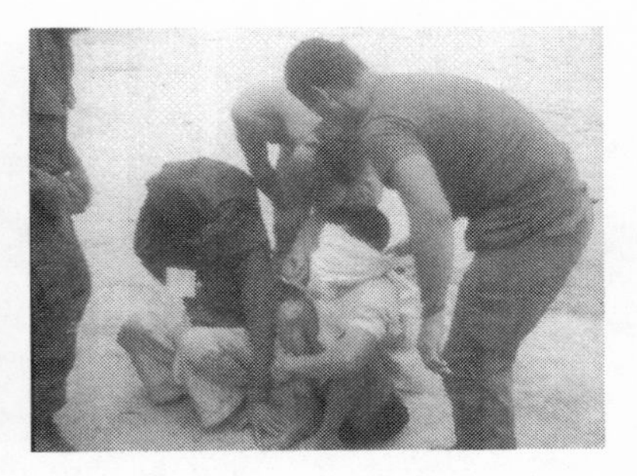

Captured Viet Cong insurgents undergo interrogation from U.S. troops.

Private First Class Hector Commacho, the classic scout and point man from the Third Brigade's Second Battalion, 12th Cavalry.

Skytroopers from the First Air Cavalry ride the skids of a UH-1 Huey during an air-assault into a new landing zone.

A machine-gunner unleashes M-60 firepower at enemy positions. If you look closely, you can see spent shells flying out of the smoking-hot machine gun.

A door-gunner on a UH-1 Huey scans the countryside below as his ship flies over an area infested with Viet Cong troops.

Firefighters work to extinguish flames on the right wing of a C-130 after the huge cargo plane ran off the runway and crashed into a truck at Khe Sanh.

Specialist Four Anthony Williams of the Fifth Battalion, Seventh Cavalry hurls a grenade at enemy positions as the Third Brigade moved toward Hue.

Part Five: Hue

(January 31, 1968–February 25, 1968)

o o o o o o o o o o o o o o o o o o o o o o o o o o o o o o o o o o o

"In February of 1966, at a strategy meeting in Honolulu, President Lyndon Johnson asked his commander in Vietnam, General William Westmoreland, what his next step might be if he were the enemy commander. 'Capture Hue,' General Westmoreland answered without hesitation, explaining that the city was the symbol of a unified Vietnam. 'Taking it would have a profound psychological impact on the Vietnamese in both the North and the South, and in the process, the North Vietnamese might seize the two northern provinces as bargaining points in any negotiations.' Two years later, almost to the day, the enemy overwhelmed Hue and held much of it for nearly a month. The only combat troops to resist the initial assault were from a depleted South Vietnamese company. The nearest U.S. troops were seven miles away."

George W. Smith
The Siege at Hue

Chapter 22
Hue falls to the enemy

While First Air Cav soldiers struggled to get squared away in I Corps, large numbers of North Vietnamese soldiers were pouring into the South, joining their Viet Cong comrades and blending into hamlets up and down the country.

We wouldn't know the true magnitude of this infiltration until after Tet.

U.S. intelligence officials had received and evaluated several enemy documents, including some captured in battle, and many of them indicated that a major offensive was imminent. Intercepted short-wave radio messages from North Vietnamese leaders echoed that information, making references to plans for a major campaign.

As Tet approached, more solid intelligence surfaced. Robert Brewer, a Central Intelligence Agency official based at Quang Tri, received a stolen document from a North Vietnamese double agent. The document focused on NVA plans to attack Khe Sanh and other allied bases at the western edge of I Corps.

On January 20, a North Vietnamese Army soldier surrendered at Khe Sanh. Speaking with interrogators there, the NVA soldier warned of an impending attack at the Marine base. The soldier, identified as La Thanh Tonc, was a senior lieutenant, and he spoke of an NVA offensive that would bring the most significant assault on allied bases since U.S. forces had arrived in South Vietnam. The assault on Khe Sanh began the very next day.

Building upon this intelligence, planning began for Operation Pegasus, a campaign intended to relieve the siege at Khe Sanh. The plan called for First Air Cavalry troops to be inserted into a number of different landing zones surrounding the Marine base.

Major General John J. Tolson, commander of the First Air Cavalry Division, had met early in January with General Creighton Abrams, MACV (Military Assistance Command, Vietnam) deputy commander, and Robert

E. Cushman Jr., III MAF (Marine Amphibious Force) commander, to draw up initial plans for Operation Pegasus.

Even as the U.S. generals talked strategy, however, NVA regulars and Viet Cong insurgents intensified their infiltration into Hue, Saigon and other major Vietnamese cities. They moved into the cities in small groups—often just twos and threes—disguised as Vietnamese workers, peasants and refugees. Some even dressed as South Vietnamese Army soldiers making their way home for the Tet holiday. Their supplies, including large quantities of weapons and ammunition, arrived hidden inside flower containers, placed beneath vegetables, rice and other foodstuffs carried on carts bound for market, even inside wooden boxes camouflaged as coffins.

ARVN Marines and U.S. soldiers continued to uncover more and more documents detailing plans by the North Vietnamese for a major offensive. Yet U.S. military leaders seemed to remain confused about the scope and the timing of the impending assault.

My own notes reflected this same confusion.

On January 16, I wrote in a letter home, "Tomorrow I leave for Chu Lai—or Landing Zone Baldy, to be more exact. While it's dangerous, I should get along pretty well. The entire First Cavalry Division is moving out." Less than a week later, I wrote that we would be moving even farther north. "Two brigades of the First Cav moved near Hue while one brigade stayed near Bong Son." Then just days later, I was making notes about riding in a truck and Jeep caravan through the city of Hue and moving on to Camp Evans.

It was becoming more and more difficult to figure out what was going on.

By the middle of January, at least 20,000 NVA soldiers had moved into positions around Khe Sanh. By late January, some 6,000 U.S. Marines had arrived to reinforce the Khe Sanh garrison. Some military analysts believe this was part of North Vietnam's master plan—to draw U.S. troops toward the western borders of South Vietnam, away from the country's major population areas.

NVA soldiers continued to move south, and as Tet approached, some 5,000 enemy troops were moving across the border into South Vietnam every week. On January 31, when the Tet offensive began, at least 12,000 NVA soldiers were hidden among the populace in Hue.

A significant number of ARVN troops had left their units, on leave because of the holiday. During October of 1967, North Vietnam's leaders had announced they would be observing a seven-day truce from January 27 to February 3, 1968, to honor Tet. Sadly, most U.S. and ARVN commanders believed that pledge had been made in good faith.

The principal architect for the Tet offensive would be General Vo Nguyen Giap, North Vietnam's most notable military leader. Giap later admitted that he had developed the plan largely by default. Another North Vietnamese general, Nguyen Chi Thanh, had been drawing up the Tet strategy. But when Thanh died in 1967, responsibility for the military blueprint fell to Giap.

Giap claimed afterward that he had opposed the plan to attack during Tet, that he planned it "reluctantly under duress from the Le Duan-dominated Politburo." Giap always favored guerrilla tactics against the United States and South Vietnam, whereas Thanh had supported military campaigns spearheaded by North Vietnam's main forces.

North Vietnam's other military leaders overruled Giap. They decided that Tet 1968 would be a perfect time to launch a major conventional offensive. They believed that the South Vietnamese government and the U.S. presence were so unpopular in the South that a broad-based attack would spark a spontaneous uprising of the South Vietnamese population, which would enable the North to sweep to a quick, decisive victory.

A multiphase plan was developed. In the first phase, NVA soldiers would attack allied bases along South Vietnam's western border to discourage U.S. reconnaissance in those regions. Following this, a second phase of widely dispersed attacks would be launched by the Viet Cong directly into the major centers of the country to prod civilians into full-fledged revolt and to bring the South Vietnamese government to its knees. With the government overthrown, the Americans and other allied forces would have no choice but to evacuate, leading to phase three attacks by the Viet Cong and NVA regulars against any remaining opposition to the Communists.

Some NVA units actually launched attacks a day early, on January 30. But those premature assaults occurred simply because some confusion existed among enemy soldiers over when the Tet attacks were supposed to begin.

On January 31, the main assault included simultaneous attacks on five major cities, 36 provincial capitals, 64 district capitals and on numerous smaller villages throughout South Vietnam.

North Vietnamese forces considered the attacks on Saigon and Hue critical to their success. In Hue, 10 NVA battalions and six Viet Cong battalions attacked and ultimately took over much of the city. Before the siege ended, thousands of civilians believed to be enemies of the Communists would be executed in what became known as the Massacre of Hue. Those slain would include government officials, police officers, religious leaders, doctors, health workers, school teachers, university professors and refugees from North Vietnam. The NVA and the Viet Cong would hold much of the city for 26 days.

The First Air Cavalry Division, which had been tapped as the primary force to help relieve the Marines at Khe Sanh, would be ordered to redeploy a number of its infantry units to the Battle of Hue. First Cav troops would be inserted into the battlefield northwest of the old provincial capital, where they would fight toward the city to help drive out the enemy forces. The soldiers would come under heavy enemy fire immediately, and, to a man, they would say this was the most intense fighting they had ever seen.

Khe Sanh and Operation Pegasus would have to wait.

Chapter 23
The battle for Hue intensifies

On Friday, February 2, First Lieutenant John J. Lewis, a platoon leader with the First Air Cavalry Division's Second Battalion, 12th Cavalry, crouched inside a cluster of coconut trees and watched several North Vietnamese Army soldiers milling in similar cover across a spacious rice paddy.

"This was the first time I had actually seen the enemy with weapons in hand, the first time I had seen them in combat," said Lewis, a six-month veteran of Vietnam.

It was two days after the Communists had taken control of Hue, and the Second of the 12th's Alpha Company had neared a picturesque village known as Thon La Chu, about five miles northwest of the imperial capital. Now the soldiers began planning an assault across a 500-meter-wide field toward the dense grove bordering the village where, unknown to the infantrymen, one regiment of NVA soldiers waited, poised in reinforced bunkers.

The 2/12th had called in aerial rocket artillery helicopters to prep the area for their assault. First Air Cav infantry battalions almost always could count on incredible firepower from helicopter gunships and from artillery batteries to support them in battle. But during the first days of their drive to help retake the city of Hue, the 2/12th would have neither. An acute shortage of supplies at Camp Evans exacerbated by heavy fog, low cloud cover and monsoon rains would plague the battalion. Before this first assault, aerial rocket ships would carry the only artillery available to them. But the initial prep went horribly wrong. One of the rocket ships fired a round at the wrong tree line, hitting U.S. soldiers crouching there. The exploding rocket killed one soldier and wounded four more.

Yet soldiers from Alpha Company continued to push into the wood line, trying to suppress heavy enemy fire while soldiers from Delta Company, on Alpha's left, Charlie Company on the right, and Bravo in back, all worked their way across the paddy.

"I've been here since April," said Sergeant Chris Jensen III, "and I couldn't believe a firefight could be this bad. After awhile I was just praying that the ARA choppers would come back, and that artillery would open up. Just drop something on them, I thought. Drop anything."

Charles A. Krohn, in his book, "The Lost Battalion," vividly described the advance of 2/12th soldiers across the rice paddy.

"Some 400 of us got up to charge," wrote Krohn, intelligence officer for the 2/12th. "A few never made it past the first step. By the time we got to the other side of the clearing, nine of us were dead and 48 wounded, cut down by accurately aimed interlocking fields of grazing fire. (Grazing fire is a military term for weapons fire that never rises in trajectory above the height of a man. Every shot has the efficient potential to kill or disable.) An estimated 50 additional soldiers received wounds that they deemed too slight to report; they did not want to interfere with the medics, who were busy treating far more serious cases."

Krohn's description conjures up memories of U.S. Civil War battles, where soldiers from one side would advance bravely across a field and be mowed down by entrenched soldiers on the other side. The charge by the 2/12th appeared to be very ill-advised. The order to charge was very unfair to those brave soldiers.

"Under the circumstances," Krohn wrote, "I thought we had done rather well. The comparison with the Light Brigade didn't escape me. I was tired but unhurt, and I felt good about it. But the facts were uncomfortable to contemplate. Fifty-seven casualties after we started the attack, and we were stopped cold—we only got 200 yards closer to Hue. I wasn't sure we had accomplished much. We made the NVA pay a price for stopping us, but not a high price: we killed only eight NVA (at best) and took four prisoners. We didn't know how many NVA wounded there were. We reported higher figures to brigade, based on wishful thinking that made us feel better, but privately we knew the enemy had scarcely been scratched. Regardless of their casualties, enough remained to fix us in place."

After the 2/12th formed its perimeter for the night, one sniper was spotted inside that perimeter. Three men from Alpha Company's First Platoon stalked him.

"When we were almost up to him," said Specialist Four David D. Dentinger, "the sniper stood up and tossed a satchel charge at one of our men, then he dived back into his hole."

While Specialist Four Stephen F. Cochran kept a rifle trained on the spider hole, Dentinger tossed in a grenade. It exploded. The Skytroopers checked the hole and found the sniper dead.

Throughout the night, NVA snipers fired some rifle rounds, but only a few mortar rounds landed inside the perimeter, and no one was hit by the mortar shrapnel.

"The night was cold and miserable, and without packs, ponchos or poncho liners, we froze," said Specialist Four Frank J. O'Reilly, a radio-telephone operator. "We had gotten less than six hours of sleep in the last 48 hours, and we had gone without food for 24 hours. We didn't have any water or purification tablets, and the river water was too muddy to drink. We were eating sugar cane, bananas and onions. The same cigarette might be smoked by 20 people."

When 2/12th soldiers had left Camp Evans to be air-assaulted into landing zones near PK-17, they had left their backpacks behind. The promise had been that the packs would be airlifted to them in short order. However, they ended up waiting days for those packs to arrive.

But hunger, lack of sleep and an absence of backpacks failed to stop the 2/12th soldiers from fighting the next day.

"We were in a crossfire," said Lewis, the platoon leader. "Finally we had about one man each in our foxholes who wasn't wounded, and there was a good chance we would be overrun. We had to get out. We blew our Claymores [directed mines]. Then on the count of three, we popped several color-smoke grenades for cover and withdrew."

The soldiers who gave Lewis and his men covering fire called the withdrawal a "psychedelic retreat." Lewis and five of his men returned to the foxholes four times to pick up weapons and bring back all the wounded men.

When the 2/12th attacked across the rice paddy, there had been nothing between them and the NVA sharpshooters except a small cemetery—just a few headstones. However, there were a couple of freshly dug graves in the cemetery, and they provided temporary cover for at least a few of the soldiers.

"When I first jumped into the grave, I was afraid I might be there permanently," said Specialist Four Brad Penrose, a Skytrooper in A Company. The shallow depression encircling the mound of the grave afforded Penrose his only cover from the enemy fire. "You might say Charlie put us right in the grave," Penrose said, "but we fought our way out of it."

One of the heroes at Thon La Chu had been Private First Class David L. Jones, 21, a medic for Delta Company. When the fighting began, Jones was a green soldier—he had been with the 2/12th just two days.

With the first call for a medic by a wounded soldier, Jones was separated from his platoon. He continued to move from one wounded soldier to another until late the first night when he finally returned to his platoon.

"That guy really had guts," Sergeant Jensen said later. "You could see he was as scared as everyone else from the way his hands were shaking when he bandaged soldiers. He never slowed down for a minute, though, and kept dodging bullets and going to everyone who needed help."

"He isn't a very big guy," said Private First Class Jerry Eaton, "but he was carrying people who couldn't walk piggyback across the open ground to secure places."

"I sure found out what combat is like fast," Jones said. "It was bad at first and kept getting worse. If I had ever stopped to really think about it, I would have looked for a hole to hide in."

Private First Class Paul A. Hunter also had a close call. A bullet fired by an NVA sniper went right through his helmet.

"We were pinned down for about 24 hours, only occasionally being able to get out of our foxholes," he said. "It was the second day of the firefight. We got word that there were some NVA soldiers approaching us, and we were told to keep our heads down. But I decided to take a peek. I just got over the edge, and I felt a big bump like a big brick or a sledgehammer had hit me on top of the head."

It was only later that Hunter pulled off his helmet to check it—and discovered the bullet hole.

Late in the evening of the second day, 2/12th leaders decided to sneak through the NVA defenses and get to higher ground behind the enemy.

"We left at about 8:15," said O'Reilly, the radio-telephone operator. "The word had gone out just before we left that there would be no smoking [light discipline]. That we didn't have to worry about because no one had any cigarettes."

The soldiers walked in a column for 10 hours in the pitch black night, through sticky rice paddies filled with water that came up to their ankles.

"During the firefight," O'Reilly said, "some of us spent 12 hours in our foxhole without ever getting out. Before we assaulted the enemy across a rice paddy, the lucky men had gotten six hours sleep in the past 48 hours, and we hadn't had food for 24 hours. When we reached the high ground two days later, most of us could claim about eight hours sleep during the last 72 hours."

Chapter 24
Three legends in Company A

The Second Battalion, 12th Cavalry included three of the most dedicated, daring and battle-experienced men I would meet in Vietnam. All three were incredibly intuitive warriors.

Captain Robert L. Helvey commanded Alpha Company of the 2/12th.

Sherman T. Anglin was Helvey's platoon sergeant.

Hector L. Commacho served as the primary point man for Alpha Company.

It was an incredible combination. To me, they were all characters out of the Old West. Three Clint Eastwoods, all assigned to the same company.

When I first met Commacho, he had been in Vietnam just four months. Helvey, who certainly recognized a good soldier when he met one, already was singing his praises.

"You've got to see this man in action to believe him," Helvey said. "He's afraid of absolutely nothing."

Helvey said Commacho displayed incredible confidence right from the start. After only two days in the field with the 2/12th, Commacho asked to walk point.

"When Commacho arrived in Vietnam," Helvey said, "he went out with an ambush squad after some of the men reported hearing movements in the brush around our perimeter. After they had been out awhile, one of the radio men called in that they were hearing lots of movement.

"They came back in. I spoke to Commacho, and he offered to go back out alone."

During the push toward Hue, Commacho demonstrated his courage at Thon La Chu. Just outside that hamlet, the 2/12th found itself in a fierce firefight with an estimated regiment of North Vietnamese Army regulars.

Two First Cav soldiers had been lightly wounded by a single sniper, and they were pinned down.

"He came racing over to me while the NVA were pouring bullets all around," Anglin said. "I told him to get down, but he insisted a sniper up there had wounded his buddies and he had to get him.

"So we put down a heavy fire while Commacho grabbed two grenades and crawled off toward the bunker."

Commacho hurled the grenades at the bunker but missed with both.

With NVA bullets slamming into the mud around him, Commacho returned to Anglin's position, picked up two more grenades and scrambled back to the enemy bunker. This time, he lofted both of his grenades into the bunker, scoring a direct hit as they exploded and took out the sniper. Later in the same firefight, Commacho took over one squad after its squad leader had been wounded and medevaced.

When Commacho's own squad ran low on ammunition, he low-crawled to the middle of his company's perimeter, where some boxes of ammo had been left. Heavy enemy fire had kept the Americans away from those ammo boxes, but Commacho managed to crawl in and grab enough for his entire squad.

"I know the enemy would try to hit me," the 23-year-old Puerto Rican said later, "but I know we need the ammo bad. If Charlie wants to stop me, he got to hit me here, in the heart, so I pick up the ammo. I make it back alright."

That night, when 2/12th commanders decided they needed to make a nighttime march, a move to higher ground, Commacho led the way.

"It was dark," Commacho said. "A cold, damp wind was blowing, but I trust myself. It was hard for all the men to walk across the river paddy because the water came up above our ankles and the ground sucked at our feet. The hardest part was finding someplace where everyone could go and making sure everyone could keep up."

The soldiers took 10 hours—from 8 p.m. until 6 the next morning—to reach the higher ground.

Two days later, when the 2/12th moved back toward the enemy positions, Commacho's luck ran out. Five enemy snipers were sitting in foxholes across a bridge, firing at the Americans and keeping them from crossing the deep river. Captain Helvey and Alpha Company decided to root out the snipers. Commacho and six other Alpha volunteers assaulted across the bridge. When they were about halfway across, enemy gunfire broke out—loud cracks that echoed along the river. The seven Alpha Company soldiers scrambled off the bridge. Commacho was the only soldier hit.

It would be Commacho's second Purple Heart. His first had come when an enemy bullet ripped into his shoulder during an NVA attempt to overrun the First Cav's Landing Zone Leslie in the Que Son Valley. Commacho had received a Silver Star Medal after that action for crawling on top of a bunker and lobbing grenades at enemy soldiers who were swarming around the LZ's perimeter.

This time, an NVA bullet tore through Commacho's boot and entered his foot. Some called this "a million-dollar wound" because it allowed the soldier to hop onto a helicopter and return to base to recuperate.

Commacho remained under cover, watching as the rest of his squad attacked the enemy snipers, finally killing four of them. The fifth one crawled away and was never found, but he left behind a trail of blood.

While Helvey boasted about his men, they also sang his praises. On one occasion, Platoon Sergeant Anglin took me aside and invited me to share his supper. While we were dining, he told me how much he admired Helvey. The man really knew how to fight this war, he said. He couldn't imagine serving with any other company commander.

Helvey was an incredible leader. He and Anglin had gained deep experience in Vietnam. Both were serving their second tours. It was fascinating just to watch them and to listen as they discussed strategy, formulating their plans to out-maneuver the enemy.

Shortly after the assault at Thon La Chu, when 2/12th commanders decided to infiltrate the enemy camp in the middle of the night, their choice to lead the midnight raid was obvious. Helvey would move out with 13 other volunteers to locate the enemy.

Slipping through the darkness in a light mist, the 14 men moved halfway across a field between the 2/12th perimeter and the NVA forces. From a graveyard in the middle of the field, Helvey used an abandoned cement building for cover and peered through his Starlight scope, scanning for enemy positions.

From the cement house, Helvey and his men worked their way behind enemy lines. There they discovered a second tree line. As Helvey explained, that meant the brigade could have attacked, moved inside the first tree line and still had NVA sharpshooters firing at them from behind that second tree line.

As Helvey's raiders returned from their reconnaissance, a recoilless rifle round slammed into the abandoned cement building. But Helvey's men were no longer there; they were all safely back behind their own lines.

Based upon the nighttime findings, 2/12th commanders decided to put an attack on hold. First Lieutenant Tony Kalbli, Alpha Company's executive officer, marveled at the midnight raid. "To attack would have been suicide," he would tell us later. "In that case alone, the 14 volunteers saved the battalion from almost complete destruction."

When Charles A. Krohn left the 2/12th to return home, Helvey would replace him as the battalion's intelligence officer.

"It is … interesting how Helvey came to be selected as my replacement, when he was so obviously qualified as a company commander, a job he loved," Krohn wrote in "The Lost Battalion." "When Scudder [executive officer for the 2/12th] confirmed that I was due to leave for the states, he sought out Sweet [the battalion commander] for a private discussion. 'Helvey's time is running out,' Scudder explained. 'If you don't replace him soon, he'll be dead.' Sweet agreed.

"Helvey missed Company A, where he was a folk hero, but remembered a story he had been told a long time before Vietnam by an old sergeant with a lot of wartime experience: 'Life in combat is like a roll of toilet paper. The more you use, the less you got left.'"

Chapter 25
The Marines fight house to house

While battalions from the First Air Cavalry Division pushed toward Hue from the northwest, U.S. Marines moved into the city from the south.

Soldiers from the First Battalion, First Marines led the counterattack, making their way north by convoy to help relieve the MACV (Military Assistance Command, Vietnam) compound, which had come under attack by North Vietnamese forces. At the same time, soldiers from the Second Battalion, Fifth Marines, air-assaulted into an area at the southwest edge of the city and also began driving north.

Until the U.S. Marines arrived on the second day of the battle, the only allied units inside the city had been South Vietnamese troops.

The low cloud cover and the heavy rains hampering First Cav units northwest of Hue also created havoc for the U.S. Marines and for the ARVN troops. The severe monsoon season made it virtually impossible for U.S. pilots to bring in air support.

During the early morning hours of January 31, the massive attack on Hue had been launched by a division-sized unit of North Vietnamese and Viet Cong soldiers. By dawn, virtually every sector of the city had fallen under Communist control. Tay Loc Airfield and First ARVN headquarters in the Citadel, and MACV headquarters in South Hue remained in allied hands, but all three of those key military installations were under siege by enemy soldiers.

Ultimately, some 12,000 Communist troops, at least 10 battalions, would be fighting in Hue. Most were highly trained North Vietnamese regular army units that had infiltrated from the north across the DMZ or from the west down the Ho Chi Minh Trail. In the city, these soldiers carried AK-47 assault rifles, RPD machine guns, and B-40 rocket-propelled grenade launchers. The NVA also had 107mm, 122mm, and 140mm free-flight rockets, 82mm and 120mm mortars, recoilless rifles, and heavy machine guns.

The North Vietnamese soldiers in Hue had been joined by six Viet Cong main force battalions, including the 12th Hue City Sapper Battalion. A typical main force VC infantry battalion consisted of 300 to 600 battle-hardened fighters. The VC soldiers were armed much like the NVA except for some of the heavier weapons. During the battle, the total Communist force inside Hue and surrounding the city swelled to almost 20 battalions. That force included three enemy infantry regiments fighting to reach Hue from the Khe Sanh battlefield.

South Vietnamese units had been depleted, some by half, by the number of ARVN troops who had been granted leave for the Tet holiday. However, those soldiers still with their units fought desperately in an effort to slow North Vietnamese and Viet Cong forces.

The elite Black Panther Company of the First South Vietnam Division battled valiantly all through the night of January 31, defending their perimeter at Tay Loc Airfield against the NVA's 800th Battalion. The NVA, in its after-battle report, credited the ARVN Black Panthers with holding their ground. "By dawn," the report said, "our troops were still unable to advance."

General Ngo Quang Truong, commander at First ARVN headquarters in the Citadel, issued a call for reinforcements, including some of his Black Panther troops from the airfield. Those troops fought back to division headquarters and were able to secure a perimeter there. General Truong also sent for his Third ARVN Regiment, his First ARVN Airborne Task Force, and his Third Troop, Seventh ARVN Cavalry to further secure his headquarters.

Soldiers from the First ARVN Airborne Task Force and the Third Troop, Seventh ARVN Cavalry responded by moving out of PK-17 along Highway 1 toward Hue. The ARVNs had called their base PK-17 because it stood almost exactly 17 kilometers from downtown Hue. The soldiers moved in an armored convoy toward Hue, but intense fire from a North Vietnamese blocking force pinned them down about 400 meters short of the Citadel wall. Unable to force their way through the enemy positions, the South Vietnamese paratroopers called for assistance. The Second ARVN Airborne Battalion moved in to reinforce the convoy, and the South Vietnamese finally penetrated the enemy lines and entered the Citadel early the next day. Initial ARVN casualties were heavy: 40 killed and 91 wounded. The convoy also lost four of its 12 Armored Personnel Carriers during the fighting.

The Third ARVN Regiment ran into intense resistance as well. Two of its battalions, the Second and the Third, advanced east from encampments southwest of the city along the northern bank of the Song Huong, but North Vietnamese firepower forced them back. Unable to enter the Citadel, the two battalions established their night positions outside the wall of the Old City.

The Third ARVN Regiment's First and Fourth Battalions, operating to the southeast, found themselves surrounded by NVA forces as they attempted to reinforce the units inside Hue. The First Battalion, commanded by Captain Phan Ngoc Luong, pulled back to the coastal outpost at Ba Long. When they reached the outpost, Captain Luong's men carried just three clips per man for their World War II-era M1 rifles, and each of those clips held only eight rounds. From Ba Long, the First Battalion soldiers commandeered some motorized junks and reached the Citadel the following day. However, they still could not penetrate the NVA perimeter. The Fourth Battalion also remained under siege and was unable to break out of its encirclement for several days.

On the morning of January 31, the ARVN Seventh Armored Cavalry Squadron set out to break an enemy stronghold. Lieutenant Colonel Phan Huu Chi, the squadron commander, led an armored column into Hue, but the squadron stalled. With the promise of U.S. Marine reinforcements, Chi's column, with three tanks in the lead, staged a second assault. This time they were able to cross the An Cuu Bridge over the Phu Cam Canal. When they reached central police headquarters in southern Hue, the tanks attempted to link up with the police defenders. At that instant, an enemy B-40 rocket landed directly on top of Lieutenant Colonel Chi's tank, killing him instantly. The direct hit stunned the soldiers driving the other tanks, and the squadron quickly pulled back.

As soldiers from Alpha Company of the First Battalion, First Marines approached Hue from the south, they came under intense sniper fire. The enemy fire forced the Marine convoy to stop several times to flush out snipers in heavy house-to-house and street fighting. NVA and VC snipers continued to lurk inside buildings, inside small sniper nests and inside makeshift bunkers. During the night, enemy soldiers from regular NVA units planned local counterattacks, and they set out explosive booby traps between themselves and the approaching Marines.

U.S. military leaders had ordered no bombing or shelling of Hue because of the city's many historic structures and because of the Citadel's symbolic value to the Vietnamese people. However, just days later, commanders rescinded those orders, and bombers, jet fighters, artillery and naval gunfire began hitting targets inside the city. The intensive bombardment turned much of the walled complex into rocky debris. Even today, visitors to Hue can see lasting evidence of the 1968 battle for the city: bullet and shrapnel marks that scarred walls and buildings, brick and stucco structures still in disrepair, and gaping holes left from bombing raids, artillery volleys, and explosions that ripped through the city.

The U.S. Marines continued to advance, recapturing precious real estate as they painstakingly made their way toward the embattled MACV compound. By the time the Marines arrived at the compound, the enemy attackers had pulled back.

As the battle raged, Lieutenant Colonel Marcus Gravel, commander of the First Battalion, First Marines, met with Army Colonel George O. Adkisson, the U.S. senior advisor to the First ARVN Division, to draw up plans for the next day's offensive. Gravel's Alpha Company, which had led the initial advance, now would remain behind to help defend the MACV compound. When dawn broke, Gravel directed his Company G in an attack across the Highway 1 bridge over the Song Huong. Gravel reinforced the attack with three tanks from the Third Tank Battalion and positioned additional tanks from the ARVN Seventh Armored Squadron on the southern bank to provide direct fire support.

As Company G began to move across the bridge, an enemy machine-gunner on the other end of the bridge opened fire, killing and wounding several Marines. Marine Lance Corporal Lester A. Tullyran miraculously reached the north end of the bridge where he hurled a grenade into the machine-gun position and took out the sniper. Tullyran later would be awarded a Silver Star for his heroics.

Two platoons of Marines following also reached the north side of the river. They turned west and immediately came under automatic weapons and recoilless rifle fire from NVA positions along the Citadel wall.

The Marines tried to withdraw. However, enemy snipers in well-dug-in positions pinned down Company G. As the Marines began taking more casualites, they commandeered some abandoned Vietnamese civilian vehicles and used them as makeshift ambulances to carry out their wounded. Among the casualties on the bridge was Major Walter M. Murphy, the First Battalion S-3 operations officer, who was hit by rifle fire and who later died of his wounds.

By that evening, the First Battalion, First Marines, in addition to securing the MACV compound, had established defensive positions at a helicopter landing zone in a field just west of the Navy LCU (Landing Craft, Utility) Ramp in South Hue. Military leaders considered the LCU Ramp crucial logistically for bringing supplies and equipment to troops within the city.

During their first day of fighting, the two Marine battalions in Hue had lost 10 soldiers killed and 56 wounded. During the night, the Marines called a helicopter into their landing zone to take out the most seriously wounded.

On February 2, the Marines brought in more reinforcements and made additional headway. The First Battalion secured the MACV communications facility that morning and, after a three-hour firefight with remnants of the

NVA, reached the campus of Hue University. After securing the campus so they could use it as a base, the Marines again pushed north. With NVA and VC forces still sniping at them, the Marines continued to fight their way building by building, block by block. It was a laborious—and dangerous—process that would go on for three weeks.

When the allies had retaken all of the city except the Citadel and the Imperial Palace on the north banks of the Song Huong, Navy A-4 Skyhawks, finally able to fly as the monsoon rains abated somewhat, began dumping bombs and napalm into the Citadel.

On February 22, as the battle neared its endgame, U.S. forces tapped Brigadier General Oscar E. Davis, the First Cav's assistant division commander, to help coordinate the forward headquarters in Hue. Davis linked up with General Truong at First ARVN headquarters. Their charge was to make a final assessment of the situation and recommend directly to General Creighton Abrams, MACV deputy commander, what they needed to secure the Citadel.

The next day, they called upon the Second Battalion, Third ARVN Regiment along with the ARVN Black Panthers to conduct a night attack inside the Citadel. Driving westward along the wall at the southeastern side of the fortress, they caught the NVA and VC soldiers by surprise and sent them reeling. By 5 a.m. on February 24, the Imperial Palace in the Citadel had been secured. The Black Panther Company ripped down the Viet Cong flag and raised a flag of their own. The Viet Cong flag had flown since the first day of the battle on January 31.

Within 72 hours after Davis arrived at Truong's headquarters, the siege of Hue had ended. By the next day, all remaining North Vietnamese Army soldiers had withdrawn from the city.

Chapter 26
The Third Brigade reaches Hue

As the fighting intensified in areas radiating from Hue, more reports surfaced of heroics by First Cav soldiers.

When troops from Alpha Company of the Second Battalion, 12th Cavalry were ambushed during their push toward the besieged city, a supporting column of Armored Personnel Carriers (APCs) rushed in to help them pull back and to provide some space for air strikes.

Specialist Four Ronald A. Kling, a squad leader for the APC unit, led one of his columns along the edge of a rice paddy that had been flooded by the rains. The enemy soldiers began firing mortar rounds as soon as Kling's company moved in, and sniper gunfire began cracking and echoing all around them.

"One platoon of Alpha Company got caught out in a rice paddy," Kling said, "and the NVA were right on top of them before they knew it." Most of the soldiers were able to move with the APCs out of the rice paddy. But when the last APC came out, NVA forces were able to close in around 47 Skytroopers who remained in the rice field. The First Cav soldiers would be trapped there until the next day.

During his time in Vietnam, Kling had served in three very important jobs. He had been a point man for five months, a fire team leader for two months, and a squad leader for one month. Even though he had come under fire from snipers and from enemy soldiers in occasional skirmishes, Kling thought of his job as more or less routine—until January of 1968 when he was among those 47 soldiers surrounded for an entire night by North Vietnamese Army regulars.

"We had been in constant action there since October 1," Kling said of the Que Son Valley. "If not in firefights, we were getting sniped at and at one point we got sniped at 17 days in a row."

No one is certain how many NVA troops had surrounded the First Cav soldiers, but Kling believed there were four different units totaling a battalion or more.

"We tried to break through the enemy, but two of our men were killed and 17 wounded, so we had to get back under cover," he said. "We called in white phosphorous and artillery all night, plotting it from 2 to 10 meters away from our bunkers."

Almost 800 high-explosive artillery rounds pounded the NVA that night, but enemy soldiers still fired off 80 mortar rounds that exploded around the American troops.

"It wasn't funny at the time," Kling said, "but they had mortar tubes on both sides and they were too close to us, so the tube would fire the mortar from one side, and it would fly over us and land on their own people. The other side would do the same thing. Our artillery eventually knocked out three of their four mortar tubes."

Sergeant Steve Martin of the 2/12th also talked about that poor marksmanship. The NVA forces surrounding the First Cav soldiers had machine guns, recoilless rifles, and a mortar position. Martin said he was thankful that 2/12th soldiers had been able to reach a hilltop where they could scramble into foxholes that had been carved out in a previous operation.

"The mortars and recoilless hit us from one direction, and the automatic weapons harassed us from the other side," Martin said. "With all the firing going on, we were confused because very few of their rounds were hitting inside our perimeter."

Martin said the enemy soldiers were so close that he didn't see how they could miss. But he and a few other soldiers craned out of their foxholes to watch where the enemy rounds were falling.

"The NVA were overshooting our positions and killing their own men behind us," Martin said. "We saw them connect with a direct hit on one of their own machine-gun positions. Their rounds kept falling on their own men and really helped us out. I didn't think anyone could shoot that bad."

Even though surrounded, the First Cav soldiers still looked out to see an NVA soldier crawl from a hedge row and edge along a shallow trench. One of the Cav troops tossed in two frag grenades, which exploded and killed the NVA soldier.

Finally, some U.S. artillery rounds began coming in, landing on NVA positions. At about 4:30 a.m., the NVA popped yellow smoke. "We thought this was it," said one 2/12th soldier, "that it meant an all-out attack, but they all took off. Our artillery really tore them apart."

The 2/12th soldiers had been fortunate to receive that artillery support. Low-flying clouds and torrential rains of the heavy monsoon season would plague the Third Brigade battalions during much of February. Helicopter pilots found bringing in supplies and ammunition especially difficult.

"The pilots who have something to fly repeatedly carry supplies to units in the field and bring in the wounded," Tom A. Johnson wrote in his book, "To The Limit: An Air Cav Huey Pilot in Vietnam."

The pilots with flyable helicopters, Johnson said, were ferrying between Camp Evans and a Navy fuel supply depot along the South China Sea coast about six miles east of the new First Cav base. Sometimes the visibility for the pilots was barely the length of a football field.

"Since the cloud layer is so low, flights must be at treetop level, and ol' Charlie soon figures out what is going on," Johnson wrote. "He moves his heaviest automatic weapons between Evans and the fuel supply. Flying in numbers makes us feel a little safer because someone who gets shot down will have a better chance of being found and rescued. We don't fly over the same ground as any of the guys ahead of us. Though we fly as a covey of 10 birds, our formation is 'helter-skelter.' Each of us uses techniques he has developed on his own to avoid being hit. We zigzag right between trees rather than fly over them. A high-speed, low-altitude engine failure will be trouble no matter how you look at it, but better that than to be running along at 300 feet and take a round in the head."

Two battalions of the First Cav's Third Brigade had air-assaulted into enemy-rich areas on day two of the campaign to relieve Hue. The Second Battalion, Twelfth Cavalry led the way, air-assaulting into a landing zone near PK-17. The Fifth Battalion, Seventh Cavalry followed, air-assaulting into a landing zone nearby.

The 2/12th ran into strong resistance almost immediately.

Ultimately, the 2/12th fought its way to PK-17. The ARVN base had been vacated by soldiers from the First ARVN Airborne Task Force and the Third Troop, Seventh ARVN Cavalry after they had been summoned to help secure First ARVN headquarters in the Citadel.

There had been occasional action at PK-17. In April of 1967, the camp, then home to some 300 South Vietnamese soldiers from the Third Regiment, First ARVN Division, was overrun. In December of 1967, enemy soldiers launched a mortar attack on the camp. During the early part of January, leading up to Tet, North Vietnamese Army regulars probed the perimeter on a couple of occasions but failed to break through the guards.

On January 31, the first night of the Tet offensive, the real barrage began. That night, eight 60mm mortars landed inside the PK-17 perimeter. Nearly every night after that, until U.S. soldiers reached Hue, the camp would receive 60mm or 80mm mortar fire, interspersed with B-40 and 122mm rockets. One night, more than 100 rounds landed inside the perimeter.

One night early in February, U.S. soldiers captured three NVA soldiers inside the perimeter at PK-17. Vietnamese interrogators discovered that the NVA soldiers were attempting to map the ARVN camp for a possible ground attack.

Soldiers from the 2/12th discovered one good thing about PK-17: most bunkers in the camp had been solidly built—they had solid concrete sides nearly a foot thick and concrete tops covered with dirt and sandbags. Despite the heavy nightly bombardment, few soldiers were hit by any of the resulting shrapnel. Although they didn't stay at PK-17 very long, most of the 2/12th soldiers agreed with Sherman T. Anglin, one of their platoon sergeants, who said of the bunkers: "I know it's the safest place I have been since I got over here."

By February 11, a Sunday, soldiers from the Fifth Battalion, Seventh Cavalry had moved into positions on the enemy's northern flank. They were receiving support from radar-controlled bombers and naval artillery, which dropped rounds on the NVA positions every day.

Late that afternoon, soldiers from the 5/7th began moving across a spacious rice paddy toward Thon Que Chu. The hamlet, encircled by dense groves of trees, stood along Highway 1 just a few miles northwest of Thon La Chu, where the North Vietnamese Army had established a regimental headquarters and where soldiers from the 2/12th had spent a night surrounded by the NVA. A Third Brigade plan to attack the regimental headquarters had been put on hold after soldiers in a 2/12th midnight scouting party spotted a huge force of heavily armed enemy troops nesting in well-fortified bunkers on the outskirts of Thon La Chu.

Skytroopers from the First Platoon of the 5/7th were told to scout the woods at the northwest corner of Thon Que Chu and "di-di" back if they received even one round of fire.

In columns 15 to 20 meters apart, the platoon began moving across the paddy.

"We had gotten within 20 meters of the wood line," said Private First Class Sam DiPolito, "when a [First Cav] soldier spotted movement and began firing. The man ahead of him turned and looked as if to say, 'What are you firing at?'"

He was still turned when an enemy sniper opened up and knocked him down. "The man who had opened fire was hit, and the man ahead of me was hit," DiPolito said. "I finally realized what was happening, and I hit the ground. If that one man hadn't opened up, we might have walked right into the North Vietnamese Army camp, and none of us would have made it back."

For two hours, the First Platoon troops maneuvered to get away from the enemy fire. With small-arms bullets and recoilless rifle rounds bouncing all around, the rest of Bravo Company opened up on the NVA while First Platoon soldiers crawled back across the paddy.

"We finally made it back by dusk," DiPolito said. "Everyone was a nervous wreck. It was a wonder any of us made it."

Two days later, the battalion would take Thon Que Chu, but during this night, the soldiers in Bravo's First Platoon didn't sleep much.

"There wasn't a rock or anything to get behind," said one First Platoon rifleman who admitted it was his most terrifying moment in Vietnam. "All we saw were bullets, bullets bouncing all over hell."

During this operation, the 5/7th also used midnight or "slash" ambush squads that ventured out under the cover of darkness to probe for enemy positions. Their goal during these missions was to locate—but evade—enemy soldiers. In the march toward Hue, some of these squads found themselves facing incredible odds.

On one midnight raid, two squads from the 5/7th, one from Bravo Company and one from Delta, moved out from their perimeter seven kilometers northwest of Hue and walked north, setting up positions just south of Highway 1. Early in the evening, lead elements of Delta Company spotted a large number of enemy soldiers carrying weapons. They called in artillery.

"The artillery started pounding the wood line," said Specialist Four Willie Calcote, who was watching the enemy soldiers through a nighttime Starlight scope. All of a sudden, "about 40 enemy with weapons and packs came tearing out of the wood line and went racing down the highway. I counted them through the scope. I saw one round of artillery fall right on one of them. The next day we found where they had buried him."

"We were only about 50 meters from Delta Company," said DiPolito, who also had volunteered for this ambush squad, "and artillery was so close that we were getting shrapnel over our heads."

The two ambush squads were supposed to return to the battalion perimeter by 2 a.m., but because of the enemy sighting and the continuing artillery fire, they were told to wait.

"We finally started back for our perimeter about 3 o'clock," said Private First Class Gary Cline, with Bravo Company. "We were walking along a dike between Highway 1 and some railroad tracks. All at once, we heard lots of ducks quacking, and heard them flapping their wings. I thought they were quacking because of us. Our front men started dropping to the ground and everybody behind followed, luckily, because about 50 enemy with weapons came running down the road toward Hue. We were 25 meters away from them."

Specialist Four Curtis W. Lantz was walking point on the way back and he was the first man to hit the ground when he spotted the enemy soldiers.

"I heard the ducks quacking," he said. "At least it sounded like ducks, but the flapping of the wings, I think, was the enemy sandals flopping against the road. I looked through the Starlight and I couldn't see anything until they got about 100 meters away. I motioned for the men in back of me to get down and they passed it back.

"If we had tried to get across the railroad tracks, they would have spotted us against the sky, so we just kept down with our weapons on bushwhack, ready for automatic fire, waiting for someone to spot us."

The soldiers stayed down for 10 minutes, then continued back to their battalion perimeter.

"It was funny in a way," DiPolite said afterwards. "They were singing and talking just like GIs do. And there was one straggler, far behind the others, who kept calling to the others, like, 'Wait for me. Wait for me.' But it wasn't funny when it happened. We were all too afraid one of the stragglers would spot us."

A couple of days later, an ill-timed whistle brought an NVA soldier so close to 5/7th soldiers that the rivals ended up in hand-to-hand combat.

A platoon from the 5/7th was working down a densely vegetated finger in a valley near Hue. The platoon had come under an intense barrage of NVA automatic weapons fire, and the soldiers had jumped into bomb craters, but they were pinned down by the bullets whining over their heads.

First Lieutenant James M. Sprayberry, the company executive officer, and several volunteers moved cautiously through the darkness toward the besieged men. The volunteers began moving at 8 p.m., and they, too, came under sniper fire from NVA soldiers nesting in bunkers and spider holes. The First Cav soldiers found themselves stalled and had to knock out the enemy positions before moving on. It was midnight before the Cavalrymen were able to advance some 200 meters, getting close enough to attempt contact with the ambushed soldiers.

"We told them we would whistle," Sprayberry said. "I told them to whistle back if they heard us."

A Cavalryman whistled. Someone whistled back.

"Once more, we whistled," Sprayberry said. "Again someone whistled back. Then, against the sky, we spotted this guy walking toward us, and I thought it was someone from the other platoon."

The man walked right up to one of Sprayberry's men and started talking—in Vietnamese. The First Cav soldier, Specialist Four Barry Tranchetti, swung up his M-16 and fired at the NVA soldier, but after he had pumped out two rounds, his M-16 jammed.

Only lightly wounded, the enemy soldier spun around and dashed into the heavy shrubbery alongside the road. But Specialist Four Delbert Mack jumped on top of the NVA, dragged him to the ground, and finally stabbed him with his bayonet.

By February 20, the monsoon deluges had eased and the heavy clouds had lifted. Supply routes had opened again for the First Cav, and well-equipped soldiers from the Third Brigade finally were ready to launch another attack on the NVA regimental headquarters at Thon La Chu.

Air Force jets had begun dropping tons of bombs on suspected enemy positions up and down Highway 1. On February 20, a Tuesday, the bombers hit enemy positions at Thon La Chu with 16 tons of bombs and five tons of napalm.

The following day, the entire Third Brigade moved in early darkness toward the NVA positions. The 5/7th and the 1/7th on its right attacked southeast while the 2/12th, from the south, attacked northwest.

In the assault, Private First Class Albert Rocha, walking point for Delta Company of the 5/7th, helped root out three enemy snipers hiding in a heavily fortified bunker. Rocha was leading his platoon in a trench along a wood line when the snipers opened fire with their AK-47 automatic rifles. Carefully working his way along a shallow trench, Rocha had almost reached the snipers when one of their bullets found its mark, ripping through the handguard on his rifle, tearing it from his hands and knocking off his helmet.

"I thought for sure he was hit," said one of Rocha's friends.

Rocha, still without a helmet, picked up his rifle again and made it to the enemy bunker.

"I could have reached up and touched their gun barrels," said Rocha, who was lying just below the bunker opening. He worked carefully around the side of the bunker, until he got on top of it. There, Second Lieutenant Frederick Krupa, Rocha's platoon leader, joined him. While Rocha unleashed a steady stream of bullets from his M-16, Krupa began tossing in hand grenades. The snipers continued to put out occasional fire so the First Platoon called for a satchel charge. Soldiers passed it up to Krupa, and he stuck it into the bunker.

"I saw it go in," Rocha said, "and I could see them trying to push it out, but the lieutenant held it right there. I watched it go off in their faces, and I was almost ready to get up and move out when one of the snipers came up, and gave me a smile. He smiled at me for half a second before I emptied my magazine into him. I had six rounds left.

"Then I was really shook up. I started to wonder, what do we have to do to kill these guys?"

Rocha left the bunker with Krupa, who had been lightly wounded in the arm by a fragment from the satchel charge, and ran with him to the medevac pad.

"I carried him," Rocha said, "and he carried me. We both got out."

The heroics of Rocha and Krupa proved significant in the capture of Thon La Chu because the three NVA snipers had been entrenched in well-fortified bunkers at the northwest corner of the village. Once the three snipers had been uprooted, other NVA soldiers were killed, captured or fled.

After the action, Rocha was unable to find his helmet.

"I looked for it after the fighting, but I still don't feel bad that I lost it. One of the sergeants told me he spotted it and it's all full of holes."

On February 22, the Third Brigade battalions moved back southeast toward Hue.

The intensity of the action seemed to be diminishing, in part because many NVA and VC soldiers had fled from Hue.

Not that the final days of February were uneventful.

Sergeant Jerry Rivera, a squad leader for Bravo Company of the 2/12th had a narrow escape when he stepped on a booby-trapped 60mm mortar round.

"I walked toward the road and just stepped on the thing," Rivera said. "The first thing I thought of was, I've blown a mine! The detonator in the round went off, causing a pop and a small amount of smoke, but the charge did not go off.

"I guess I was just lucky, that's all. It makes you think about a lot of things, mostly how good it is to be alive."

Even a squad of First Cav engineers got into the act in their support of the 2/12th.

Soldiers from C Company, Eighth Engineers Battalion, found themselves in the middle of some intense action, exchanging gunfire with NVA regulars near Hue.

Engineers in the battalion low-crawled around the battlefield, blowing up trees and stumps to clear an area for a medevac helicopter.

Not only did the engineers have to try to avoid enemy fire, with bullets slamming into the dirt all around them, but they had to scramble to reach a trench line some 40 meters away to make sure they weren't injured by flying debris from the time-fused plastic explosives they planted near the trees and the stumps.

In addition to carrying their demolition and construction equipment, the company of engineers carried a machine gun, a grenade launcher, an anti-tank weapon and their M-16s. During their short stint with the 2/12th, the engineers recorded 12 kills of enemy soldiers.

One pilot from the First Cav's 227th Aviation Battalion had a harrowing experience inside the city itself. Chief Warrant Officer Fredrick E. Ferguson flew his craft into the Citadel on a medivac mission, even as the Viet Cong flag still flew from the main flagpole there.

Ferguson flew right past that flagpole to set his helicopter down in a tiny courtyard inside the ARVN compound. Wounded Vietnamese and U.S. soldiers were loaded into the helicopter, then Ferguson winged back out past the Viet Cong flag, with just a few feet of clearance between his rotor blades and the buildings in the Citadel.

The compound had received virtually constant small arms and mortar fire during Ferguson's daring mission. As the First Cav pilot brought his ship up and out of the compound, a couple of the wounded passengers looked back to see an 81mm mortar round explode on the ground right between the skid marks that had been left by Ferguson's helicopter.

On February 22, the main 5/7th force made contact with a column of NVA soldiers moving out of Hue. Meanwhile, Skytroopers from Bravo Company of the 5/7th were able to air-assault into Hue to link up with Armored Personnel Carriers from Bravo Troop, Third Squadron, Fifth Armored Cavalry. The following day, the rest of the 5/7th moved past an NVA force that had been pounded during the night by artillery, and they rejoined Bravo Company and the APC troop. The northwest wall of Hue had been secured. The next morning, the First Cav's 1/7th linked up with the 5/7th, which had moved to secure the city's southwest wall. Once this wall had been secured, NVA and VC resistance within Hue collapsed.

On February 25, 2/12th Skytroopers moved almost to the Hue Citadel, completing the barrier that sealed off the enemy soldiers from the northwest, the west and the southwest.

The city of Hue once again rested in allied hands.

During the First Cav's drive to the city's northwest wall, three of us from the division's Public Information Office had spent nearly three weeks covering the Third Brigade battalions. Two of the best PIO photographers, Richard Conrad and Steve Robinson, captured some incredible action from the battlefield.

Conrad and I would be with the 2/12th as it neared the city.

Robinson was with the First Cav's 5/7th when that battalion reached the northwest wall. One of Robinson's most striking photographs—and one of the most disturbing—showed First Cav soldiers walking across a bridge between two walls in Hue. The stone walls had crumbled under the incredible bombardment. There was rocky debris everywhere. Robinson's photograph was a graphic and tragic illustration of what had happened to the city many of us considered the most beautiful in South Vietnam.

Today, when I look at that photograph, I'm reminded of a quote now attributed to Captain Myron Harrington, who commanded the 100-man Delta Company, First Battalion, Fifth Marines during the Battle of Hue. On the day after Hue once again had been secured, Harrington surveyed the absolute devastation within the city and asked, "Did we have to destroy the town in order to save it?"

Chapter 27
The Massacre of Hue

On February 25, 1968, the First Cav's Second Battalion, 12th Cavalry made its way south from the northwest wall of Hue.

When the Skytroopers had nearly reached the wall, they discovered an abandoned area that had been used as an NVA hospital and supply depot. They also discovered bloodstained boats on the nearby Song Sau, indicating that wounded enemy soldiers had been brought here from Hue. Strewn about the hastily abandoned hospital facility were assorted medical supplies including blood expander, gauze bandages and antibiotics. In a supply area alongside, First Cav soldiers uncovered more than 600 pounds of ammunition, grenades, uniforms, field stoves and web gear. They also found three field phones, a hand-operated generator, a 60mm mortar tube, a B-40 rocket launcher, an SKS rifle and several 82mm mortar rounds.

Nearby, the First Cav's 1/7th found more equipment: a B-40 rocket launcher with three rockets, one .50-caliber machine gun, one SKS rifle, six 60mm mortar rounds, some Chi-Com claymores and grenades plus assorted web gear. The abandoned items were a strong indication that NVA and VC soldiers had fled Hue in disarray, leaving much of their gear behind.

As the First Cav's 2/12th continued south along the wall, it would be linking up with Companies Alpha, Bravo and Delta of the 2/501st Infantry of the 101st Airborne Division. The 2/501st had been operating under the control of the First Cav's Third Brigade.

As the two units neared one another, their lead elements made a grisly discovery. In a freshly dug mass grave near the western wall, the U.S. soldiers found the bodies of 30 people, all Vietnamese civilians. Each of the civilians had been shot in the head. For First Cav soldiers, it was the first gruesome find in what would come to be called the Massacre of Hue.

The city of Hue was home to some 140,000 people, about half of its population today, when the North Vietnamese launched their Tet offensive. When the Battle of Hue ended on February 24, 1968, at least 3,500 civilians had been reported missing. Some of those civilians died in the fighting or were buried under the rubble from bombings and artillery barrages. But countless others had been executed by NVA or VC soldiers. As more and more mass graves were discovered, the estimates of civilians killed or missing would rise to 5,800.

In the first mass grave excavated within the city, more than 150 bodies were found. Many of those civilians had been bound together with wire and bamboo strips. For many, their hands had been tied behind their backs. Some of their skulls had been bashed in with rifle butts, others had been shot, still others apparently had been buried alive with dirt rapidly replaced on top of the shallow graves.

The search for bodies would go on for months. Even a year and a half after the Battle Of Hue, some 250 skulls and stacks of bones were discovered along a shallow creek in a gorge about 10 miles south of Hue. Some woodcutters walking in the thick groves stumbled across the ghoulish scene after a heavy rainstorm had swelled the currents, exposing bodies and skeletons in a shallow grave along the banks of the creek. An October 31, 1969, report in *Time Magazine* described the grisly find in Nam Hoa Province: "The eyeholes were deep and black, and the water flowed over the ribs."

The woodcutters reported their find to their hamlet chief who contacted province officials in Hue. Volunteers from the South Vietnamese Popular Force, sent in to exhume the bodies, found more than two dozen mass graves in the area.

When NVA and VC soldiers had gained control of Hue, they took as captives a number of civilians. Viet Cong death squads systematically executed South Vietnamese government leaders and employees, police officials, Catholics, intellectuals and prominent business people. Viet Cong cadres, sweeping through the city, carried detailed documents listing enemies to the Communist cause.

Further, NVA and VC soldiers randomly executed farmers, older women, elderly men, young girls, school teachers and school children.

"They had no reason to kill these people," said Le Thi Bich Phe, one Vietnamese woman whose husband had been executed.

Because of Hue's historic value, U.S. and ARVN troops initially waged their battle to retake the city with surgeon-like precision, using nothing more powerful than naval gunfire and extremely accurate eight-inch howitzers. But when the fighting intensified, and allied troops stalled, commanders decided to unleash more powerful weapons on suspected enemy positions.

By the time the Battle of Hue ended, almost half of the city had been destroyed or substantially damaged, including much of the Citadel and the palaces and tombs of the former Annamese kings. Some estimates said at least 80 percent of all homes in Hue had sustained damage or been destroyed during the fighting. An estimated 116,000 civilians had been left homeless. U.S. Marines would report finding old men, old women and children crawling out from beneath the rubble, waving pieces of white cloth attached to sticks. The allied forces provided temporary housing for the refugees at Hue University and at a makeshift complex near the MACV compound. U.S. and South Vietnamese officials worked to restore electricity and other city services, provide potable drinking water, ensure that everyone had food, and reduce health hazards, including taking care of bodies found throughout the city. Catholic leaders in Hue and South Vietnamese government leaders, aided by U.S. personnel and resources, worked diligently to restore order to the city. By the end of February, a full-time administrator was in place to coordinate aid for refugees in Hue.

Some observers suggested that the refugees were the lucky ones.

One month after the Battle of Hue ended, a farmer working his fields southeast of the city tripped across a heavy strand of wire. The farmer tugged on the wire and lifted a skeletal hand out of the soil. The South Vietnamese government launched an immediate investigation. Volunteers digging in spots near the farmer's discovery, where some of the crops seemed to be growing taller and greener, uncovered more than 20 mass graves and 809 bodies. When residents of Hue heard of the find, scores of them flocked to the site in nearby Phu Thu to sort through the remains of clothes, shoes and other personal effects of missing relatives—and to help identify the victims.

However, it was the gruesome 1969 discovery of human remains along the shallow creek in Nam Hoa Province that recalled one of the most vicious atrocities during the Battle of Hue. On the fifth day of the Tet offensive, Communist soldiers had appeared at the Catholic Cathedral in Hue's Phu Cam district, where a number of Vietnamese men had sought refuge with their families. The NVA and VC soldiers took 398 of those men as captives and marched off with them, saying they planned to indoctrinate the men. Their families never saw the men again. Documents found later showed that all of the men had been shot or bludgeoned to death at the foot of the Nam Hoa Mountains, some 10 miles from the church, then buried in common, shallow graves.

The dead discovered along the creek all had been among those men marched away from the Cathedral.

Don Oberdorfer, author of the book "Tet!: The Turning Point of the Vietnam War," spent five days in late 1969 with Paul Vogle, an American English professor at Hue University, interviewing several people in Hue who had witnessed the NVA and VC occupation.

Oberdorfer classified all the killings into two categories: the planned execution of government officials and their families, political and civil servants, and collaborators with Americans; and those civilians not connected to the government who tried to avoid questioning, spoke harshly about the occupation, or who were believed to have "a bad attitude" about the Communists.

Oberdorfer reported that in the Phu Cam district, virtually every able-bodied man over the age of 15 who took refuge in the Catholic Cathedral ended up taken away and killed. Oberdorfer interviewed Ho Ty, a Viet Cong commander who helped with the advance planning to promote a general uprising. Oberdorfer quoted Ty as saying that the Communist Party "was particularly anxious to get those people at Phu Cam.... The Catholics were considered particular enemies of ours."

Part Six: Khe Sanh

(March 29, 1968–April 15, 1968)

o o o o o o o o o o o o o o o o o o o o o o o o o o o o o o o o o o

"Khe Sanh Combat Base, site of the most famous siege (and one of the most controversial battles) of the American Vietnam War, [today] sits silently on a barren plateau surrounded by vegetation-covered hills often obscured by mist and fog. It is hard to imagine as you stand in this peaceful, verdant land that in this very place in early 1968 took place the bloodiest battle of the Vietnam War.... But little things help you picture what the history books say happened here. The outline of the airfield remains distinct (to this day nothing will grow on it). In places, the ground is literally carpeted with bullets and rusting shell casings."

Robert Storey and Daniel Robinson
Vietnam, A Lonely Planet
Travel Survival Guide

Chapter 28
We fly into Khe Sanh

The clouds hung low in the western sky as our helicopters neared Khe Sanh. Our pilots strained to see their way through the pea-soup fog.

Then, all at once, there was Khe Sanh. We could see the Marine base through a break in the fog. The pilots brought their Hueys closer to the ground as we neared the landing strip.

As we skimmed over the ground, we could see all those NVA diggings we had heard about—the complex of tunnels and trenches carved out of the red earth by North Vietnamese soldiers. We also could see the craters and the pock marks that had been left by B-52 bombing strikes and U.S. Marine artillery barrages. The red craters resembled Mars; everything had been destroyed, and there wasn't a tree to be seen. It was incredible to think about what must have gone on here as the U.S. Marines hunkered down and had to sit tight as NVA soldiers carved into the clay, creating their tunnels and trenches, at least a few of them nearly reaching the perimeter of the Khe Sanh base.

Late in March of 1968, the First Air Cavalry Division had launched Operation Pegasus to help relieve some 3,500 Marines and 2,100 ARVN troops surrounded and under siege by some 20,000 NVA troops at this garrison just below the DMZ at the extreme northwestern edge of the country. I had first mentioned Khe Sanh on March 10, writing, "We've been reading about the Marines at Khe Sanh, and it seems to be going really bad for them now with NVA within 50 yards of the perimeter. I read someplace where the NVA had fired a rocket that landed just outside the perimeter and it had collapsed the ground into what looked like a freshly dug bunker or a tunnel so now the Marines are walking around with thin rods poking into the ground inside of their perimeter checking for tunnels. It's definitely bad news."

Little did I know that in just weeks, I would be standing inside that perimeter.

On March 25, units of the First Air Cavalry began preliminary reconnaissance for Operation Pegasus. Pegasus had been chosen as the code name for the operation, referring to the mythological flying horse "Pegasus," because elements of the First Cav would be at the heart of the operation.

On March 28, I wrote, "Tomorrow at 10 a.m., we are going to Khe Sanh! Well, not quite Khe Sanh, but we'll be about 10 miles east and south of there. The Third Brigade is supposed to take charge of LZ Stud, which will also be the headquarters for the First Cav's forward command post. I'll be going there with two of our photographers to cover the Third Brigade; Graham will be going with another photographer to cover the rest of the Division. We don't know how tough it'll be, but I'm hoping things will slack off a bit. I doubt Khe Sanh will ever be overrun, and had said that before without realizing the First Cav would be helping to take off the pressure. Right now, the NVA have quieted a bit, but every once in a while they rise up again, so we never really know how effective our Operation Jeb Stuart is.

"This place is really nice," I wrote of LZ Stud. "It's about 15 miles east of Khe Sanh, but we're digging deep bunkers so we're pretty safe for the most part. They've got swimming and showers all around. A river runs through the middle of the camp so we've finally got somewhere to wash again."

On April 8, Specialist Five Fred Fiallos, one of our photographers, and I joined the Third Brigade's Second Battalion, Seventh Cavalry in its move from LZ Stud into Khe Sanh. The pilots of our helicopter brought the craft down on the west end of the Khe Sanh runway, and we scrambled out with our few possessions. We sat down on the reddish clay of the landing strip, and we leaned back against our backpacks. The soil here was dusty. Even with the low cloud cover, there had been no moisture.

We seemed to be sitting in some sort of turnaround and taxiing area for cargo planes so we realized that we might have to move at a moment's notice. We could see the bulk of the base off to our right, to the south, running east and west parallel to the runway. I looked back at the area where we had settled in and noticed a small trench in front of us—not a deep trench, but an impression large enough to hold a couple of people. It was not a moment too soon, as it turned out.

In the distance, through the haze, I could see a C-130 lumbering toward the half-mile-long runway, lining up to land from the east. The four-engine cargo plane settled into its approach with wheels extended, touched down, then rumbled toward us. Suddenly, I heard an explosion as a mortar round hit the runway just a few yards from the plane. For a moment, the pilots lost control of the craft. The plane veered sharply to its left and dropped off the runway. As the pilots fought to regain control, the C-130 headed right toward a First Cav Chinook helicopter that had been unloading some supplies.

Then all I saw was dust—a huge red cloud billowing up, obliterating everything—and all at once, there was the Chinook, its two giant rotors straining to gain altitude, rising up over the C-130 as the huge cargo plane came through the cloud. The plane finally came to a stop when it ran into a three-quarter-ton truck that had been standing in the unloading area. One engine well along the right wing burst into flames, but it was quickly extinguished by base firefighters.

Only total alertness and quick action by the Chinook pilots had averted a major disaster. I had kept the trench in front of us in mind as the C-130 drew closer, but it stopped a safe distance from us. Not that the trench would have saved us from a runaway cargo plane. Anyway, welcome to Khe Sanh.

The two-engine C-123s and the larger four-engine C-130s coming into Khe Sanh to deliver supplies were popular targets for mortar, rocket and artillery rounds. The Marines referred to the cargo planes as "mortar magnets," and safely landing those planes demanded high-level pilot skills.

Because NVA units had surrounded the base and had cut off Route 9, the main road into the garrison, the Marines could not be resupplied by ground. The supplies came by air, most of them from Da Nang, a 30-minute flight away. Fairchild C-123s and Lockheed C-130s delivered almost all of the cargo. Transport crews used speed-offloading techniques to minimize their time on the ground. When weather or hostile fire prevented planes from landing at the airstrip, parachutes and various cargo-extraction systems were used to pull off supplies from planes flying low over the base.

I heard later that one soldier had died on the C-130 that we watched come in and crash. I heard that the soldier had not been strapped in and that he was thrown against a steel piece inside the plane when it ran off the runway and crashed into the truck. However, I was never able to verify that story.

Chapter 29
The NVA soldiers retreat

Fred Fiallos and I walked from the airstrip to the main base area inside Khe Sanh and immediately began scoping out the bunkers left behind by the Marines. The fortress we commandeered was the most incredible bunker I would see during my year in Vietnam. These Marines really knew how to build a solid structure.

The Marines who designed this bunker had carved out a basement of sorts, digging deep into the red clay. The basement appeared to be at least five feet deep in a square shape with all four walls about eight feet long. Then they had constructed a frame using large beams, 6-by-6 timbers, at the corners and across the top, to support the sandbags they would stack over their heads. For additional support, they had placed a fifth upright 6-by-6 timber smack dab at the center of the bunker. They had built solid walls, using two thicknesses of sandbags from the basement up to the roof to form all four walls. They also had placed wooden ammunition boxes filled with red dirt inside the bunker atop all four of the sandbag walls. The heavy beams they used for their ceiling and the lumber on top of those beams supported a roof with so many sandbag layers that I finally quit counting.

The Marines also built what they called "outer blast walls," rows of sandbags outside any door or window opening. The Marines found that these outer blast walls helped keep shrapnel from entering their bunkers and bouncing off inside walls.

After we hauled our meager belongings into the bunker, I took a quick tour along the walls. Atop one of those ammo boxes filled with dirt, I discovered an unopened can of tomato juice. I shook the can. It was full, and I could feel the liquid sloshing around inside. Great, I thought, tomato juice. I hadn't tasted tomato juice in months. I took out my church-key opener, cut into the tin can and took a swig. If you've ever run across leftover spaghetti sauce inside your refrigerator after it has started to sprout green or black bacteria, you can imagine my reaction at the first taste. The tomato juice had turned sour. Though still a liquid, this stuff had been hiding here under the rafters for way too long.

It was understandable that the Marines would construct such elaborate bunkers. North Vietnamese Army soldiers lobbed in mortar, rocket and artillery rounds with great regularity. Major impetus for those incredible bunkers came on February 23 of 1968, when the North Vietnamese launched more than 1,300 artillery rounds into the base at Khe Sanh and its outposts, more than on any previous day of attacks. Almost all of the bunkers at Khe Sanh were reinforced in hopes they could withstand such shelling. Not that it always worked—plenty of Marines died when mortar, rocket or artillery rounds landed directly on top of their bunkers.

The Marines learned to always know the location of the nearest trench or bunker. Some pilots said Khe Sanh from the air looked like a giant ant farm because trenches on the base itself, some up to 6 feet deep, were dug connecting almost all bunkers on the perimeter. The Marines called their network the "trenchway" highway.

One of those trenches proved a potential lifesaver for me the next day. When morning broke, I decided to take my own little tour around the Marine base. I was about halfway through my scouting mission when the first artillery round slammed into the base.

There's no question that these were artillery shells. Soldiers learned early on to recognize incoming mortars, rockets and artillery rounds in an instant. With mortars, you would hear a pop, much like a bottle of champagne being opened, as the round was fired. A few moments later, you would hear a dull thud, a hollow explosion, as the round hit the ground. With rocket rounds, I don't remember so much noticing the report as they were fired, just a very pronounced whistling as they came through the air, then a very solid explosion as they hit the ground. With artillery rounds, you could hear an echo-like report when they were fired, then moments later you would hear the shells whining toward you, then the ear-splitting explosion as they plowed into the ground.

With artillery rounds, you could follow the sound of the shells coming in. I had heard the artillery report, but I just assumed it was a U.S. artillery unit firing, which it almost always was. But when I heard the first shell whine in and explode, I dove into one of the deep trenches the Marines had dug here.

Most of the trenches at Khe Sanh ranged from four to six feet deep, and they were a couple of feet wide. The one protecting me had to be more than six feet deep. I am 6-foot-3 and I could not see out over the top.

I waited. A few moments later, I heard another shell being fired, then followed the sound of the round as it whined in and exploded. I knew the rounds had not landed close to me, but you always worry that the next one might.

About five rounds exploded into the base. Then nothing. I waited a few minutes, then started to worry about something that might be just as deadly as an artillery shell—a venomous king cobra or one of those legendary Khe Sanh rats.

Finally I crawled out of the trench and managed to find my way back to our bunker.

We slept in our bunker at Khe Sanh for eight nights. Operation Pegasus ended on April 15, and we shipped out with a First Air Cav unit leaving the base.

I hadn't heard about the Khe Sanh rats until later—probably a good thing; otherwise, I would have freaked out. We slept on cots in sleeping bags with our usual mosquito netting pulled around us. If there were rats rustling around, they didn't wake us—or bother us.

Not so for many of the Marines. The stories of the Marines and their rats at Khe Sanh became the stuff of legends.

The U.S. Special Forces had been the first to reach Khe Sanh, arriving by truck in 1962. One of the first to settle in was Weapons Specialist Frank Fowler, who complained bitterly about the rat population.

"One time we went into the village and bought some metal rat traps because it was so bad," Fowler said. "We were using mosquito nets on our bunks to keep the rats off. I remember one night there was a big metal rat trap with teeth on it. And I remember the first rat we got. When [the trap] snapped, it woke me up. And then the rat started dragging the thing off!"

The U.S. Marines joined the Special Forces at Khe Sanh in 1966. More outrageous stories of the rat population made their way into military lore. Even the leader of the Marines at the combat base, Colonel Tom Horne, chimed in: "My memory of that place is waking up with 15 or 20 rats on the bed with me!"

In 1967, the year the buildup of soldiers escalated significantly on both sides, a Catholic chaplain told of his first night at the base when a rat lost its footing on the dirt ledge atop the inside wall of his bunker, fell on his chest, and bounced to the floor with a squeal.

Protestant Chaplain Ray Stubbe marveled at how most of the U.S. Marines at Khe Sanh remained calm under the onslaught of mortars, rockets and artillery shells. "It's a modus vivendi," he said. "The men run for shelter, but they don't cringe when they get there." It was the rats, he said, that would become frantic under fire. When incoming rounds landed, the rats would race for the bunkers and wildly run up into the ceilings where they tried to hide in between the sandbags.

One U.S. Marine sergeant at the base claimed he had killed 34 rats. His fellow Marines gave him credit for establishing the base record.

In his book, "Welcome to Vietnam, Macho Man," former U.S. Marine Ernest Spencer provided a vivid description of his experience with rats.

"There were always rats at Khe Sanh," he wrote. "Not your stereotypical Asian variety of chopstick-using rat. Khe Sanh rats are snarling suckers with big heads. Having evolved in a jungle environment, those rats are capable of fighting anything.

"The rats began exerting themselves several breeding cycles into the siege. A rat jumps on my chest one night. On my back on my cot, I slap at him with my left hand while I try to shield my face with my right. He is grinning at me, I swear.

"Rats love the sandbag walls. Since the walls are several layers thick, the rats have a lot of room for their quarters. You can hear them in there screaming, eating, fucking, and kicking each others' asses. Rats are nasty—they are always fighting.

"Rats behave more logically during the siege than we do. They let their feelings out. You can hear them squeaking and going berserk during a barrage. Us macho men just sit there quietly and take it."

By April 8, U.S. forces in Operation Pegasus had retaken Route 9. That, in essence, meant most of the NVA forces had retreated. On April 15, the U.S. Command announced that the operation for the relief of the base had been concluded and all objectives had been met. The siege had lasted 77 days. It would be the longest single battle of the Vietnam War.

U.S. intelligence officers considered Operation Pegasus a major success. They suggested that the operation had caught the NVA units largely by surprise, leaving them very badly beaten. The enemy soldiers were forced to retreat without burying their dead, and they had to leave large numbers of their wounded behind.

In June of 1968, U.S. military leaders announced that Khe Sanh would be abandoned. The Marines proceeded to dismantle the base, ripping open sandbags, blowing up their fortified positions, filling in trench lines with bulldozers, and hauling away everything of possible use to the enemy.

The last Marines left on July 6. It's likely that most of them agreed with Michael Herr, who wrote in "Dispatches," one of the Vietnam War's most celebrated books, "There is no feeling in the world as good as being airborne out of Khe Sanh."

With the U.S. Marines gone, only the rats stayed behind. They would thrive, at least for a time, with no incoming artillery, no soldiers around to set traps or otherwise harass them, and plenty of garbage, food scraps and tomato juice left behind by the Americans. But when they had devoured this food supply, the rats, too, would be forced to take their leave of Khe Sanh.

Chapter 30
A 77-day siege is lifted

The siege of Khe Sanh had begun on January 21.

Early that morning, North Vietnamese gunners had scored a direct hit on the combat base's main ammunition dump. More than 90 percent of the dump's contents, 1,500 tons, went up in smoke in the ensuing secondary explosions. It was the first attack in what would become almost daily artillery, rocket and mortar shelling.

Some 20,000 NVA soldiers surrounding the Marines were under the direct command of General Vo Nguyen Giap, North Vietnam's most famous military leader. Khe Sanh attracted enormous attention in the United States, and the siege would draw obvious comparisons to the 1954 Battle of Dien Bien Phu, a siege that lasted 55 days during the Indochina War. At Dien Bien Phu, a village in northwestern Vietnam near the Laotian and Chinese borders, French military commanders chose to make their stand against the Ho Chi Minh-led Vietminh. But the French ended up being surrounded, then defeated by the North Vietnamese Army. Giap had been the top general in that siege, too, and his triumph there had elevated him to government prominence second only to Ho Chi Minh.

As troops from the First Air Cavalry Division entered Khe Sanh on April 8 of 1968, there were no enemy soldiers in sight, although an occasional mortar, rocket or artillery round still would slam into the Marine base.

One day before we arrived at Khe Sanh, I had written about Third Brigade plans "to secure the base from the Marines so they can push to the surrounding hills and try to clear the area of NVA. Actually, this has been a much easier task than we thought it would be at first. The 1/7th has had most of the contact. Other contact has been light.

"When I think how the Cav has moved around in just three months, helping clean up Hue and now Khe Sanh, it's amazing we have anyone left. The Marines are supposed to be clearing a road [Route 9] into the camp so they can receive some supplies by road convoy rather than getting all of their supplies by air."

An article in the Friday, April 12, 1968, edition of *Time Magazine* provided an excellent overview of the First Air Cavalry's role in relieving the siege.

"Operation Pegasus [was conducted] under the command of Major General John J. Tolson, 53, commander of the 1st Cavalry Division (Airmobile) in Viet Nam," the magazine reported. "It was launched from Landing Zone Stud in the Khe Sui Soi river valley 11 miles northeast of Khe Sanh; its first task was to open Route 9, which had been in enemy hands since last August. Its overall goal: to create a ground supply line to Khe Sanh and to destroy the enemy around the Marine camp. To do the job, Tolson had 19,000 of his own Air Cavalrymen with their nearly 300 helicopters and 148 heliborne artillery pieces, plus 10,000 U.S. Marines and three battalions of the South Vietnamese Army.

"While the Air Cavalrymen leapfrogged ahead to seize high ground and set up artillery protection, the Marines marched on either side of Route 9 and straight down the potholed road itself, clearing mines and repairing bridges. Accompanied by M48 tanks and truckloads of ammunition, rations and bridge girders, they marched toward Khe Sanh.

"Overhead, five-string formations of Huey helicopters carried the Air Cavalrymen, giant Chinook choppers hauled slings of artillery, and Flying Cranes brought in bulldozers. When the lead units of Pegasus were within a mile of Khe Sanh's perimeter, they halted to let the Air Cav's rocket-firing helicopters pound away at North Vietnamese gunners still dug into surrounding hills. Once the guns were silenced, Air Cavalrymen were lifted in to seize the high ground around the base. But the Marines inside Khe Sanh drew first blood in that mission. Breaking out of their own perimeter for the first time since the siege began, they stormed and took Hill 471, two miles from their base."

After four days of tough fighting, soldiers from the Third Brigade's Second Battalion, Seventh Cavalry reached Khe Sanh to take over the defense of the battered base. At about 8 a.m. on April 8, Private First Class Juan Fordoni, from Puerto Rico, reached out over the barbed wire to clasp hands with a Marine lance corporal. Other Skytroopers were right behind him. Some erected signs on the base that read, "Under New Management, compliments of the First Air Cav."

First Air Cav soldiers fanned out to clear Khe Sanh's perimeter of any remaining NVA soldiers, jumping into trenches dug out and stocked with supplies by the enemy during the 11-week siege. A battalion of South Vietnamese Rangers, helping in the sweep just outside the perimeter, discovered NVA trench and bunker complexes extending right up to the concertina wire surrounding the base.

The first meeting to plan Operation Pegasus had occurred early in January. That conclave included Tolson, General Robert E. Cushman Jr., III MAF commander, and General Creighton Abrams, MACV deputy commander. But then the North Vietnamese launched their Tet offensive and the Battle of Hue forced everything to be put on hold.

Operation Pegasus finally began on April 1.

On that day, pilots from the First Cav's First Squadron, Ninth Cavalry found themselves socked in by a heavy morning fog. But when the midday sun burned off that fog, the helicopter pilots finally were able to move out and begin their reconnaissance operations. The pilots proved to be very effective in pinpointing and destroying NVA anti-aircraft positions, a major plus for Pegasus. While the pilots kept NVA soldiers occupied, First Cav engineers were able to construct an airstrip at LZ Stud, which would serve as the division's forward command post.

North Vietnamese gunners shelled LZ Stud once. They also shelled LZ Tom, a Second Brigade fire base, once. At both bases, Skytroopers spotted small groups of enemy soldiers, thought to be forward observer parties, as the artillery rounds were coming in. First Cav units fired back and ripped up these enemy soldiers, who were dug in on nearby hills. Neither LZ Stud nor LZ Tom would be shelled again during Pegasus.

When Operation Pegasus ended on April 15, U.S. Army forces had suffered 315 casualties, including 59 soldiers killed and five missing in action. The cost to the NVA was at least 1,300 killed. At Khe Sanh and surrounding bases of operation, some 1,000 U.S. Marines and 750 South Vietnamese soldiers had lost their lives during the 77-day siege.

Some military leaders estimated that at least 12,000 North Vietnamese Army soldiers had been killed during the siege, including thousands wiped out by U.S. bombing missions. U.S. and South Vietnamese soldiers on patrol around Khe Sanh discovered hundreds of shallow NVA graves. They also found hundreds of NVA bodies lying scattered right where they fell.

Two of the North Vietnamese divisions in the siege had been all but annihilated. The 304th and 325th NVA Divisions were driven back so quickly that they had been unable to bring along their supplies and equipment in their retreat.

There had been contact every day of the operation, much of it heavy. Whenever the First Cav soldiers drove back NVA units, they were amazed at the weapons and equipment they found as they scoured the battlefield. Elements of the First Cav turned up many large enemy supply caches every day of the fighting. One cache discovered by the First Brigade contained 50,000 rounds of AK-47 ammunition and 1,600 mortar rounds.

Under normal conditions, North Vietnamese soldiers rarely left anything behind, not even a rifle bullet. But in their haste to flee the First Cav, they left piles of valuable equipment. In one sweep of the area, Skytroopers discovered 182 rockets and mortars, 260,000 rounds of small-arms ammunition, 13,000 rounds of larger-caliber ammunition and 8,700 hand grenades and mines. Several hundred North Vietnamese even discarded their AK-47 rifles as they ran, violating one of the most basic principles of war—that a soldier never gives up his weapon even in retreat. Whether shell-shocked, battle weary, or just plain terrified, the fleeing North Vietnamese soldiers had been forced to leave all of this behind.

Operation Pegasus marked the first time that First Cav soldiers had fought within range of enemy tube artillery. But the duel of the batteries turned out to be very one-sided. The First Cav's artillery batteries pumped out an incredible volume of shells, and the division's Chinooks, from the 228th Assault Support Team, kept hauling in the ammunition—an incredible 500 tons of artillery shells every day.

When the First Air Cav began Operation Pegasus, there had been many unknowns. NVA soldiers were well dug in around the Marine base, and no one knew for sure what they might be planning. Just two weeks later, the Skytroopers had assaulted into the area, had linked up with the Marines at the garrison, had helped reopen Route 9, and had helped chase a most formidable enemy out of the area.

On the day following the end of Operation Pegasus, many First Cav soldiers were told they now would be air-assaulted into the A Shau Valley, a region extending 22 miles between two mountains in I Corps just six miles from Laos. The code name for the campaign in the A Shau, also known as the Valley of Death, would be Operation Delaware.

The A Shau Valley was another suspected hotbed for North Vietnamese Army soldiers, and the air-assault made perfect sense. The First Cav's work at Khe Sanh was done. The siege had been lifted.

Part Seven: The World

(May 31, 1968–July 15, 1968)

o o o o o o o o o o o o o o o o o o o o o o o o o o o o o o o o o o

"I was that which others cared not to be. I went where others feared to go and did what others failed to do. I asked nothing from those who gave nothing. And, reluctantly, accepted the thought of eternal loneliness—should I fail. I have seen the face of terror, felt the chill of fear, warmed to the touch of love. I have hoped, pained, cried. But, foremost, lived in times others would say best forgotten. At the very least, in later days, I will be able to say with greatest pride, that I was indeed a Soldier."

George L. Skypeck
173rd Airborne Brigade
Dak To

Chapter 31
Visiting Hawaii for R&R

Kay and I planned to meet in Hawaii during May for Rest and Relaxation (R&R).

We purposely had delayed our R&R until later in my tour. I hated the idea of going to Hawaii halfway through my year in Vietnam, as many of our troops did, and having to return for six more months. I wanted to return to Vietnam "short," with just a few weeks left before I could again touch U.S. soil.

Also, Kay was pregnant with our first child, and she hoped she would have the baby before meeting me in Hawaii.

Because of the pregnancy, I had set up our trip to Hawaii for the middle of May. Our son, Christopher Michael, was born on April 4, 1968. Kay endured 32 hours of labor, a record for our family, and one that we don't care to see broken. The doctors said Christopher "came breech," which means that the baby's bottom chooses to emerge first. I had never heard the term before. Obviously, after 32 hours of labor, Kay needed some rest and relaxation of her own.

As we neared the date of our R&R, both the U.S. Army and the North Vietnamese Army seemed to be plotting against us.

First, the Army informed us that the date for our R&R had been moved back. Now, instead of May 15, we were scheduled to arrive in Hawaii on May 31. I was in Khe Sanh when we were trying to reschedule and there was no way I could get back to headquarters to make any changes. This meant that Kay had to call to change her flight plans and our hotel reservations.

Second, on May 19, a couple of weeks before I was scheduled to leave Camp Evans to begin my journey to Hawaii, North Vietnamese soldiers decided to fire a couple of 122mm rockets into our base.

The first rocket slammed into the Camp Evans ammo dump, and the second hit a diesel fuel bladder. The midnight sky filled with black smoke. The secondary explosions would keep us up the rest of the night.

Four of us had been sleeping in our Third Brigade PIO tent, and all of us rolled off of our cots in a flash, slid across our wood floor and dove headfirst into the bunker abutting our tent. We had cut out a corner of our wooden floor so we would be able to slide right into our bunker without leaving the tent. All four of us sat in the bunker, shivering each time the ground trembled from another explosion.

Finally, we decided we needed to find a bigger bunker to protect us. All of us scrambled out of our bunker, dashed out the door of our tent and did a hands-and-knees crawl to a tent next-door to ours. We knew soldiers in the neighboring tent, and we knew they had constructed a large and very solid bunker.

When we reached our destination, still hugging the ground, we looked up at several soldiers standing near the tent-flap opening. I remember vividly that at least a couple of them just started laughing at us.

As it turned out, only the first couple of explosions had been from incoming NVA rounds. The rest had been from our own ammunition going off after the direct hit there. The soldiers laughing at us had been standing outside their own tent, watching the fireworks as our ammunition cooked off in the ammo dump.

We had located our Third Brigade PIO tent quite some distance from the division PIO tent. We liked it that way because we were away from most of the officers, no one harassed us, and we enjoyed staying close to soldiers in the Third Brigade. The division PIO tent stood much closer to the ammo dump, and on this night we were thankful we had decided to dig in some distance away.

Soldiers closer to the ammo dump were just as terrified as we were.

"I remember sitting on the floor of our bunker and feeling the vibration in my butt as each explosion rocked the compound," one soldier said. "Pallets of eight-inch powder bags were exploding all at once, and when the things would go off, I could feel the ground shake against my ass before the concussion invaded the bunker. The roof seemed to lift up with each explosion and dirt would fall all over the place. I was never so damned scared in all my life as I was that night."

The NVA rockets also wiped out some of the First Cav's helicopters. Shrapnel ripped through a number of the engines and rotors, making the machines unflyable. No helicopters would be available to fly until they could be repaired during the next few days.

Someone suggested that the NVA soldiers had launched their rockets to celebrate the birthday of Ho Chi Minh, who had been born on May 19, 1890. The NVA certainly celebrated. One First Cav soldier later talked about watching a fireball that rose several thousand feet into the air when the 6,000-

gallon fuel bladder erupted. "Someone told me later that the fireball topped out at 15,000 feet and was quite beautiful," the soldier said. "From underneath, it certainly was spectacular—multicolors, with stuff flying out in all directions. I admired it for a time, then the old brain turns over once. It says to me, 'Everything that goes up must come down. Get under something.'"

The soldiers who had to fight the fires weren't quite so admiring.

"We had to put on protective masks to keep from being burned," said Sergeant Warren Carlstadt, who headed the Camp Evans Crash and Rescue Team. Parking their truck a safe distance from the flames, a four-man team began hosing down the conflagration that resulted from the rocket hit on the fuel bladder.

"Luckily, no one was hurt," Carlstadt said. "The flames climbed to skyscraper height."

The four-man team from Headquarters Company, 11th Aviation Group, fought steadily to put the fire down until their truck ran low on water. "Our truck holds 400 gallons of water and 40 gallons of foam concentrate, which mixes with water for these types of fires," Carlstadt said. "It only took 10 minutes to empty, and we headed for the water point for more water."

When the four men returned, they found additional help—a tractor and trailer water truck. After fighting the blaze for a solid two hours, they finally tamed the fire.

Once I managed to climb aboard the jet that would bring me to Hawaii, everything went like clockwork.

I believe I slept during much of the flight. All I remember is that as we neared Honolulu International Airport, the pilot came on the intercom to say, "We're starting our final descent, and we will be landing in 15 minutes. The temperature in Honolulu is 80 degrees. Aloha."

I don't recall exactly where our jet ended up at the airport, but I do remember we had to board a bus to ride from the taxi area to Fort De Russy at one end of Oahu. That's where the wives and girlfriends were waiting. The room was filled with the women anxious for their men to climb off the bus. Kay said she knew I would be the last one off. I was. I'm usually pretty laid back, and I'm not usually big on rushing to get off of boats, buses or airplanes.

Kay also said she was shocked at how red my hair had become—she prefers blonds—and at how dry it had become. I've thought since that maybe in Vietnam I had immersed myself in some Agent Orange, but just didn't realize it.

Kay had changed our hotel one more time. The hotel she had reserved had been very unimpressive, she said, and she wanted everything to be nice for us. She appreciated our very special R&R rate, but she said the "pool-level" room had an odor of mildew, it seemed very humid, even damp, and it featured avocado-colored walls.

The clincher came when Kay walked into the room and spotted a fat little lizard climbing up one of the walls. The lizard closed its paper-thin eyelids over its bulbous eyes and froze in position. The reptile blended quite nicely with the avocado wall, but Kay was not impressed. The bellboy who had brought Kay to the room walked over, grabbed the lizard and plucked it off the wall; Kay returned to the front desk and got her money back.

We ended up in an extremely nice hotel, settling into a room on a higher floor, one with a balcony that overlooked the surf off Diamond Head.

We spent our first couple of days relaxing on the beach. We also visited some of the shops and ate a couple of meals in restaurants along the Ala Moana Center, advertised as the world's largest outdoor shopping mall. We knew we wanted to experience some of the usual Oahu activities such as swimming, shopping, touring Pearl Harbor, and spending an evening with Don Ho, but we had a whole week.

I do remember participating in a luau—I believe it was at twilight on our second day. We marveled at the show the Hawaiian people put on. Obviously they were paid to perform hula dances, to serve drinks and to make sure each of us had a taste of the various foods—a roasted pig, baked bananas, coconut meat, pineapples and poi. I had never tasted poi before, and I have not tasted it since. To me, it tasted much like the homemade paste our country school teacher stirred up for our creative paper projects.

I remember enjoying our evening much more a few nights later when we sat in Duke Kahanamoku's Club at the International Market Place in Waikiki listening to Don Ho sing "Tiny Bubbles." I remember both of us sipping on Mai Tai cocktails, made with Bacardi rum poured over crushed ice and topped off with colorful straws and miniature, brightly colored umbrellas.

On our second day in Hawaii, we had signed up for an all-day tour of the islands, which we would take a couple of days later. Touring in the smaller two-engine plane would allow us to see several islands, including Kauai, Maui and the Big Island. Obviously we would be subjected to a number of takeoffs and landings.

I especially wanted to visit Kauai, the island where Rodney Oshiro, one of my roommates at the University of Minnesota, had grown up. I knew he would not be there, of course, but I wanted to see what this island looked like. Oshiro had described it to us as a Garden of Eden.

During our time at the University of Minnesota, Oshiro had told me of his father, who fought on our side during World War II against the Japanese. Following the bombing of Pearl Harbor on December 7, 1941, many Japanese Americans found themselves facing incredible animosity, in most cases pure vitriol. When the U.S. government agreed to allow some people of Japanese ancestry to join special fighting units, Oshiro's father stepped forward. He had enlisted with a special segregated unit, the all-Japanese 442nd Regimental Combat Team, and he had been killed in combat.

Oshiro also had told me on one occasion to grab my ear with my fingers if I unexpectedly touched anything too hot. It's strange how we develop these habits, but this one has always worked for me. Even today, when I burn my fingers on something, I grab my ear lobe. It's much like a habit I developed in Vietnam. Another soldier told me that before you put on your combat boots, you should turn them upside down and shake them—you never know what might be lurking inside. To this day, before I slip my shoes on, I shake them to make sure there's nothing unsavory inside.

On the morning we were scheduled to board our Hawaiian Islands tour plane, we ordered room service for breakfast. I don't know why, but I decided to enjoy a large meal. I had heard somewhere that you shouldn't fly on an empty stomach so I dined on eggs, toast, pancakes and a slab of ham—all washed down with plenty of coffee and orange juice.

It didn't take long for me to realize my breakfast menu had been a huge mistake. Shortly after taking off from Oahu on our way to the first island, my stomach began to churn. I had been pointing our camera out one window, trying to take photos of Hawaiian scenery, photos that would be partially obscured by the wing of the plane. The small plane started to bounce a bit as it passed through air turbulence, and, suddenly, I turned to Kay and said I couldn't take any more pictures. I was feeling deathly ill.

I filled the first vomit bag in short order. Kay also began feeling sick, and she, too, deposited part of her breakfast. But I was by far the worst.

Before it was over, all the other passengers on that little plane, about 10 of them, were passing vomit bags back to us, and I was dreading all the take-offs and landings we would be making before the day was over. I would write to Kay on June 10, after I had returned to Vietnam: "Have you gotten over Hawaii yet? Tonight we had pineapple for dessert and I could barely stand it. Surely no comparison to the fresh, unsweetened type we had in Hawaii. Maybe there's a place at home where we can get fresh pineapple.

"But that plane ride! I guess we won't forget that for awhile. I managed to fly all the way back here without getting sick once. Pretty good, huh? Especially after I filled three of those bags!"

It bothered me that here I was, a First Air Cavalry Division soldier who rode in helicopters nearly every day, and I'm the only one who got sick on a tour of the islands.

During our last days in Hawaii, we visited the USS Arizona Memorial, the final resting place for many of the battleship's 1,177 crew members who lost their lives when Japanese planes attacked Pearl Harbor. The Memorial commemorates the site where World War II began for the United States in the Pacific. It was a sobering experience to think of these U.S. soldiers caught by surprise when the Japanese pilots brought their planes in to destroy and sink the U.S. ships.

We were further sobered—shocked might be more accurate—by the news we heard when we arrived at the airport to catch our return flights.

When we walked into the terminal, we saw the headlines and the newspaper reports of Robert F. Kennedy being shot shortly after midnight on June 5 following his primary win in California over Eugene McCarthy, the former U.S. senator from Minnesota. Up until then, we hadn't been listening to radio or watching television.

Just two months earlier, on the very day our first son had been born, an assassin had shot and killed Dr. Martin Luther King. Now we were being forced to deal with yet one more national tragedy.

My first reaction was, "This can't be happening." Then I remember thinking, "I'm sure he can't be hurt that badly. We can't have another Kennedy assassinated."

The three major television networks, CBS, NBC and ABC, all had begun coverage at the scene only moments after the shooting at the Ambassador Hotel in Los Angeles. The first broadcast included footage of a large crowd of supporters gathered in the ballroom, awaiting Kennedy's address.

A still photograph of Kennedy sprawled on the floor was televised as reporters noted in voice-over that he had been shot by an unknown assailant. About two hours after the shooting, supplemental footage was shown of Kennedy from behind as he earlier had stepped up to the podium, with a crowd around him. Shots were heard, camera angles were jolted in the confusion, but one camera managed to focus on the senator lying injured on the floor.

Intermittent reports provided updates of Kennedy's medical condition. Reporters at the scene first noted his condition by sight only, saying he had been shot repeatedly but was conscious and had "good color." Those initial reports gave us hope that Kennedy's wounds would not be life-threatening. One physician at the scene said the extent of his injuries was unknown.

But reports that followed sounded more and more somber. On June 6, some 26 hours after the shooting, it was announced that Robert Kennedy had died.

Chapter 32
Digging in for the final days

My last month in Vietnam would be spent in a bunker.

It made me recall what one soldier had said when I first arrived for my tour, that soldiers generally are scared during their first couple of months in country, and they're definitely scared during their last month.

Immediately after returning from Rest and Relaxation in Hawaii, I had gone back into the field with the infantry.

"I'm going back out for four reasons," I wrote on June 10. "First, I want to get rid of any anxieties I might have for the last 30 days over here. Second, the time goes faster when I'm out there—and I know it would drag back here. Third, I want to keep the people back here from messing with me. In the back of my mind, I have the feeling that someone back here might want to harass me. Fourth, I want to get a few last pictures, ones that I haven't taken and ones I might want to have just to remember the guys over here."

I spent about a week in the field, and then returned to my bunker.

Those of us in Third Brigade PIO had paid dearly to have a much larger bunker built next to our tent. We had bribed an engineer who operated a backhoe by giving him a 12-pack of Budweiser. In our PIO office, we really weren't huge beer drinkers anyway, and he carved out a huge hole for us.

But we had never used that large bunker—until I returned from my last foray into the field and finally decided to sleep there. Nesting inside that deep bunker, I could burrow into my sleeping bag atop my canvas cot and pull the mosquito netting all around me.

We had never completed the bunker so it had no roof. I would sleep there at night with the stars twinkling in the sky. Even without a bunker roof, I figured, it would take a direct hit from an NVA rocket or mortar round to get me. I did have visions of a cobra or a python someday falling into my pit, but that never happened, either. Those possibilities—and occasional rains—were my main concerns. When the rains did come, I had to crawl out of the bunker and seek shelter in our PIO tent, where my fellow soldiers still slept.

Sleeping inside the Camp Evans perimeter didn't guarantee safety, of course. One of our PIO members, Sergeant Paul Hughes, who had worked with me at three other First Cav landing zones, suffered a wound while walking along one of the dirt roads inside Camp Evans. An NVA mortar landed near Hughes and a piece of shrapnel caught him in the leg. Winning a Purple Heart that way held no allure for me.

While I tried to lay low during my last days in country, not everyone else always cooperated.

During my final weeks, General William Westmoreland, commander-in-chief of U.S. forces in Vietnam, decided to visit First Cav headquarters. The general would spend a day at Camp Evans, shake hands with some of the top brass and present medals to a number of division soldiers. I planned to attend the ceremonies, and we scheduled a couple of PIO photographers to record the event.

The day before Westmoreland arrived, a top Third Brigade sergeant summoned me to his tent. He would be in the receiving line to shake hands when the four-star general reviewed the troops, he said.

"I'd like you to take my camera and get a couple of shots when he shakes my hand," the first sergeant said. He handed me his Polaroid.

I had not used a Polaroid since my days at Letterman General Hospital, but I figured I could handle the assignment. When the general grabbed the first sergeant's hand, I took one picture, cranked out the print, then shot one more. When the Polaroid prints began to develop, I realized I had a problem. With a four-star general standing in front of me, I knew my hands had been shaking, but I didn't realize how much. Both of my photos had captured the first sergeant and General Westmoreland from their necks down. I had cropped off their heads completely.

After the ceremonies, and after everyone else had left, I showed the photos to the sergeant. You could see the blood rise in his face, beginning at his neck and quickly moving up to the top of his sunburned head. I don't remember ever seeing anyone so totally furious. He threatened to send me "to the infantry," even while I was apologizing profusely, with tears welling in my eyes, as I recall, and trying to explain how I had missed the shot he wanted.

Such a scenario, being sent to the infantry, actually had happened just a few weeks earlier to a friend of ours, a very likable second lieutenant who often joined us evenings to play bridge or hearts. The second lieutenant, who had spent several weeks in a desk job at Camp Evans, received orders to join one of the First Cav's infantry units. Just a couple of weeks later, we received word that he had been seriously wounded in a firefight. An Army chaplain, also a friend who often played cards with us, went to visit the second lieutenant in the hospital, and he returned to tell us, "I talked with him, but he's not good. I don't think he's going to make it." A few days later, we heard that our friend had died.

I no longer remember the top sergeant's name—if I ever did know it. But to this day, it strikes me that even though I was "short," I was about one mistake away from walking point for an infantry company.

General Westmoreland certainly had more important business at Camp Evans. He awarded medals to some of the real heroes in the First Cav.

One of them, First Lieutenant Thomas M. Lutchendorf, received the Distinguished Service Cross, the nation's second highest award for valor.

Lutchendorf, with Delta Company of the First Cav's Second Battalion, Seventh Cavalry had flown in on the first wave of an air-assault into a one-ship landing zone near Phan Thiet. The fourth helicopter that came in crashed, leaving 18 men stranded on a 906-meter-high hill. As the men scrambled for cover, automatic weapons opened up on them from NVA positions on two sides of the LZ. Punji stakes lined the other two sides of the LZ.

While the First Cav soldiers worked their way over the side of the hill, Lutchendorf remained behind to direct air strikes, aerial rocket artillery and gunships on top of the enemy positions. "He exposed himself to the heavy gunfire as he hurled grenades at the NVA and threw smoke grenades to mark friendly positions," his citation read.

"There were eight enemy bunkers," Lutchendorf said after he had received his medal, "and all had automatic weapons positions. I had the men attack with hand grenades, but we knocked out only one bunker."

After scrambling down the side of the hill, the platoon was hit by an enemy mortar barrage. Lutchendorf continued to crawl among his men, aiding the wounded. Lutchendorf suffered two wounds himself—a nick in the leg and a bullet that went through his left arm as he was dragging another wounded man to cover.

Napalm bombs and ARA strikes directed by Lutchendorf wiped out a number of enemy fortified positions. As darkness approached, he helped form a perimeter, then returned to throw more grenades at the bunkers. He called in a final air strike only 10 feet from himself.

During the night, Lutchendorf maintained radio contact with 2/7th headquarters. He also positioned his men so they could keep pressure on the enemy positions. At dawn, Lutchendorf ordered five men to secure an LZ for the medevac helicopter. The chopper dropped in, picked up the more severely wounded first, and continued to fly until everyone had been evacuated. Lutchendorf was the last man to crawl into the medevac ship. Only six men from the platoon had escaped injury.

When a patrol searched the hilltop the following day, they found that the NVA had fled during the heavy allied bombardment, leaving behind six bodies.

Sergeant Paul James Rock also received a Distinguished Service Cross from General Westmoreland.

Rock had volunteered for a seven-man killer team, a squad that operates at night searching for enemy activity.

With Bravo Company in the First Battalion, 12th Cavalry, Rock and his squad were scouting out an area of enemy activity near Bong Son. Moving toward a small village, the team passed through a sugar cane field and waded knee-deep into a rice paddy. When the team was about 300 meters from the village, the soldiers climbed out of the rice field and began walking on one of the two parallel dikes bordering the paddy.

"We walked about 20 meters on the dike," Rock said. "The point man was right in front of me and I could hardly see him. It was so dark. I had been looking into the ditch between the two dikes, and all of a sudden, I thought I spotted someone in the ditch. The point man must have missed him. I was almost past him." What Rock spotted turned out to be three NVA soldiers. Rock and the NVA soldiers opened fire on each other simultaneously. Rock and the rest of the team dropped to the ground just as a grenade exploded.

Rock, wounded by four enemy bullets and grenade fragments, got up and charged the NVA soldiers, killing one and wounding the other two. After the fight, Rock applied first aid to a wounded comrade, and then stayed back to cover the team's withdrawal.

In presenting the medal, Westmoreland said, "I have pinned on many Distinguished Service Crosses, heard many citations read. This one supports in full measure this award. Sergeant Rock is a combat soldier and an Air Cavalryman of the highest order."

It was the kind of heroism I was going to miss when I left the First Air Cavalry Division.

On June 28, just a couple of weeks before I would leave Vietnam, I wrote of traveling to "Da Nang to get most of the material for a story on the 15th T.C. (Transportation Corps) Battalion. They fix our helicopters.

"Now I just have to get it written before I leave this place. Just a little more than two weeks.

"Da Nang has a real nice U.S.O. Club—milkshakes, hot dogs, even bacon-lettuce-and-tomato sandwiches for the asking. At their mess hall, they have ice in the Kool-Aid, and you can come in any time you're thirsty and get all the Kool-Aid you want! I sort of hated to leave that place." Obviously, soldiers in Da Nang were living better than we were at Camp Evans.

Chapter 33
Finally, back on U.S. soil

One of the greatest fears among U.S. soldiers in Vietnam was to be "short" and have something disastrous happen.

With all of the aircraft coming into and flying out of the airfield at Camp Evans, I certainly had thought of the possibility that two aircraft could collide.

That kind of disaster did occur later in the year, on October 3, 1968. I had returned safely to American soil by then, but when I heard about the crash, I wondered if anyone who had served with me had been on board. I didn't recognize anyone on the list of casualties, but that didn't make the crash any less tragic.

The crash involved a U.S. Air Force C-7A Caribou and a CH-47 Chinook helicopter.

The Air Force pilots had taken off from Camp Evans using the longest runway, Runway 36. The last message from the Caribou pilots was succinct: "Rolling." The official accident report said the plane "was observed to break right prior to reaching the end of the runway."

The Chinook pilots had lifted their helicopter out of nearby Landing Zone Nancy just a few minutes before. The Chinook flew along Highway 1 in a shallow descent. The pilots were making a scheduled daily passenger and mail shuttle and were headed to a helicopter landing pad just east of the centerline of Runway 36.

As the pilots brought their Chinook down toward the landing pad, located about 1,000 feet south of the approach end of the runway, the Air Force pilots continued to bank their C-7A to the right and began gaining altitude.

The Chinook was coming in at about 100 knots. Officials estimated that the C-7A, with climb power, probably had hit about 105 knots.

No one knows exactly what happened, but the two aircraft collided at an altitude of about 1,100 feet. The C-7A pilots had steepened their bank to the right, probably in a last-minute attempt to avoid the collision, but the front of the plane smashed into the rear rotor of the helicopter. The Chinook features two large rotors atop its fuselage, one in front and one in back, and it needs both of them whirling to maintain stability. At least one of the helicopter's gigantic rear rotor blades sliced through the cockpit of the airplane at a downward angle from the top of the co-pilot's windshield to the bottom of the pilot's windshield, destroying all engine controls. The rotor blade killed both pilots instantly.

The accident report filed by the division said that "one of the rotor blades, or debris from the cockpit struck the left propeller of the C-7A. One of the blades was severed from the propeller and passed through both sides of the fuselage of the airplane. The left propeller then separated from the engine and fell to the ground."

The C-7A fell away to the right, went into a steep descent and crashed into the ground outside of the air field. Upon impact, the airplane disintegrated. There was no fire and no explosion, but all passengers on board died.

When the collision occurred, the Chinook lost all of its rear main rotor blades. "Once these blades were broken and distorted by the collision," the accident report said, "they chopped into the top of the helicopter's fuselage before finally separating from the hub. They dislodged two sections of the synchronizer drive shaft, which also fell to the ground."

With the back rotor gone, the front rotor sent the Chinook spinning. With no thrust, the helicopter simply fell out of the sky. It landed nose-first on its top left side, and exploded.

While the Chinook tumbled toward the earth, "the rear rotor mast and pylon separated from the fuselage and landed 150 meters short of the fuselage," according to the accident report. Two soldiers jumped or were thrown out of the helicopter as it went spinning through the air. Both were killed when they hit the ground. All other passengers in the helicopter died when the craft exploded.

Eleven First Cav soldiers had been riding in the helicopter. Thirteen soldiers, including the pilots, perished in the Caribou.

Our fears of such a tragedy made most of us feel uneasy during fixed-wing takeoff until the plane's landing gear had thumped up into the wheel wells and until we were well away from the base.

Many soldiers coming home from Vietnam also had another fear—How would they be treated once they had returned to American soil? Many would find themselves battling "post-Vietnam syndrome" or Posttraumatic Stress Disorder (PTSD) and find themselves plunged into deep depression.

A few years after returning home, I would find myself writing about one soldier whose life had crashed and burned following his return from Vietnam. Wayne Bertilson was a good friend of mine. He also was a shirt-tail relative on my father's side of the family. He was three grades behind me in high school, but he was a gifted baseball player, a pitcher his father once described as throwing "like a rifle." We played together on St. James town teams for a few summers. When I played first base, my gloved hand would be raw after handling his pickoff throws, which had almost as much velocity as his bullets to batters.

Our tours in Vietnam were nearly parallel, although we were at opposite ends of the country—he served with the Ninth Infantry Division in the dangerous Delta region. Bertilson suffered wounds twice in the same leg, and the two wounds left a cross on the outside of his left thigh. They brought him two purple hearts, one presented by Hubert H. Humphrey, the late U.S. senator and vice president from Minnesota. Humphrey wrote Bertilson a letter praising his service to his country. His wounds also brought him a letter early in December of 1967, from Odin Laingen, then Seventh District congressman from Minnesota. Laingen had been visiting Vietnam, and he had run across the 21-year-old soldier in South Vietnam's Third Field Hospital.

Bertilson had written a note thanking the congressman for talking with him. Laingen's response emphasized that the young soldier "shouldn't be thanking us. Rather, we should be thanking you for the fine service you are performing for your country."

While in Vietnam, Bertilson also received some psychological wounds. His first leg wound occurred when his point man stepped on a land mine and some of the shrapnel hit Bertilson. The point man died. Later, while Bertilson was on a week's leave in Thailand, his unit got hit very hard, and several of his best friends were either killed or wounded.

When Bertilson was scheduled to return home on Feb. 24, 1968, five months before I would return, he wrote to his mother that he didn't "want any fuss—no parades or anything like that."

"Well, he didn't have to worry about parades," she said, speaking of the anti-war sentiment that existed then. "There wouldn't be any."

Upon returning home, Bertilson discovered first-hand the unpopularity of the Vietnam War. "He figured he was a hero when he was there," his father said. "But when he came back from Vietnam, people couldn't have cared less."

Bertilson had attended Mankato State University for two years, from 1965 to 1967, before being drafted. When he returned to school after his discharge, the anti-war protests had become intense.

"I think he'd have been a lot better if he hadn't gone back to college right away," his mother said.

The student protests had a great impact upon Bertilson. Though a bright and articulate young man who cared about people, he found himself struggling under the dark cloud of PTSD. He turned to alcohol, to drugs, and to crime. He was convicted of a number of burglaries. When he stole something, his mother said, there seemed little question he would be caught. It was as if he wanted to be caught, "as if he were crying out for help."

Bertilson's family went through incredible agony during the last decade of his life. Said his father, "We cried and we prayed. We prayed and we cried. We sometimes wondered where God was."

I last saw Bertilson in December of 1979. I was managing editor at *The Free Press,* the daily newspaper in Mankato, and he was seeking signatures for a large card he planned to send to the American hostages in Iran. We managed to recognize one another. We spent some time talking about the good old days, and he said he wasn't playing baseball anymore. When we parted, I made a mental note to get back to him for a status report on how he was coming with his personal demons.

In late February of 1980, Bertilson died after he fell down a flight of steps outside his apartment in Mankato. The fall was an accident, the coroner told the Bertilsons. Their son had fractured his skull.

It seemed fitting that at his funeral, his age would be written out to the day—33 years, 3 months, 25 days. It seemed a reflection, somehow, of Bertilson's concern about the American hostages in Iran, and of the daily vigil many U.S. citizens kept during their captivity.

Bertilson's death occurred just as it seemed he might be turning himself around. He was just a few credits from earning his degree in political science, and he had been spending a few weeks as a political science student intern with Blue Earth County. Although he wasn't working at the time of his accident, Bertilson had been excited about his job. "He said he enjoyed it so much," his mother recalled. It was Bertilson's kind of job, his father added. "He loved people. He could work with anyone."

His parents had been excited about his new prospects. They lived in constant hope that the best traits of their son would resurface and become dominant again, so he might ultimately find a better life.

As his father put it, "When you really love someone, it's hard to give up."

My return to the United States would be much different. My expectations were much more modest. I simply wanted my life to be what it had been before I left for Vietnam—to luxuriate in the warmth and comfort and security of being surrounded by family and friends. I certainly expected no parades. Though I had heard of U.S. soldiers being taunted or spat upon when they returned to American soil, I certainly didn't obsess about the prospect.

For the trip home, I rode in a C-123 Caribou to the Vietnam air base at Cam Ranh Bay. Then all of us, soldiers from several different units, climbed aboard a Boeing 707 that would carry us to Tokyo, then on to Seattle. I remember being greeted by real flight attendants, all women, who during our flight would serve us cold sodas, hot coffee and real food.

At Cam Ranh Bay, the pilots taxied the Boeing 707 to the main runway. They applied and held the brakes while they revved the engines. Within moments, the jet began rolling down the runway, pressing all of us back into our seats as the craft gained speed, then lifted off the concrete and climbed into the sky.

I remember looking out the window over the wing and watching the coastline and the South China Sea fall behind us. I recall little about the flight except that, once again, I would sleep during much of it. After refueling in Tokyo, we took off again, and we settled back for the 10-hour trip to Seattle.

I had been dozing when we made our approach into McChord Air Force Base. I don't remember the exact time, but it was Monday, July 15, 1968, and it was pitch black. It must have been early morning. We climbed off the jet at an Air Force terminal and boarded buses that would take us to the Logistics Center. Many of us would be leaving active duty immediately, and we would be processed through Fort Lewis.

This was a homecoming of sorts for me. I had gone through basic training at the Army Training Center at Fort Lewis, and I remember straining my eyes each day through those low-flying Seattle clouds to drink in Mount Rainier. I loved that beautiful, snow-covered landmark, and I honestly believe it helped me survive in Seattle.

I also liked the idea that Fort Lewis, a 70,000-acre site dating from World War I, the product of a $2 million gift from the residents of Pierce County, had been named for Captain Meriwether Lewis, who with William Clark led the Lewis and Clark Expedition of 1804 to 1806, which sought a Northwest Passage to the Pacific Ocean. The role of Fort Lewis as a processing center for soldiers traveling to and from southeast Asia would end in 1972, and it became home to the U.S. Army's Ninth Infantry Division.

At Fort Lewis, we would be fitted for new dress uniforms, be served a breakfast of steak and eggs, be offered showers after our long flight home, and fill out all the necessary paperwork to be released from active duty—with no requirement to serve in the U.S. Army Reserves.

When we had finished the paperwork, our new uniforms were ready for us. I remember looking at the shirt and realizing that my First Air Cav patch was no longer on my left shoulder; now it was on my right. That switch symbolized a soldier who had served in combat and had returned home. That dress uniform—and the patch—still hangs in my closet today.

A group of us boarded a bus bound for Sea-Tac Airport, where we would spend a few hours waiting for our final flights. Minneapolis-St. Paul International Airport then served as the hub for Northwest Airlines so I would board one of their 727s for the final leg home.

I remember my wife and my parents meeting me in Minneapolis. This was long before two airliners had been commandeered and flown into the twin towers of the World Trade Center so there was no heightened security. They were able to come right to the gate. My most vivid recollection is of Kay running to me and of us standing there for several minutes just holding on to one another. I also remember looking up and seeing my mother, and standing beside her, my father holding my son. My father had this special look on his face, a look of total pride—not in me, but in his grandson. Even at three months, the two of them had developed a special bond, a special bond they never lost.

My next few weeks would be spent looking for a job as a newspaper reporter. I finally settled on a job as regional editor for *The Sentinel,* a daily newspaper in Fairmont, Minnesota. The pay would be $150 a week. In nine months, I would move on to *The Free Press* in Mankato, Minn., the newspaper where one day I would become the top editor.

During my trip home, no one harassed me and no one spat upon me. I had heard of one soldier in uniform who, while in San Francisco, had been approached by a woman who went out of her way to tell him, "I hope you're not proud of yourself. You're just a murderer." But nothing like that ever happened to me—and I never saw it happen to anyone else.

Even today, my thoughts of Vietnam are positive. I have incredibly fond memories of spending one year in that theater with some incredible people.

My feelings about the Vietnam War mesh exactly with what Michael Norman wrote in his book "These Good Men: Friendships Forged From War"—even though Norman's heroes served in the U.S. Marine Corps and mine served in the First Air Cav.

In recalling his tour in Vietnam, Norman wrote:

"I did not pick these men. They were delivered by fate and the U.S. Marine Corps. But I know them in a way I know no other men. I have never since given anyone such trust. They were willing to guard something more precious than my life. They would have carried my reputation, the memory of me. It was part of the bargain we all made, the reason we were so willing to die for one another."

Part Eight: Reflections

o o o o o o o o o o o o o o o o o o o o o o o o o o o o o o o

"Rarely has contemporary crisis journalism turned out, in retrospect, to have veered so widely from reality. Essentially the dominant themes of the words and film from Vietnam ... added up to a portrait of defeat for the allies. Historians, on the contrary, have concluded that the Tet offensive resulted in a severe military-political setback for Hanoi in the South. To have portrayed such a setback for one side as a defeat for the other—in major crisis abroad—cannot be counted upon as a triumph for American journalism."

Peter Braestrup
"Big Story"

Chapter 34
North Vietnam finally prevails

Most military analysts today say the 1968 Tet offensive proved a major military defeat for the North Vietnamese Army and for the Viet Cong.

During Tet and in the allied campaigns that followed early in 1968, thousands of troops from the North had been killed or captured. Modest estimates placed those numbers at 32,000 killed and 5,800 captured.

Some assessments today say the NVA and the VC had been so damaged during the battles of Tet that leaders in Hanoi would be unable to mount any sustained offensive for the next four years.

Building upon its momentum in finally helping drive enemy forces from Hue, the First Air Cavalry Division, first at Khe Sanh and then in the A Shau Valley, continued to pursue enemy troops, forcing swarms of them to flee back to the North. After many of the battles, First Cav soldiers discovered just how desperate the NVA were to escape—uncharacteristically, the enemy left behind huge quantities of munitions, supplies, and bodies of fallen comrades.

Some NVA and VC soldiers tried valiantly to regain momentum through a series of isolated attacks, but many of these were directed at cities in Vietnam's Delta region. NVA soldiers, armed with rifles and rockets, did launch one more significant attack on Saigon, in May of 1968.

The Communists wanted to maintain their military presence in order to strengthen their position in any peace talks. Initial plans called for formal talks to begin in January 1969. Those talks, scheduled for Paris, would include representatives from the United States, South Vietnam, North Vietnam, and the National Liberation Front (NLF or the Viet Cong).

Those of us in the First Air Cav certainly were aware of the plans for peace talks, even if we were off the mark with some of the details. We heard a lot of discussion about what shape the table would be in Paris. I do understand that where a negotiator sits can strengthen or weaken a position so we weren't surprised when we heard that the table for the talks would be an oval or a circle.

In one of my last notes before leaving Vietnam, dated May 14, 1968, I wrote, "We see by the papers that the Americans and the North Vietnamese have excluded South Vietnam from preliminiary peace talks. Now if all things work out alright, the South Vietnamese probably will force all Americans to leave their country."

I wrote that the Viet Cong would not be in on the negotiations, either. "Most everyone here agrees that it's a wise move. We don't have to recognize the NLF that way."

We would learn later, in June of 1969, that the NLF and its allied organizations had reorganized and renamed itself the Provisional Revolutionary Government of the Republic of South Vietnam (PRG). The PRG would be recognized by Hanoi as the legal government of South Vietnam, and it would be included in the Paris peace talks. I have never understood why the Americans at the peace table allowed that. Nor have I ever understood why the signed peace accord would allow North Vietnamese troops to remain in South Vietnam.

The sides that would try to reach a peace agreement first met in Paris on May 10, 1968. The North Vietnamese delegation was headed by Xuan Thuy. Thuy would remain the official leader of his country's negotiating team throughout the process, although it would be Le Duc Tho, the fifth-ranking member of North Vietnam's ruling Politburo, who would carry most of the clout in hammering out the peace proposal. The U.S. delegation was headed by ambassador-at-large Averell Harriman, although Henry Kissinger ultimately would become the team leader as negotiations proceeded.

The military losses by the North Vietnamese and the Viet Cong during Tet should have provided a scenario for peace talks heavily favoring the United States and the South Vietnamese. However, the real impact of the Tet offensive had been to shock the American public. The stunning images U.S. citizens saw during the military battles caused more and more of them to severely question sending more young men to fight in Vietnam. In the end, U.S. politicians and diplomats negotiated from a position of weakness—they wanted the United States out of Vietnam at all costs.

In his book "The Price of Power: Kissinger in the Nixon White House," Seymour M. Hersh presents a damning portrait of President Richard Nixon and Kissinger fumbling their way through the peace process.

"Kissinger and Nixon would repeatedly claim that the failures in South Vietnam and Cambodia were not their responsibility but the fault of Congress, which had cut off funding for the war," Hersh wrote. "Even the public release of the secret Nixon-Thieu commitments in the spring of 1975, as Saigon fell, failed to provoke a reexamination of the Nixon-Kissinger war strategy. America proved a sore loser in Vietnam, and quickly turned its back not only on its policies but also on its young men who had fought, suffered, and died there.

"In the end, as in the beginning, Nixon and Kissinger remained blind to the human costs of their actions—a further price of power. The dead and maimed in Vietnam and Cambodia—as in Chile, Bangladesh, Biafra, and the Middle East—seemed not to count as the President and his national security advisor battled the Soviet Union, their misconceptions, their political enemies, and each other."

In 1978, I would meet Henry Kissinger during a party at the Georgetown home of Katharine Graham, then the publisher of *The Washington Post.* Most of us were riveted by this man who had negotiated the peace settlement in Vietnam. It was fascinating to listen to the heavily accented basso of the former secretary of State. Little did I realize then that Kissinger may have sold us down the river—and South Vietnam along with us—at the Paris peace table.

The Paris Peace Accords finally were signed on January 27, 1973, by the United States, the Democratic Republic of Vietnam (DRV or North Vietnam), the Republic of Vietnam (RVN or South Vietnam), and the PRG, which still represented indigenous South Vietnamese revolutionaries, primarily the Viet Cong.

The accords ended direct U.S. military involvement in Vietnam and temporarily ended the fighting between north and south. In signing the accords, the United States showed incredible trust in North Vietnam and in the PRG, the new Viet Cong. Today, that trust still amazes me. Most U.S. and South Vietnamese forces had trusted enemy troops during Tet. Mutual cease-fires for Tet had been observed since 1963. By 1968, those cease-fires had become a standard and understood practice. In November of 1967, Viet Cong leaders said they would be observing a seven-day cease-fire for the upcoming Tet holiday. On Jan. 25, just days before launching their Tet offensive, the Viet Cong made a public appeal for all soldiers to observe the Tet cease-fire.

In fairness, U.S. military leaders anticipated that NVA and VC soldiers might violate the truce. But they didn't communicate that concern very well to their front-line troops. General Westmoreland did recall 15 combat battalions from border assignments to reposition them closer to Saigon. U.S. military leaders also persuaded South Vietnamese President Nguyen Van Thieu to reduce the formal Tet cease-fire to 36 hours.

But even with the concern over a possible ceasefire double-cross, virtually half of all South Vietnamese troops remained on leave. That left all ARVN units short of manpower when enemy forces launched their offensive.

In making a mockery of the Tet truce, proposed in the first instance by the Viet Cong and reluctantly agreed to by the allies, the Communists, as U.S. Ambassador Ellsworth Bunker said later, made it highly unlikely that there would ever be a holiday truce again. By demonstrating the strength of their manpower, the flexibility of their communications and command networks and the diversity and depth of their weaponry in the Tet attacks, the Communists also made it highly unlikely, as President Lyndon Johnson all but said, that there would be any bombing pause over North Vietnam.

Even with the Paris Peace Accords signed in 1973, Richard Nixon's declaration of "peace with honor" would hold up only a couple of years. In 1973, with the peace accords signed, the last U.S. troops left Vietnam.

For those who had seen the slaughter of civilians during and after the Battle of Hue, it can only be imagined what fate awaited civilians of South Vietnam following the departure of U.S. forces. As General Westmoreland said about the atrocities in and around Hue, "This was a terrifying indication of what well might occur should the Communists succeed in gaining control of South Vietnam."

An estimated 225,000 South Vietnamese soldiers had died during the war. Historians today say another 65,000 were murdered or shot after the country fell to the North Vietnamese. The Communists forcibly relocated or sent to "reeducation camps" a substantial percentage of South Vietnam's population; large numbers of those people, as many as 250,000, died of disease, starvation, or overwork. Some of these civilians were kept in captivity until 1986. Great numbers of South Vietnamese civilians tried to flee from South Vietnam by venturing into the South China Sea. Many of those died aboard their boats or were lost at sea.

With U.S. soldiers now out of the picture, North Vietnamese leaders, supported by remnants of the Viet Cong, intensified their efforts to overthrow President Thieu and remove what they considered a U.S.-supported puppet-government. Thieu soon resigned. In his farewell speech on April 21, 1975, Thieu accused the United States of betrayal.

Following the signing of the peace accords, North Vietnamese soldiers again filtered into South Vietnam and ultimately took control of the southern provinces. Within two years, North Vietnames forces were in position to capture Saigon and form a government of national unity. In April of 1975, North Vietnamese soldiers moved into Saigon and took control of the city. Those soldiers, under the command of Senior General Van Tien Dung, began their final assault on the evening of April 29, launching a ground attack after a heavy barrage of artillery.

The South Vietnamese forces, commanded by General Nguyen Van Toan, quickly collapsed under the intense assault. By the afternoon of April 30, North Vietnamese troops had captured nearly every important installation within the city, and they had raised the North Vietnamese flag over the Independence Palace. South Vietnam capitulated shortly thereafter, and Saigon would become Ho Chi Minh City.

Chapter 35
This was their finest hour

We have had 40 years to dissect the Vietnam War—and to assess what went wrong for the United States.

The easy answer is that a growing discontent over the war cost this country a military victory.

But analyzing Vietnam becomes much more complicated than that—and there's no consensus even today on what went right and what went wrong.

One of the most extensive analyses of the Vietnam War can be found in a book written by Peter Braestrup, a former U.S. Marine in Korea and a former bureau chief in Saigon for *The Washington Post.* In preparing his 1977 book, "Big Story: How the American Press and Television Reported and Interpreted the Crisis of Tet 1968 in Vietnam and Washington," Braestrup dug into his topic with incredible energy and conducted some amazing research. Braestrup put together a detailed content and photo analysis of both print and television reporting. He read every article published during the Tet battles by three media groupings: the Associated Press and United Press International; the *New York Times* and *The Washington Post*; and *Time* and *Newsweek.* He also viewed video tapes of every newscast from Tet aired by the three major networks: ABC, CBS and NBC.

It's a staggering accomplishment.

In his book, 740 pages of text in two volumes, Braestrup concludes that the American media largely misreported what had occurred during the Tet offensive—to the detriment of the U.S. soldier.

"Essentially," Braestrup wrote, "the dominant themes of the words and film from Vietnam ... added up to a portrait of defeat for the allies. Historians, on the other hand, have concluded that the Tet offensive resulted in a severe military-political setback for Hanoi in the South." In their reporting of the Tet offensive, Braestrup said, "the media tended to leave the shock and confusion of early February, as then perceived, as the final impression of Tet, even after NVA and VC forces had been soundly defeated."

"Drama was perpetuated at the expense of information."

The negative tone of the reports from Vietnam, Braestrup wrote, "added to the distortion of the real situation on the ground in Vietnam."

Some of the misreporting occurred because the majority of war correspondents in the Vietnam theater spent most of their time in or near Saigon. Certainly, some of the more daring reporters, such as battle-hardened Peter Arnett of the Associated Press, spent time with troops in more dangerous areas such as Hue and Khe Sanh. But even for the reporters who ventured into these war zones, these were extraordinary events and not at all what was going on throughout the rest of the country. Further, many of the correspondents lacked any extended experience in warfare. Braestrup estimated that only 40 of 354 print and TV journalists covering the war at the time had seen any real fighting. Their own fears deeply biased their reporting, which suggested that the Communist assault had thrown Vietnam into chaos. So when NVA and VC forces brought Saigon under fire, it was natural that most of those journalists would be alarmed, even confused, and that they would allow their own panic to seep into their reports—often with incomplete or misleading information.

The editors and news directors at home seized on the distorted reporting to question the military's version of events. As Braestrup writes, the Viet Cong insurgency may very well have been in its death throes, just as U.S. military leaders were telling the American people at the time. Yet the press painted a very different picture.

Braestrup concludes that during Tet, the reporting evolved into an extreme case of crisis-journalism. The result was a "portrait of defeat" for the U.S. and South Vietnamese forces because "the special circumstances of Tet impacted to a rare degree on modern American journalism's special susceptibilities and limitations." Such reporting by the U.S. media left the public with an image of U.S. and South Vietnamese forces struggling to survive—an image, for the most part, contrary to what was actually occurring. The reports back in the United States further fueled the antiwar protests, undercut support for the troops in Congress, and eroded President Lyndon Johnson's own confidence in the war effort.

When I think of antiwar protesters, I always think of people such as Jane Fonda, Tom Hayden, Joan Baez, Abbie Hoffman, and, maybe unfairly, Senator John Kerry. I also wonder, could they have been wrong? They would never admit that, of course.

I also think of Walter Cronkite, the longtime CBS news anchor who had become widely known as "the most trusted man in America." Cronkite in 1968 decided the United States and the South Vietnamese could not win the Vietnam War. In fairness, Cronkite made his pronouncement after he had visited South Vietnam and observed war activities for himself. He even visited Hue near the end of the battle there. But, again, what Cronkite saw in Hue was not at all what he would have seen throughout the rest of South Vietnam.

Cronkite's initial words in his famous "Report from Vietnam" on February 27, 1968, showed an incredible misreading of the actual situation in Vietnam.

"Tonight," he said, "back in more familiar surroundings in New York, we'd like to sum up our findings in Vietnam, an analysis that must be speculative, personal, subjective. Who won and who lost in the great Tet offensive against the cities? I'm not sure. The Viet Cong did not win by a knockout, but neither did we. The referees of history may make it a draw. Another standoff may be coming in the big battles expected south of the Demilitarized Zone. Khe Sanh could well fall, with a terrible loss in American lives, prestige and morale, and this is a tragedy of our stubbornness there; but the bastion no longer is a key to the rest of the northern regions, and it is doubtful that the American forces can be defeated across the breadth of the DMZ with any substantial loss of ground. Another standoff. On the political front, past performance gives no confidence that the Vietnamese government can cope with its problems, now compounded by the attack on the cities. It may not fall, it may hold on, but it probably won't show the dynamic qualities demanded of this young nation. Another standoff."

As with the antiwar protesters, I'm sure Cronkite, even today, would never admit he may have been wrong. But his words carried incredible weight. Following Cronkite's editorial report focusing on the Tet offensive, President Johnson reportedly said, "If I've lost Cronkite, I've lost America."

When I think of Walter Cronkite, I also think of his unwavering support for the National Aeronautics and Space Administration (NASA). Cronkite developed incredible expertise on the U.S. space program, and he became one of the most knowledgeable people in the media reporting on NASA. I do wonder, even today, what impact Cronkite might have had on the Vietnam War effort if he had championed U.S. soldiers the same way he championed U.S. astronauts.

But the disillusionment over the war went well beyond Jane Fonda and Walter Cronkite. The erosion of support in Congress and in the White House signalled a propaganda defeat for the United States.

Lost in the confusion was the solid progress of the allied troops. On the battlefield during Tet, the NVA and VC had suffered huge losses. Even in Hue, where battles raged for 26 days, South Vietnamese troops, the U.S. Marines and the First Air Cavalry Division by March 2 had crushed the last pockets of NVA resistance. At Khe Sanh, ARVN troops, the U.S. Marines and the First Cav successfully uprooted a well-entrenched enemy and chased the survivors home.

U. S. and South Vietnamese forces during Tet not only neutralized some powerful North Vietnamese military divisions, they also recorded victories that ultimately would bring significant drops in U.S. casualties—from almost 15,000 in 1968 to 9,414 in 1969 to 4,221 in 1970, by which time the Viet Cong, from many accounts, had almost ceased to exist as a major fighting force in South Vietnam. More and more Vietnamese provinces were seeing new peace and stability. By the end of 1969, an estimated 70 percent of South Vietnam's population had come under government control, compared with 42 percent at the beginning of 1968. In 1970 and 1971, American ambassador Ellsworth Bunker estimated that at least 90 percent of the Vietnamese populace lived in zones free of NVA and VC control.

Although many U.S. reporters in Vietnam missed the mark on what allied soldiers were accomplishing there, I continue to believe that foreign correspondents should be allowed to operate as unfettered as possible, even in war zones. U.S. foreign correspondents draw upon the First Amendment to the U.S. Constitution for much of what they report from overseas. I admire the First Amendment. I certainly have used it to my advantage—and I have defended it when necessary.

In journalism classes I teach, I often recite the First Amendment out loud, so the students can better appreciate the words hammered out by the founders of America and finally edited and written by James Madison:

> "Congress shall make no law respecting an establishment of religion, or prohibiting the free exercise thereof; or abridging the freedom of speech, or of the press; or of the right of the people peaceably to assemble, and to petition the government for a redress of grievances."

Five freedoms beautifully detailed in 46 words. It's an incredible document. As American journalists, although we tend to highlight freedom of speech and freedom of the press, we firmly support the First Amendment in its entirety. I would not relinquish any of those freedoms, even though I do recognize that in wartime, some of those rights lay bare the soft underbelly of a democracy.

I know that happened during the Vietnam War. The words guaranteeing "the right of the people peaceably to assemble" and "to petition the government for a redress of grievances" certainly cost our soldiers. The people peaceably assembling, or the war protesters, and the people petitioning for a redress of grievances, or the people lobbying before Congress, ultimately turned the tide of the war.

The Vietnam War offers us important lessons—even beyond the obvious lesson that reporters, editors, news directors and news anchors must strive to cover war activities objectively, fairly and accurately.

Many Americans who have strong feelings about the Vietnam War cling rigidly to their opinions. They do not want to discuss the topic, and they refuse to consider new findings.

My opinion has changed, however. Even during my year in Vietnam, my view evolved. Early in my tour, during August of 1967, I wrote that "the war should end or at least fizzle out within the year." By May of 1968, I was writing that "if things work out alright with the peace talks, the South Vietnamese probably will force all Americans to leave their country," and I was referring to that as a good thing.

I always have believed that we should not have been in Vietnam in the first place. But that's a moot point. We were there. The United States should have given its soldiers everything they needed to prevail. That's a good lesson for our future. When we do send our young people onto the battlefield, we should do it with our full support. First, the cause should be just. Second, we should be fully committed to succeed. That lack of support is why so many soldiers who returned home from Vietnam felt so betrayed by their leaders—and by the American people.

Our soldiers deserve solid support from the generals, from the Congress, from the White House, and from the people. Our soldiers deserve unwavering support from their president, from their generals and from the diplomats negotiating the peace.

How satisfying it must have been for the men in the Royal Air Force to hear Winston Churchill say during World War II: "I look forward confidently to the exploits of our fighter pilots—these splendid men, this brilliant youth—who will have the glory of saving their native land, their island home, and all they love, from the most deadly of all attacks."

Certainly you can argue that the soldiers of Great Britain were fighting for survival. But all soldiers fight for survival.

During my time with the First Air Cavalry Division, I watched U.S. soldiers perform incredible acts of bravery. It would have been so appropriate for someone to praise these soldiers as Churchill had praised his before the House of Commons on June 18, 1940:

"Hitler knows that he will have to break us in this Island or lose the war. If we can stand up to him, all Europe may be free and the life of the world may move forward into broad, sunlit uplands. But if we fail, then the whole world, including the United States, including all that we have known and cared for, will sink into the abyss of a new Dark Age made more sinister, and perhaps more protracted, by the lights of perverted science.

"Let us therefore brace ourselves to our duty, and so bear ourselves that if the British Empire and its Commonwealth last for a thousand years, men will still say, 'This was their finest hour.'"

U.S. soldiers in Vietnam deserved no less.

I found these troops to be well-trained and highly skilled. They displayed tremendous courage under fire. Beyond the battles, many of them spent incredible amounts of time forging friendships with and striving to help the South Vietnamese people. And they sustained all these efforts even when they felt betrayed by their fellow citizens back home.

These young men found themselves in situations where they easily could have folded. But they did not. They refused to wilt even in the face of insurmountable odds, all with the expressed purpose of bringing ultimate peace and freedom to another people in a faraway land. These men displayed a rare blend of bravery, compassion, perseverance and professionalism. It's these decent and courageous warriors who will always be my heroes.

The PIO Players

John Bagwell

"Hey, Bagwell! You're so skinny that if you tried to thread a needle, you'd hang yourself!"

That's the kind of commentary John Bagwell encouraged from his listeners on Armed Forces Vietnam (AFVN) radio.

Bagwell, better known to his First Air Cavalry Division radio audience as "The Scrawny Thing," used his wit, his incredible energy, and what some of his listeners would call his "acid humor" to win a huge audience. Broadcasting out of An Khe, Bagwell became the favorite disc jockey of thousands of American soldiers in the Central Highlands of Vietnam.

The "Hey Bagwell!" jokes perhaps proved the greatest catalyst behind the young announcer's popularity.

"They developed just by accident," Bagwell said. "One of the men here in the Public Information Office and I were doing some promotions and he cut a couple 'Hey, Bagwells!' just for fun. I ran them and it just grew. It wasn't intentional."

Some of Bagwell's listeners didn't like his brand of humor, but most of them did, and everywhere he went, Bagwell was besieged by soldiers yelling, "Hey, Bagwell! Hey, Bagwell!"

When Bagwell reported for one evening of guard duty, another soldier spotted him and ran to the 15th Administration Company mess hall, calling out, "Hey, Bagwell's on guard duty." Enlisted men and officers alike filed from the mess hall to watch as Bagwell stood inspection.

Through it all, he remained the quintessential Bagwell.

"When the inspecting officer stopped in front of me," Bagwell said, "I managed to get the bolt on my rifle open after two or three tries. He looked at my rifle a while, then handed it back to me and went on. After I carefully put my rifle back over my shoulder, the officer looked at me and said, 'You can close your bolt now.'"

During my time at An Khe, I worked on several programs with Bagwell. It was fun duty.

We created one series of humorous broadcasts based upon a character called Chickenman. The Chickenman series had been developed in 1966 by disc jockey Dick Orkin at WCFL Radio in Chicago. The series lampooned the then-popular Batman TV series. I worked at the Presidio in San Francisco in 1966 and 1967, and the series was broadcast in the Bay Area on KSFO Radio by Don Sherwood, who absolutely owned the 6 to 10 a.m. drive-time slot.

In An Khe, we called our hero Ted Turtle. My primary job was to write the scripts. Bagwell and fellow broadcaster Steve Stroub performed the production work for the series. Other members of our PIO crew played the various parts in the script.

When I left the safety of An Khe to join the Third Brigade at Bong Son, the series ended. I don't believe Ted Turtle ever emerged from his shell again.

Before entering the Army, Bagwell, from Ardmore, Okla., attended the University of Oklahoma and worked at the student radio station. He also did spot news reporting for KOMA radio and for United Press International. It was at the University of Oklahoma radio station that Bagwell began developing what became one of his top assets in An Khe, his in-studio engineering skills. His ability to cue up music and ad-lib with ease pulled him through a variety of tight spots.

When he arrived in Vietnam in March of 1967, Bagwell was assigned as a clerk at the First Air Cav's 15th Administration Company.

"They weren't very impressed with me at first," Bagwell remembers. "I get very upset when I enter an airplane. I had been flying for several days when I got to 15th Admin and had just started recovering from the flight to An Khe on a C-130 when I reported for my first day of work."

"'You're Bagwell?' someone asked me. 'Right,' I answered. 'Which way do I go for sick call?'"

Bagwell worked three months at the 15th Administration Company before being transferred to AFVN radio, where he initially went on the air with the late Charge-of-Quarters (CQ) show.

After doing the night show for awhile, Bagwell moved to the Saturday evening slot, then began his morning "Scrawny Thing Happening." During his prime, he had to be at the station by 7:30 a.m. to begin preparing his program. He put on the First Cav news at 8:05, and then he came on the air with his program at 8:15. His show ran to 11 a.m. In the afternoon, he would keep busy as An Khe radio's program director, doing newscasts, preparing audio tapes and "Top 40" surveys, conducting interviews and scheduling programs.

"I don't try to pattern myself or my show after anyone," he said. "Naturally, you pick up different things from different people. My best is being myself.

"I don't consider anything I do difficult. If it was, I wouldn't be able to do it."

During his time at An Khe, Bagwell received some special awards from soldiers at the 15th Administration Co. One of them came in the form of an official certificate of achievement that read: "Bagwell's wit and quick humor and good music make mornings pass by quickly … for all of Camp Radcliff and the broadcasting area of AFVN An Khe."

Bagwell said appreciation such as that gave him his greatest satisfaction.

"This was just their way of saying they enjoyed the show and thought I had a good program. The most satisfying part of the job for me is when somebody says they heard you this morning and you were great. Then you know you're getting across."

Today, Bagwell owns and operates Bagwell Marketing, a full-service advertising, public relations and marketing company based in Dallas, Texas.

LARRY COLLINS

Larry Collins served as an artist and a photographer with the First Air Cavalry at Camp Evans, Phu Bai and Phuoc Vinh. His tour with the First Air Cavalry Public Information Office began in April of 1968. He had arrived in Vietnam in February of 1968 as an infantry soldier with Delta Company of the 5/7th.

Collins created some wonderful artwork for *The Air Cavalry Division* magazine. Donald Graham, who edited that magazine, kept in touch with Collins. A few years ago, while I was in Minot, N.D., working as editor of the *Minot Daily News,* a huge package arrived from Graham. Inside was a large framed reproduction of a Larry Collins photograph. Graham said he had gone to an art show featuring Collins' work and he had purchased three of the framed photographs. Obviously, I felt incredibly honored to be remembered. The photograph sent to me shows our tents, our sandbags, our helicopters and our overhead power lines at Camp Evans. It's titled "Wire Webs," and today it's displayed on my office wall.

On October 8 of 2006, Collins sent another photograph to Graham with the comment, "Here are copies of a picture I took at the pond outside Camp Evans in 1968. I think it was after you left. On the left is Mike Larson, I think. Would you forward this to him?"

It certainly does appear to be me in the photograph, although I had no recollection of swimming in that pond. Then, while researching for this book, I ran across two passages in which I mentioned the pond. On June 19, I wrote, "Some of us went swimming last night in a makeshift pond here—dirty but the best we've got—and fun!" On June 23, I wrote, "We just came back from swimming, but already I'm starting to get sweaty again." So Collins was correct, I was swimming in that pond.

"This was a skinny dipping party we had (and, I think, outside the wire)," Collins wrote in his note to Graham. "Turns out it was in a mine field. I found out when I went to an infantry reunion this summer of Delta 5/7th that one of my comrades was killed there by a mine within months of this picture."

Such an event makes me thank my lucky stars. It reminds me of something Graham wrote to me in June of 2006: "My feeling about the year is the same as yours—since we returned in one piece, it was the best education I ever had. But I was lucky as hell."

Today, Collins owns and operates his own business, Larry Collins Fine Art, located at 145 Commercial St. in Provincetown, Mass.

Richard Conrad

Richard Conrad may have been the purist combat photographer I worked with during my year in Vietnam. He certainly was one of the most daring.

He's the only photographer who tried to get into a combat zone with me—and was refused. Usually we would just hop onto a helicopter. There was nowhere Conrad would not go. On one attempt to join the Second Battalion, 12th Cavalry, the helicopter pilots told us they couldn't fly us out. The landing zone out there was too hot, one pilot said, and he had drawn fire from enemy soldiers when he lifted out of that LZ. That was during the Battle of Hue, and the 2/12th was under siege from North Vietnamese soldiers. Thinking back on that incident, Conrad and I probably were fortunate that the pilot used great common sense and declined to bring us into a hot LZ.

My introduction to Conrad came in January 1968 when I moved from Bong Son to Landing Zone Baldy. "I think I'll enjoy myself here," I wrote. "A Specialist Four [Paul] Hughes, who I was with at Bong Son, is here, and so is a Specialist Five [Richard] Conrad, who, although I haven't met him, has so few faults, Graham said, that he doesn't seem human. So they should be good to work with."

Conrad and I traveled together with a number of First Cav units. On one occasion, we were traveling near Thon Que Chu with one of the Seventh Cavalry companies when a young soldier named Anthony Williams rose up to hurl hand grenades at an NVA sniper. Williams threw grenade after grenade, each time yelling, "Fire in the hole!"

Conrad and I each snapped several photos. When we returned to base, we began editing our negatives, which had been developed in a common darkroom. We began debating over one specific frame on a strip of negatives, which had captured a grenade just leaving Williams' hand.

We sat down and reconstructed the scene, actually diagramming our positions when we had been shooting the pictures. I had been shooting from one side, and Conrad was shooting from a different angle. Conrad finally realized that it had to be my photo, and he graciously said so.

Without question, I considered Conrad not only one of the finest and most daring photographers I worked with during my tour—but also one of the classiest.

Herb Denton

Herb Denton died on April 29, 1989.

Born on July 10, 1943, in Muncie, Ind., Denton grew up in Little Rock, Ark. He attended public schools there and completed his secondary education at the Windsor Mountain School in Lenox, Mass.

He attended Harvard College. There he worked in the college library to help pay his way, and he served on the editorial board of the *Crimson*, the student newspaper. Donald Graham was president of the *Crimson* during that same time and the two of them became best friends. Denton graduated cum laude in 1965 with a bachelor's degree in American history.

Denton joined *The Washington Post* in April of 1966. A few months later, he was drafted into the Army. During his service with the First Air Cavalry in Vietnam as a public information specialist, he received the Bronze Star for Meritorious Service.

He returned to *The Washington Post* as a reporter in 1968. In 1974, he was named assistant Maryland editor, and in 1976, he became District editor.

Denton joined the *Post's* national staff in 1980, where he covered urban affairs and state and local government. He also helped cover activities at the White House.

In January of 1983, he was sent to Lebanon, and he reported from there for two years. Then he opened the *Post's* bureau in Toronto, where he was working at the time of his death. He was an honorary member of the Museum Guild of Toronto.

Survivors included his mother, Lucille D. Denton of Little Rock; a brother, Stanley, of Pittsburgh, and a sister, Jacquelyn Alton of Houston.

In 1980, when my wife and I visited Washington, D.C., with two of our children, Christopher and David, Herb Denton became our tour guide. He brought us to several of the many tourist attractions in Washington, D.C., and its suburbs. It stunned me a bit on this visit when he first greeted me with, "Hi, Mike." Denton had never called me Mike. During our entire year together in Vietnam, he always called me "Larson." I considered him a close friend, but it was always "Larson."

During our visit to Washington, he also bought me a book featuring the artwork of Pablo Picasso. "I want to do this for you," he said. He knew I loved art and that I tried to create artwork of my own. I still have the book. Inside the cover is my inscription: "Nov. 1, 1980. From Herb Denton."

A booklet put together for Herb Denton's funeral included some of his best writing from the *Post*. In that same booklet, Juan Williams, the FOX News political analyst who was then writing for the *Post,* commented, "There are all kinds of ways to deal with being a black man in America. My friend and mentor Herbert H. Denton Jr., who died here Saturday, never shouted a mouthful of rhetoric or spent time pointing fingers at whites. He did not condemn the futility of black anger. What he did was to build a potent legacy—a generation of black journalists at *The Washington Post.*

"As a reporter he was intense but often felt unappreciated, resented, in fact, as Don Graham's black buddy or treated as an outsider in the glitzy white world of big-time Washington journalism. He wanted to make something happen and saw the opportunity in editing. He made a good enough impression as a reporter to become an editor. He began coaching a group of reporters of all races, but he focused special energy on a few blacks.

"Most frequent was his fierce criticism. Any mistake I made was reason for shouting and threats. He was more critical of me than any white editor. But when my career was threatened once, it was Herb Denton—who by then had left editing and had become a foreign correspondent—who traveled back to this country to defend me.

"What Denton did was to establish black journalists at the *Post* and make a way for black journalists in the future in a way no lawsuits and no rhetoric have ever approached. And in the process he increased the newspaper's awareness of black Washington. This is his legacy, and it puts him among the legends of journalism."

Fred Fiallos

Fred Fiallos worked with me in a couple of locations, including Camp Evans.

From Honduras, Fiallos possessed a wonderful disposition, and he was a great companion in the field. In addition to shooting some superb photographs, he also wrote a few stories for the *Cavalair*.

Fiallos always seemed calm and collected. The only time I saw him exasperated was when a fellow photographer, Steve Robinson, mispronounced his name. Fiallos' name was pronounced "Fee-Eye-Ohs." Without fail, Robinson would call him "Free-All-Eez." Fiallos tried to correct him virtually every time he heard his name mispronounced, but Robinson never did get it right.

Fiallos won our hearts during the middle of his tour when he took his Rest and Relaxation trip to Tokyo. Before he left, Fiallos asked if any of us wanted him to pick up camera equipment for us. I piped right up that I wanted to buy a good camera that I could use when I returned to the United States. I gave Fiallos the money he estimated it would cost. From Tokyo, he mailed out an Asahi Pentax camera and a leather camera bag filled with all the extra lenses and accessories I would need. I use that camera to this day.

I did feel concern when a U.S. Air Force C-7A Caribou and a CH-47 Chinook helicopter crashed in midair at Camp Evans on October 3, 1968. I figured Fiallos would have been leaving Vietnam about that time, and I was relieved when I didn't recognize any names on the list of casualties.

I haven't heard from Fiallos since, but I trust he made it back safely to his home in Honduras.

DONALD GRAHAM

For a person of such prominence, Donald Graham maintained what could be called a modest profile.

But a modest profile didn't mean a low profile. During our time in Vietnam, it seemed Graham often was blazing the trail for the rest of us. More than once, Graham would join a unit, then I would replace him when he moved to a new and often more dangerous area.

In 1984, Rudy Maxa wrote an article about Graham, then publisher of *The Washington Post,* for *Gentlemen's Quarterly* magazine. Maxa called me in Mankato, Minn., where I was then managing editor for *The Free Press.*

"I don't think he got any special treatment," I told Maxa, "with the exception of one incident. In the course of a visit, Edward Kennedy made a special request—he wanted to see Don. Here we were out in the field, and we had to come bouncing back in the back of a truck to an airfield so Don could catch a plane to meet the senator. I think he was embarrassed for the Army to go to all that trouble."

I can still remember that trip, sitting in the bed of a three-quarter-ton U.S. Army truck, dressed in our combat fatigues, holding our M-16s between our legs and hell-bent on getting him to see Kennedy. At one point I looked at Graham and just smiled, "You're sickening." He looked a bit sheepish.

Maxa, who worked 13 years at *The Washington Post* as an investigative reporter and personalities columnist, also wrote of "Graham's low-key personality, his controlled way of speaking and acting that some suggest is a studied opposite to his father, who cut a brash path through Washington. Unlike his father, Donald Graham keeps his own counsel and works to blend in with the crowd."

"I was amazed," I had said to Maxa, "when I found out who he was—that he had been sent to Vietnam and drafted like the rest of us who couldn't afford to buy our way out."

Graham had told Maxa that only a short while before completing his two years in the Army had he decided to join the family business. But there was little doubt where he would end up. Graham's grandfather, Eugene Meyer, had purchased the *Post* for $825,000 in June of 1933 at a bankruptcy sale. Some 21 years later, in 1954, when Graham was 8 years old, the company was able to swing a deal for the *Washington Times-Herald,* which at that time actually was larger and more profitable than the *Post.* After the purchase of the *Times-Herald*, Meyer was quoted as saying, "This will make the paper safe for Donny."

When he returned to Washington after his year in Vietnam, Graham could have gone right to work at the *Post.* Instead, he decided to join the

Washington Police Department because he wanted to get to know the city better. He served for 18 months in Washington's Ninth Precinct, then a predominantly black area that was considered one of the city's most dangerous.

Before becoming publisher of the *Post,* Graham decided to go through a rigorous management-training program. Over an eight-year span, he worked in a variety of jobs, including city reporter, makeup editor on the news desk, clerk in the accounting department, assistant home-delivery manager in circulation and ad salesman. He also spent time as a reporter in the Los Angeles bureau of *Newsweek,* the magazine also owned by the Post company, and he spent time working for the magazine in New York, first in the editorial department, and then in the business department. Finally, he spent one year as sports editor at the *Post.* In Vietnam, we had spent hours debating sports personalities and sports teams, and Graham was so obviously a Washington-team fanatic that it came as no surprise when he called his stint as sports editor "one glorious year."

During his career, Graham gained a reputation for knowing the name of virtually every person working at *The Washington Post.* To me, that's an incredible testament to the way he treated his employees.

After becoming general manager of the *Post* and then publisher, Graham continued to rise steadily through the executive ranks, ultimately taking the top leadership position for the Graham family's media properties. He succeeded his mother, long-time publisher Katharine Graham, as chief executive in 1991 and as chairman in 1993. Mrs. Graham died at age 84, on July 17, 2001, after suffering a head injury when she tripped and fell on a sidewalk while attending a conference of media executives in Sun Valley, Idaho. Graham also had been attending the conference, and he was with his mother when she died at a hospital in Boise.

Today Graham is chairman of the board and chief executive officer for the Washington Post Company.

Paul Hughes

I worked with Paul Hughes in four locations—An Khe, Bong Son, Landing Zone Baldy and Camp Evans.

In at least a couple of those locations, we made tape recordings for my parents. Each time we performed, we could count on Hughes to ask my mother to send more goodies, especially donuts and cupcakes.

Hughes became a sergeant in our PIO camp. Why he became a sergeant and the rest of us rose through the ranks as specialists, I have no idea.

Hughes received a Purple Heart after he was wounded by flying shrapnel. An NVA mortar round exploded near him as he was walking along a dirt road inside our Camp Evans base.

Before entering the U.S. Army, Hughes had worked as a ski instructor. He told us his main job was to capture other skiers on film. In doing that, he had to ski ahead of them, backwards, and shoot them as they were coming down the ski slopes. Did skiing photographers actually do that? It sounded pretty incredible, and I found it an absolutely fascinating image, but I took Hughes at his word.

Robert Kirk

One of the first soldiers I mentioned in letters home was Robert Kirk, my first roommate in An Khe. He was a very deep thinker with an incredibly dry sense of humor. In one letter home, I referred to him as "profound" and "extremely brilliant." He was a delight to have around, even though he always crushed me when we played chess.

I remember him saying things such as, "Stan Laurel had a lot to stand on—his name." Standing on his laurels, I guess. On another occasion, I gave Kirk 500 piasters, the equivalent of five U.S. dollars, to pick up two color rolls of film for me. He left the film for me along with a note that read, "Two rolls of color film, $2.80 per cartridge. Thanks for the tip! Kirk." I believe I paid him back.

Kirk would remain at An Khe for much of his tour. He performed a number of essential clerk duties for the Public Information Office, and he wrote a few stories from our base camp. He had taken three years of French in high school, and he was there to help me when I decided to study some French.

Kirk had told me that he hoped to be a doctor someday. However, I lost contact with him after Vietnam, and I don't know whether he achieved his goal.

MICHAEL LARSON

Michael Larson spent most of his life in Mankato, Minn., first as an editor at *The Free Press* newspaper and then as a professor of journalism at Minnesota State University, Mankato.

Larson began his career in journalism as a reporter for the *St. Paul Dispatch*, where he worked during his senior year at the University of Minnesota, then full-time after his graduation until he was drafted into the U.S. Army.

After returning from Vietnam in July of 1968, Larson took a job as regional editor for *The Sentinel* in Fairmont, Minn. He left in April of 1969 to become a reporter, then associate editor at *The Free Press* in Mankato, Minn.

In April of 1972, he left to become managing editor for *The Herald* Newspapers, a group of weekly newspapers published by Paddock Circle, based in Libertyville, Ill. He went on to serve as managing editor for *The Journal* in New Ulm, Minn., in 1975 and the *Red Wing Republican Eagle* in 1977.

In August of 1979, Larson returned to Mankato to become managing editor for *The Free Press.* He was promoted to editor in 1984. While at *The Free Press*, Larson earned his Master's in Business Administration in 1986 from Mankato State University School of Business. In 1995, while still at *The Free Press*, he began teaching reporting and writing classes at the university, which had changed its name to Minnesota State University, Mankato.

In 1997, he began a three-year sabbatical, moving to Minot, N.D., where he served as editor of the *Minot Daily News.*

In 2000, he and his wife Kay returned to their home state of Minnesota, and Larson accepted a position as metro editor and business editor at the *St. Cloud Times.*

In 2001, armed with his MBA, Larson took a job as assistant administrator for Melrose Area Hospital, part of the CentraCare Health Network, based in St. Cloud. He left there in 2003 to resume teaching at Minnesota State University, Mankato. That year, he also began teaching journalism classes at St. Cloud State University.

During his years of teaching, Larson introduced thousands of college students to the mystery of "Rosebud," the famous dying words of Charles Foster Kane. He taught reporting and writing courses in both Mankato and St. Cloud, but he always called his Introduction to Mass Communications course his favorite class. He developed the class for students at Mankato and also taught it at St. Cloud. Teaching in a large auditorium setting, he enhanced his lectures each term by showing several movies, including "Citizen Kane," the 1941 Orson Welles masterpiece that many producers, directors and critics in Hollywood still consider the greatest movie ever made.

As a newspaper reporter, Larson won a number of awards at both the state and national levels for in-depth reporting and writing. His investigations focused on a wide variety of topics ranging from death and taxes to poverty and from teen-agers to senior citizens. A series of articles on death and dying, which he wrote with John Lampinen, now the top editor for Paddock Publications in suburban Chicago, won a first-place national award for investigative reporting from the Suburban Newspapers of America.

As he moved into the 21st century, Larson turned from newspapers to books. He worked with his sister, Jill Larson Sundberg, on a number of titles including *My Red Hat, My Red Hattitudes, Babes Remember, Cozy Cozy* and *Sunday Drives*. He also wrote books of his own, including *There's Magic All Around Us* and *A Murder in Mundelein.*

Steve Robinson

Steve Robinson captured my attention during First Air Cav battles northwest of Hue and at Khe Sanh.

Robinson was a daring photographer. At Hue, he took some of the most memorable photos from the war. In one series, shot while he was traveling with the First Cav's Fifth Battalion, Seventh Cavalry, Robinson's photographs showed the absolute devastation of Hue.

Later, Robinson traveled with us to Khe Sanh, and he traveled with Seventh Cavalry soldiers in the A Shau Valley, another hotbed for North Vietnamese Army soldiers. He also shot a superb series of portraits while spending a day with Major General John J. Tolson, commanding officer of the First Air Cavalry.

Robinson always struck me as a "good-ol' boy." He grew up in Oklahoma, he spoke with a Southern drawl, and he chattered incessantly about catching crawdads, a type of crayfish, in the creeks near his hometown. "The North has lobster," he would say, "the South has crawdads."

Robinson also drove fellow photographer Fred Fiallos crazy with his Oklahoma accent. Fiallos' name was pronounced "Fee-Eye-Ohs." Without fail, Robinson would call him "Free-All-Eez." It was not intentional. It was hilarious to hear Robinson mess up the name without fail and even more hilarious to watch the grimace on Fiallos' face every time it happened.

John Root

John D. Root died on September 24, 2004.

Dr. Root, who retired in 2001, was professor emeritus of history at the Illinois Institute of Technology in Chicago, Ill., where he had worked for 32 years. His funeral and burial took place in Michigan City, Ind.

Even though he had developed multiple sclerosis, Root served the school both as a history professor and as chair of the Humanities Department.

"I had the pleasure of working with him for many years in his role as chairman," said Lew Collens, president of the school. "I will long remember and value John's dedication to his students, his department and the university."

Survivors included one brother, two nieces, two nephews and nine great-nieces and nephews.

Dr. Root was a 1962 graduate of the University of Notre Dame and earned master's and doctoral degrees from Indiana University.

Serving with the First Air Cavalry Division in Vietnam, he received two Bronze Stars while attaining the rank of captain.

Dr. Root published many articles on Vietnam and was writing a book at the time of his death. His family asked that memorial donations be sent to MS Research in care of the Root Funeral Home, 312 E. Seventh St., Michigan City, IN 46360.

Dan Stoneking

Dan Stoneking died on January 29, 2007, in Mexico.

Stoneking had risen through the ranks to become executive sports editor for the *Minneapolis Star* after his *Star* career as a sports writer, and he had been a radio sports talk personality on KSTP Radio in St. Paul.

Stoneking had lived most of his 64 years in Burnsville and in St. Paul, but he had moved permanently to Chetumal, Mexico, a few years ago.

He died of pneumonia. He had suffered from cancer for a dozen years.

In Vietnam, Stoneking worked in our office at An Khe until early in December of 1967, and then he traveled to Japan to become editor of the *Cavalair*.

We called him "Stoney," just as people did back in Minnesota. In one letter home, I referred to him as "a really swell guy who worked as a sports writer for the *Minneapolis Star.* He has a chance to be the Twins baseball writer but doesn't seem all that interested because it would take him away from home and family six months each year."

In that same letter, I made mention of the World Series going on between the Boston Red Sox and the St. Louis Cardinals, which the Cardinals won in seven games. We were able to listen to a live broadcast of each game. The broadcast began about 12:45 a.m. Vietnam time. Most of us would retire to our cots and mosquito netting, planning to listen to a rebroadcast at 3 p.m. the following day. But not Stoney. He stayed up for every broadcast because, as he put it, "I can't even stand an instant replay!"

I also sang the praises of Stoney in December, shortly after he left for Tokyo. In a letter dated Dec. 13, I wrote, "I learned more about writing from Sergeant Stoneking (Master's in journalism from Northwestern) than from most of my writing instructors. He wouldn't accept my stuff until he thought I had done my best, and he suggested practical improvements. Really great."

Stoneking's departure for Tokyo also brought an end to his radio programs on AFVN radio out of An Khe. He and Staff Sergeant Dick Wade had gained a nice following for a program they had initiated, a program devoted to sports. It was a precursor of sorts for the radio talk show Stoneking would host on KSTP radio when he returned to the Twin Cities.

Stoneking had joined the *Minneapolis Star* in the early 1960s after receiving his master's degree in journalism from Northwestern University in Evanston, Ill. After returning from Vietnam, Stoneking rejoined the *Minneapolis Star* and ultimately became the newspaper's executive sports editor.

After the *Star* merged in 1982 with the *Minneapolis Tribune*, its stronger morning sister, Stoneking continued to write sports. While reporting on the

Minnesota Twins for the *Star Tribune* in 1984, he was suspended for an incident of plagiarism and did not return to the paper. He had lifted some words and phrases from an article by Thomas Boswell, the noted baseball writer of *The Washington Post.*

Stoneking loved hockey, and he covered the Minnesota North Stars as a radio reporter for a number of years after he left the *StarTribune*. His car once sported a vanity license plate reading "Mr. Puck."

In the *StarTribune* article announcing Stoneking's death, the newspaper quoted Lou Nanne, a former general manager for the North Stars. Nanne said Stoneking was more than a reporter to the team, that Stoneking was trusted with secrets and was an honorary teammate, one who was subjected to player pranks.

"He was a friend to the players and the management group," Nanne said. "People really enjoyed his writing and company. He could watch hockey or talk hockey all day long. He never seemed to tire of it."

Stoneking also was an early supporter of girls and women's sports in Minnesota, setting up a 1978 exhibition game to display the talents of the University of Minnesota women's hockey team. He also pushed for female reporters to be allowed into team locker rooms, and coached his daughter, Shannon, of Burnsville, in youth soccer. She played hockey for Providence College from 1988 to 1992.

In addition to his radio work after he left the *Minneapolis Star*, Stoneking became sports editor for the *Stillwater Gazette* in Minnesota. He also did freelance writing, and some of his work appeared in *Sports Illustrated* magazine.

In the mid-1990s, Stoneking taught English and mass media courses at a Mexican college.

In addition to his daughter, Shannon, Stoneking was survived by his wife, Irma Sanchez, of St. Paul; a son, Scott, of Lakeville; a former wife, Sarah, of Farmington, and two grandchildren.

Steve Stroub

Steve Stroub died on February 5, 1968. He was summarily executed by North Vietnamese soldiers after he had been captured in the city of Hue.

I enjoyed working with both Stroub and his close friend, John Bagwell. The three of us worked together on some humorous sketches that we played on the air for Armed Forces Vietnam (AFVN) listeners. Stroub's family lived in Austin, Minn. He was one of three members of our Public Information Office from Minnesota, the other two being Dan Stoneking, from the Twin Cities, and me, from St. James. Stoneking had been tapped in December to become editor of the *Cavalair*, and he spent much of his tour in Japan, editing and publishing that paper. Stroub was a husky soldier on a fit frame. His face was dark and his teeth gleamed white when he spoke and when he smiled. And he smiled often.

"One of my real good friends was killed here last week," I wrote in a letter dated Feb. 14. "He was Steve Stroub, a radio man who worked closely with me and John Bagwell, another radio man, when we were doing the Ted Turtle series—I think I told you about it. Stroub was our announcer and production man. We were doing the serials for Bagwell's morning radio show.

"Stroub and Bagwell were at the Hue TV station when NVA and VC attacked Hue. They received lots of small-arms fire and finally decided to make a run for it. A civilian with them led the way and got cut down. Bagwell, following, had a bullet rip into his toe, but he escaped, seeing a satchel charge go off in front of the house as he crawled away. He said the house collapsed. He never saw Stroub.

"Bagwell got to a Catholic church where a priest hid him and cared for his wound and buried his weapon. A couple nights ago, he got out and arrived here today.

"Marines found a body two days ago with a billfold full of identification showing him to be Stroub. Bagwell was to identify the body, but Marines took the body to Da Nang, and he hasn't seen the body yet.

"They both are great guys, and you don't really understand why things have to be this screwed up. I'm going to see Bagwell again tonight and talk some with him, maybe find out more about what happened. It's a lot more vivid when someone you know gets hit."

We found out later that six men assigned to the AFVN station had been taken prisoner. Five of them would spend about five years in captivity before being released. The sixth, Stroub, was shot shortly after his capture. His execution was witnessed by Sergeant First Class Harry Ettmueller, one of the other men taken captive.

Infantry battalion table of organization

Charles A. Krohn, in his book "The Lost Battalion," provided the clearest explanation of infantry organization I found during my research.

Below is the table he provided:

Unit	Plus	Totals	Commanded by
One rifle squad		10 men	Sergeant
Three rifle squads	One platoon HQ (three men) and weapons squad (11 men)	44-man platoon	Lieutenant
Three rifle platoons	One company HQ (13 men) and one mortar platoon (11 men)	171-man company	Captain
Four rifle companies	One battalion HQ (33 men) and one HQ support company (146 men)	862-man battalion	Lieutenant colonel

An infantry battalion, Krohn wrote, "is supposed to have a total strength of 862, but this is only the authorized strength, and not the number actually assigned and available for combat, which is called the 'foxhole strength.'"

Krohn emphasized that his unit, the First Cav's Second Battalion, 12th Cavalry "was a lightly equipped infantry battalion, able to conduct only limited sustained combat. It had to have substantial support and reinforcement from brigade and division assets.

"A typical infantry division of the Vietnam era would have a total of nine rifle battalions, a reconnaissance battalion (squadron), four artillery battalions, plus various combat support and combat service support battalions."

A Vietnam glossary

AFVN: Armed Forces Vietnam Network radio and television.

AHB: Assault helicopter battalion.

Airborne: Refers to soldiers who are qualified as parachutists.

Air Cav: Air cavalry; helicopter-borne infantry; foot soldiers supported by helicopter gunships.

Airmobile: Rapid-response helicopter-borne infantry.

AK-47: A Soviet-manufactured Kalashnikov semi-automatic and fully automatic combat assault rifle; fires a 7.62mm bullet at 600 rounds per minute. The basic weapon of North Vietnamese Army soldiers, it made a distinctive popping sound. Another distinctive feature was its curved clip.

AK-50: Newer version of the AK-47. Some of these rifles had a permanently mounted "illegal" triangular bayonet that left a sucking wound that would not close.

AO: Area of operations.

APC: Armored Personnel Carrier; a track vehicle used to transport Army troops or supplies, usually armed with a .50-caliber machine gun.

Arc Light: Code name for B-52 bomber strikes along the Cambodian-Vietnamese border. When these bombs landed, U.S. soldiers could feel the earth tremble up to 10 miles away from the target area.

Artillery: Larger and heavier shells fired from larger guns or cannons; see battery.

Arvin: Soldier in Army of the Republic of Vietnam units.

ARVN: Army of the Republic of Vietnam; the South Vietnamese Regular Army.

A-team: Basic 10-man team of the U.S. Special Forces. The A-teams often led irregular military units that were not under the control of the Vietnamese military command.

B-52: The gigantic Boeing-manufactured U.S. Air Force high-altitude bomber.

Bac-si: Vietnamese for doctor; also used to refer to a medic in the U.S. Army.

Backhaul: To carry by helicopter from a company's position to the battalion base camp; for example, water would be brought to the company in five-gallon metal cans; the empty cans then would be backhauled.

Band-aid: Radio call sign for a medic.

Base camp: A resupply base for field units and a location for headquarters of brigade- or division-size units, artillery batteries and airfields; also known as the rear.

Battery: An artillery unit equivalent to a company; six 105mm or 155mm howitzers or two eight-inch or 175mm self-propelled howitzers.

Beaucoup: French term for "very much"; Vietnamese slang for "many" or "much."

Beehive round: An explosive artillery shell that delivered thousands of small projectiles, "like nails with fins," instead of shrapnel.

Bird: A helicopter or any aircraft.

Bird dog: Forward air controller, usually riding in a small aircraft.

Blood trail: A trail of blood left by a fleeing soldier who has been wounded.

Blue: The rifle platoons of the First Air Cavalry's First Squadron, Ninth Cavalry; also, a body of water, referred to as blue because that's its color on a map. A radio transmission to an infantry company might include the question, "Have you crossed that blue yet?"

Body bag: A heavy-duty plastic bag used to transport dead bodies from the field.

Body count: The number of enemy killed, wounded, or captured during an operation.

Boom-Boom: Vietnamese slang for sex; also, slang for a Vietnamese prostitute (Boom-Boom Girl).

Boonies: Infantry term for the field; jungles or swampy areas.

Bouncing Betty: An antipersonnel mine with two charges: the first charge propels the device upward, and the other sets off an explosion at about waist level.

Bronze Star: U.S. military decoration awarded for valor or meritorious service. Most soldiers in the First Air Cavalry Division's Public Information Office were awarded a Bronze Star for Meritorious Service.

Bush: Infantry term for the field.

Care package: A container mailed from home in the United States filled with lots of goodies.

C-4: A plastic, putty-textured explosive carried by infantry soldiers. The material burned when lit and would boil water in seconds instead of minutes; used to heat C-rations in the field and to blow up bunkers.

C-7; C-7A: Small cargo airplanes; referred to as Caribous.

C-123: A Fairchild-manufactured two-engine propeller-driven cargo airplane; popularly called the Caribou, it was in fact a larger version of the C-7.

C-130: A large four-engine propeller-driven Air Force plane used to carry people and cargo; also known as the Hercules C-130.

C-141: Large cargo airplane; also known as the C-141 Starlifter.

CA: Combat assault. The term describes dropping troopers into an LZ.

CH-47: Chinook cargo and transport helicopter.

CH-54: Largest of the American helicopters, strictly for cargo; also called the Flying Crane or the Skycrane.

Cache: Hidden supplies.

Cav: Cavalry; the First Cavalry Division (Airmobile).

Charlie: Viet Cong or NVA. "Charlie" (or "Charles" or "Chuck") was short for the phonetic representation "Victor Charlie" for "VC."

Chicom: Chinese Communist.

Chieu Hoi: Vietnamese "open arms"; enemy soldiers who choose to give up.

Chinook: CH-47 cargo and transport helicopter.

Chop chop: Vietnamese slang for food; also, slang meaning to move quickly.

Chopper: A helicopter.

CIB: Combat Infantry Badge; U.S. Army designation for men assigned to the infantry for being under enemy fire in a combat zone. The badge could be worn on both fatigues and dress uniforms.

Clacker: A small hand-held firing device for a claymore mine.

Claymore: An antipersonnel mine. When the mine is detonated, small steel projectiles fly out in a 60-degree fan-shaped pattern to a maximum distance of 100 meters.

Click: See klick; sometimes written as click, one klick equals one kilometer.

Clip: Infantrymen in Vietnam carried several clips that could be inserted quickly into their M-16 rifles. The clips could be popped in and out of the rifle's loading port during firefights. Most of the clips contained 20 rounds of ammunition, although many Skytroopers used just 18, to prevent jamming.

CMB: Combat Medical Badge; awarded to medics who served with the Infantry while under direct enemy fire.

CMH: Congressional Medal of Honor; the highest U.S. military decoration awarded for conspicuous gallantry at the risk of life above and beyond the call of duty.

Cobra: An AH-1G attack helicopter, heavily armed with rockets and machine guns, which made its first appearance in Vietnam late in 1967.

Code of Conduct: Military rules for U.S. soldiers taken prisoner by the enemy.

Commo bunker: Bunker containing vital communications equipment.

Compound: A fortified military installation.

Concertina wire: Coiled barbed wire with razor-type ends; the barbs along the wire are razor sharp.

Connex container: A corrugated metal packing crate, approximately six feet in length.

Contact: Firing on or being fired upon by the enemy.

CONUS: Continental United States.

Counterinsurgency: Anti-guerrilla warfare.

CP: Command post. In a company, this is the cluster of radiomen and others who remain with the company commander at all times. It often includes the first sergeant or executive officer (sometimes both), a medic and a man who supervises the log for the company.

CP pills: Anti-malarial pills.

CQ: Charge of Quarters. An officer or a soldier officially in charge of a unit headquarters at night.

C-rations: Combat rations; canned meals for use in the field. Each cardboard package typically consisted of a can of some basic course, a can of fruit, a packet of some type of dessert, a packet of powdered cocoa, sugar, powdered cream, coffee, a small pack of cigarettes (usually four smokes), a piece or two of chewing gum and toilet paper.

Crew chief: The senior door-gunner on a UH-1 Huey assault helicopter; also the door-gunner charged with the responsibility of keeping the helicopter mechanically sound.

CS: A riot-control gas that burns the eyes and mucus membranes.

DEROS: Date of expected return from overseas; the most-anticipated day for most soldiers in Vietnam.

Det-cord: Detonating cord used with explosives.

Deuce-and-a-half: Two-and-a-half ton truck.

Di-di: Slang from the Vietnamese word di, meaning "to leave" or "to go."

Di-di-mau: Vietnamese slang for "go quickly."

Dink: Derogatory term for an Asian.

Dinky dau: To be crazy, from "dien cai dau."

Distinguished Service Cross: The nation's second highest medal for valor.

DMZ: Demilitarized Zone; the dividing line between North Vietnam and South Vietnam established in 1954 at the Geneva Convention.

Doc: Medic or corpsman. Medics were known as "Doc Smith," for example. Medics also were called Band-Aids or Ben Caseys.

Door-gunner: Soldier who sat in the open doorway of a UH-1 Huey assault helicopter. Door-gunners would fire their machine guns at enemy soldiers or suspected enemy positions.

D-ring: A D-shaped metal snap link used to hold gear together, used in rappelling from choppers.

Dust-off: Medical evacuation by helicopter.

Eagle flights: Large air-assault of helicopters.

Early-Outs: A drop or reduction in time in service; a soldier with 150 days or less remaining on his active duty commitment when he DEROSd from Vietnam or ETSd from the Army under the Early-Out program.

Eleven Bravo: Army designation for an infantry soldier; the MOS of an infantryman.

EM: Enlisted man.

EOD: Explosive ordinance disposal; a team that disarms explosive devices.

E-tool: Entrenching tool; a folding shovel carried by infantrymen.

ETS: Date of departure from an overseas duty station; estimated time of separation from military service.

Fatigues: Standard combat uniform, green in color.

Field Surgical Kit: A small container carried by medics for minor surgery and suturing.

Fire base: Temporary artillery landing zone used for fire support of forward infantry operations.

Firefight: A battle, or exchange of small-arms fire with the enemy.

Fire in the hole: Shout by a soldier when he would pull the pin on a grenade and launch it toward an enemy position, usually a bunker, a tunnel or a trench.

Flak jacket: Heavy Fiberglas-filled vest worn for protection from shrapnel.

Flare: Illumination projectile, hand-fired or shot from artillery, mortars, or air.

Flying Cranes: The CH-54, largest of the American helicopters, used strictly for carrying or lifting cargo; also called Skycranes.

FOB: Forward Operations Base; the place where a company spends the night.

Forward observer. A person attached to a field unit to coordinate the placement of direct or indirect fire from ground, air, and naval forces.

Frag: Fragmentation grenade.

Fragging: The assassination of an officer or NCO by his own troops, usually by a grenade.

Freedom Bird: The plane that carried soldiers from Vietnam back to The World.

Free-fire zone: Free to fire upon any forces you may come upon; you do not have to identify any moving person or creature; sometimes called free-kill zones; within this zone, everyone and everything is deemed hostile and a legitimate target.

Friendly fire: Accidental attacks on U.S. or allied soldiers by other U.S. or allied soldiers.

G-3: Division-level tactical advisor; a staff officer.

Gook: Derogatory term for an Asian; derived from Korean slang for "person."

Green Berets: U.S. Special Forces.

Grids: A map broken into numbered thousand-meter squares.

Grunt: Infantryman.

GSW: Gunshot wound.

Gung ho: Enthusiastic soldier (usually about military matters and killing people).

Gunship: An armed helicopter.

GVN: Government of South Vietnam.

Hamlet: A small rural village.

Hammer and anvil: An infantry tactic of surrounding an enemy base area, then sending in other units to drive the enemy out of hiding.

H&I: Harassment and interdiction; artillery bombardments used to deny the enemy terrain that they might find beneficial to their campaign; general rather than specific, confirmed military targets; random artillery fire.

Heat tabs: Flammable tablets used to heat C-rations; these often took a long time to heat the food and gave off harsh fumes.

HHC: Headquarters and headquarters company; higher-higher—the honchos; the command.

Hoi Chanh: Kit Carson scouts; Hoi Chanh Vien in Vietnamese, loosely translated, means "members who have returned." Kit Carson scouts were enemy soldiers who had defected and now scouted for U.S. troops.

Hootch: A hut or simple dwelling, either military or civilian.

Hootch pole: Infantry soldiers in Vietnam could create a makeshift hootch in the field by cutting three long hootch poles, using pieces of bamboo or other strong straight pieces of wood. Two of the pieces would be pounded into the ground, and a cross-pole would be tied to both, three or four feet off the ground. Two ponchos snapped together would be draped over the cross-pole. Loops of string would be passed through the corner eyelets of the ponchos, then be pegged to the ground. Sometimes a fourth hootch-pole, perpendicular to the cross-pole, would be connected to the poncho-hoods to keep the sides of the hootch from sagging inward.

Horn: The telephone; also a PRC-25 radio.

Hot: An area that's under enemy gunfire or known to be infested with enemy soldiers.

Hot LZ: A landing zone receiving fire from enemy positions. Red smoke grenades were used to alert incoming pilots to a hot LZ.

Hots: Hot food ferried by helicopters into the field.

HQ: Headquarters.

Huey: Nickname for the UH-1 series of Bell helicopters.

Hump: Grunt term for walking or marching in the field carrying a rucksack or a backpack.

I Corps: The northernmost military region in South Vietnam.

II Corps: The Central Highlands military region in South Vietnam.

III Corps: The densely populated, fertile military region from Saigon to the Central Highlands.

IV Corps: The marshy Mekong Delta southernmost military region.

IG: Inspector General .

Immersion foot: A condition resulting from walking in water for a prolonged period of time, causing cracking and bleeding of the feet.

In-country: Being inside Vietnam.

Insert: To be deployed or dropped into a tactical area by helicopter or by parachute.

Iron Triangle: A Viet Cong-infested area between the Thi-Tinh and Saigon rivers, next to the Cu Chi district.

JAG: Judge advocate general; the legal department of the Armed Services.

JP4 jet fuel: The jet fuel used by most of the helicopters in Vietnam.

KIA: killed in action.

Kit Carson scout: A former Viet Cong who acted as a guide or interpreter for U.S. military units.

Klick: One klick equals one kilometer; sometimes written as click.

LAAW: A shoulder-fired, 66mm rocket. The launcher is made of Fiberglas and is disposable after one shot.

LBJ: Long Binh Jail, a military stockade in Long Binh.

Lifer: A soldier making the military his career; also a soldier who had more time remaining in Vietnam than you did.

Lima-lima: Land line; refers to telephone communications between two points on the ground.

Litters: Stretchers used to carry wounded soldiers.

Lit up: Fired upon.

Log: Short for logistics. It meant resupply. Under ideal conditions, a company would "get logged" twice a day. If your air mattress sprang a leak, for example, you could "put it on log"; in other words, you requested that a new air mattress would be sent with the day's resupply.

Logbird: The helicopter that brought log.

LP: Listening post; usually a four-man position set up at night outside the perimeter away from the main body of troopers; the LP acted as an early warning system against attack.

LRRP: Long Range Reconnaissance Patrol; an elite team usually made up of five to seven men who would venture deep into the jungle to observe enemy activity without initiating contact; this describes the nighttime behind-enemy-lines scouting missions led by Captain Robert L. Helvey of the First Air Cav's 2/12th.

LSA: Lubricant for small arms; lubricant for small weapons.

LT: Lieutenant.

LZ: Landing zone; usually a small clearing secured temporarily for the landing of resupply helicopters; some LZs became more permanent and eventually became base camps.

Machine gun: A rapidly firing automatic weapon, often mounted, that delivers rapid and continuous firepower as long as the trigger is pressed. In Vietnam, the standard lightweight machine gun used by U.S. forces was the M-60.

MACV: Military Assistance Command, Vietnam.

MAF: Marine Amphibious Force.

Mm: Millimeter, usually referring to the size of shells shot from guns.

M-14: A 7.62mm-caliber rifle that fired on semi- and full-automatic; a rifle used early in the Vietnam War.

M-16: The standard U.S. military rifle used in Vietnam beginning in 1966; successor to the M-14.

M-60: The standard lightweight machine gun used by U.S. forces in Vietnam.

M-79: A U.S. military hand-held grenade launcher.

MARS: Military Affiliate Radio Station; used by soldiers to call home via Signal Corps and ham radio equipment.

MASH: Mobile Army Surgical Hospital; field hospitals.

Marker round: The first round fired by mortars or artillery; used to adjust the following rounds onto the target.

Medcap: Medical Civil Action Program in which U.S. medical personnel would go into villages and hamlets to offer medical aid to the local populace.

Medevac: Medical evacuation from the field by helicopter.

MFW: Multiple frag wounds.

MIA: Missing in action.

Mike-mike: Millimeter, as in "81 mike-mike mortar."

Minigun: Rapid-fire electronically controlled machine gun with multi-barrels, capable of firing up to 6,000 rounds a minute, primarily used on helicopters and other aircraft.

Mr. Charles: The Viet Cong or the NVA.

Montagnard: A French term for several tribes of mountain people living in the hills of central and northern South Vietnam. Vietnam was a former French Colony and some of the Montagnard phrases and customs carried over from French Colonial days.

Mortar: A mortar consists of three parts—a steel tube, a base plate, and a tri-pod. A round is dropped into the tube, striking a firing pin, and causing the projectile to leave the tube at a high angle. We usually referred to them as 120mm mortars.

MOS: Military occupational specialty; the training specialty of a soldier.

MP: Military Police.

MPC: Military payment currency; the scrip U.S. soldiers received as pay in Vietnam.

Mule: A small, motorized platform often used to transport military supplies and personnel.

Nam: Short for Vietnam.

Napalm: A jellied petroleum substance that burns fiercely; used against enemy equipment and personnel.

NCO: Noncommissioned officer.

NLF: National Liberation Front.

NPFF: Vietnamese National Police Field Force.

Number One: The best.

Number Ten: The worst.

NVA: North Vietnamese Army.

OCS: Officer Candidate School.

OD: Olive drab.

OH-6A: Light Observation Helicopter. The pilots would sit in Plexiglas bubble cockpits, which had room for only two people.

OH-13S: A Light Observation Helicopter brought into Vietnam by the First Air Cavalry Division.

P-38: A tiny collapsible can opener.

P-39: A tiny beer can or soda can opener; also referred to as a "church-key."

Perimeter: Outer limits of a military position; an outer circle of soldiers or guards around a military position.

PF: Popular Forces; South Vietnamese National Guard-type local military units.

Phoenix: Intelligence-based campaign to eliminate the Viet Cong infrastructure.

PIO: Public Information Office.

Point; also, point man: The first soldier or lead element on a combat patrol.

Poncho: A plastic sheet rolled up and strapped beneath our backpacks; most often used to make a lean-to or a pup tent for sleeping at night.

Poncho liner: A nylon insert for the military rain poncho, used as a blanket.

Pop smoke: To ignite a smoke grenade to signal an aircraft; to mark a company's position for an incoming helicopter, for example.

POW: Prisoner of war.

PRC-25: Portable Radio Communications, Model 25; a back-packed FM receiver-transmitter used for short-distance communications. The range of the radio was 5 to 10 kilometers, depending upon the weather, unless attached to a special, nonportable antenna that could extend the range to 20 to 30 kilometers

PsyOps: Psychological operations.

Public information specialist: A soldier assigned to the Public Information Office; writers and photographers who often traveled with the infantry in the field.

Puff the Magic Dragon: The AC-47, a propeller-driven aircraft with three miniguns capable of firing 6,000 rounds per minute per gun for a total of 18,000 rounds per minute. The miniguns were on one side of the plane. The plane would bank to one side to fire.

Punji stakes: Sharpened bamboo sticks used in a primitive but effective pit trap. The stakes often were smeared with excrement to cause infection.

Pup tent: A small tent we erected in the field. Most soldiers used their ponchos to make a pup tent.

Purple Heart: U.S. military decoration awarded to any member of the Armed Forces wounded by enemy action. Any soldier who received three Purple Hearts was allowed to leave Vietnam.

Push: Radio frequency; frequency of a PRC-25 being carried in the field.

PX: Post Exchange; a department store-like shop that operates on U.S. military installations worldwide.

QUAD-50s: A four-barreled assembly of .50-caliber machine guns.

RA: Regular Army; prefix to the serial number for enlisted men.

Rack: A bed or a cot.

R&R: Rest and recreation, rest and recuperation or rest and relaxation. All three terms were used interchangeably by soldiers. There were two types in Vietnam—a three-day in-country R&R and a seven-day out-of-county R&R. Some infantry soldiers would receive a special in-country R&R for the entire company, usually after a major firefight.

Rangers: Elite commandos and infantry specially trained for reconnaissance and combat missions.

React Force: A unit that would come to the aid of another unit under enemy fire.

Rear: To the foot soldier, this was any place except the boonies.

Rear job: Any job that took the grunt out of the field; a job at a division's base camp.

Recon: Reconnaissance; venturing into the field away from the main unit for the purpose of identifying enemy activity or mapping enemy positions.

Red alert: The most urgent form of warning; signals an imminent enemy attack.

Red Legs: Slang for men in the Artillery.

Rock 'n' roll: Firing a weapon on full automatic.

Rockets: Usually 122mm rounds shot from rocket launchers.

Rocket ships: Helicopter gunships armed with miniguns and 2.75-inch rockets.

ROK: Soldier from the Republic of Korea.

Rotate: Returning to the United States after serving a one-year tour in Vietnam.

RPG: A rocket-propelled grenade; a Russian-made portable antitank grenade launcher.

RTO: Radio telephone operator.

Ruck/rucksack: The backpack issued to foot soldiers in Vietnam.

S-1: Personnel.

S-2: Intelligence.

S-3: Operations.

S-4: Supply.

S-5: Civil Affairs.

Saddle up: Put on one's pack and get ready to move out.

Salvo: Firing an artillery battery in unison.

Sapper: A Viet Cong or NVA solder who got inside an allied perimeter, armed with explosives.

Satchel charges: A pack of explosives used by enemy soldiers. The pack could be dropped or thrown, and it was more powerful than a grenade.

Scout ships: Smaller helicopters used for reconnaissance, usually OH-6A or OH-13S Light Observation Helicopters with Plexiglas bubble cockpits carrying one or two people.

Seabees: Navy construction engineers.

SEAL: A highly trained Navy special warfare team member. The acronym stands for Sea, Air and Land.

Search-and-destroy: An operation in which U.S. soldiers searched an area and destroyed anything the enemy might find useful.

Sham: Malingering; fake or slack. The World War II term was "goldbrick." Someone who was wounded slightly and spent a week in the hospital might say, "I got a seven-day sham." Some soldiers also called a rear job a sham job.

Ship: In Vietnam, a helicopter; a helicopter gunship.

Short: A Vietnam tour of duty close to completion.

Short-timer: Soldier nearing the end of his tour in Vietnam.

Shrapnel: Pieces of metal sent flying from an explosion.

Silver Star: U.S. military decoration awarded for gallantry in action.

Sixty: An M-60 machine gun (Never a 60mm mortar).

Skids: Hollow metal tubing on Huey helicopters that acted as a landing gear; First Air Cavalry soldiers often would stand on the skids and leap from the craft as it neared the ground when they were being airlifted into a new area.

Sky Crane: A huge double-engine helicopter used for lifting and transporting heavy equipment; in the sky, it resembled a huge mosquito.

SKS: A Chinese-manufactured rifle used extensively in Vietnam by the Viet Cong.

Skytrooper: Any soldier assigned to the First Air Cavalry Division.

Slack man: The second man on a patrol; the man walking directly behind the point man.

Slick: A UH-1 helicopter used for transporting troops in tactical air-assault operations. The term "slick" refers to the fact that the helicopter, used to carry troops, is streamlined, lighter, and carries no external weapons. Slicks were armed only with the M-60 machine guns used by the door-gunners.

Sling: To carry in a sling underneath a helicopter; also to prepare to be carried in such a manner as in, "We're going to sling our packs today," which meant transporting those packs by helicopter.

Smoke grenade: A grenade that released brightly colored smoke, used for signaling helicopters where to land; yellow was a safe LZ, and red was a hot LZ.

SOP: Standard Operating Procedure.

Sortie: A flight by a helicopter or a plane in Vietnam.

Spec 4: Specialist Fourth Class. A U.S. Army rank immediately above Private First Class.

Spec 5: Specialist Fifth Class. Equivalent to an E-5 sergeant.

Spider hole: A camouflaged enemy foxhole.

Starlight scope: A viewing scope that intensifies images at night by magnifying reflected light from the moon, stars or any other source of light.

Steel pot: The standard U.S. Army steel helmet.

Strobe: A hand-held strobe light for marking landing zones at night.

Sundries: Cartons distributed to soldiers from time to time containing candy, cigarettes, pipe tobacco, chewing tobacco, shaving gear, writing paper, ball-point pens, etc.; also called PX rations or SPs (Sundry Packages). We called a package from home with similar contents a care package.

TACAN: Tactical Air Navigation devices, used to help military pilots navigate their planes in Vietnam.

Tangle foot: Single-strand barbed wire strung in a patchwork pattern at about ankle height; a barrier designed to make it difficult to cross the obstructed area by foot; usually placed around permanent defensive positions.

Tango-Charlie: Time check; in other words, "What time is it?"

Tet: The Buddhist lunar New Year; Buddha's birthday.

Tiger Fatigues: Camouflage fatigue uniforms.

TOC: Tactical Operations Center; the command post and information center for troop operations.

Top: a top sergeant.

Tracer: A round of ammunition chemically treated to glow so that its flight can be followed; usually fired with other bullets to help the shooter assess the accuracy of his weapon.

Triage: The procedure for deciding the order in which to treat casualties.

Trip flare: A ground flare triggered by a trip wire; used to provide warning that the enemy might be approaching.

UH-1H: A Huey helicopter.

US: Prefix to the serial number of U.S. Army draftees.

USO: United Service Organization, which provided some library resources, limited refreshments and a variety of entertainment for the troops.

VC: Viet Cong.

Victor Charlie: The phonetic designation for Viet Cong; the enemy.

Viet Cong: South Vietnamese Communist.

Vietnamese Popular Forces: South Vietnamese local military forces.

Vietnamization: U.S. policy initiated by President Richard Nixon late in the war, attempting to turn fighting responsibilities over to the South Vietnamese Army during the phased withdrawal of American troops.

Wake-up: The last day of a soldier's Vietnam tour; example for six days: five days and a wake-up.

Walking wounded: Wounded who are able to walk without assistance.

Wasted: Killed.

White phosphorus: An explosive round from artillery, mortars, rockets or grenades; also, a type of aerial bomb. When the rounds explode, a huge puff of white smoke appears from the burning phosphorus. When phosphorus hits the skin, it will continue to burn. Water will not put it out. It has to be smothered (in Vietnam, mud was used to seal off the wound) or it will continue to burn until it exits the body.

Willy Peter: The phonetic designation for white phosphorus.

Wood line: A row of trees at the edge of a field or rice paddy; a tree line.

The World: The United States.

WP: White phosphorus.

Xin loi: A Vietnamese phrase meaning "sorry about that."

XO: Executive officer; the second in command of a military unit.

Zapped: Killed.

Research Sources

Books

Archer, Michael, *A Patch of Ground: Khe Sanh Remembered.* L&R Publishing, Melbourne, Australia. Copyright 2005.

Braestrup, Peter, *Big Story.* Presidio Press, Navato, CA. Copyright 1994.

Butler, David, *The Fall of Saigon.* Simon & Schuster, New York, NY. Copyright 1985.

de Chaunac, Jacques-François, *The American Cavalry in Vietnam: "First Cav."* Translated from the French. Turner Publishing, Paducah, KY. Copyright 2003.

Fall, Bernard B., *Street Without Joy.* Stackpole Co., Harrisburg, PA. Copyright 1961.

Gilmore, Donald L., with Giangreco, D.M., *Eyewitness Vietnam, Firsthand Accounts from Operation Rolling Thunder to the Fall of Saigon.* Sterling Publishing Co., Inc., New York, NY. Copyright 2006.

Hammel, Eric: *Khe Sanh: Siege in the Clouds, an Oral History.* Crown Publishing, New York, NY. Copyright 1989.

Herr, Michael, *Dispatches.* Alfred A. Knopf, New York, NY. Copyright 1977.

Hicks, Ned B., *Revelation: A Novel of the Vietnam War.* iUniverse, New York, NY. Copyright 2005.

Hersh, Seymour M., *The Price of Power: Kissinger in the Nixon White House.* Summit Books, a division of Simon and Schuster Inc., New York, NY. Copyright 1983.

Humphries, James F., *Through the Valley: Vietnam, 1967-1968.* Lynne Rienner Publishers, Inc., Boulder, CO. Copyright 1999.

Isaacs, Arnold R., *Without Honor: Defeat in Vietnam and Cambodia.* Johns Hopkins University Press, Baltimore, MD. Copyright 1983.

Johnson III, Lawrence H. *Winged Sabers: The Air Cavalry in Vietnam, 1965-1973.* Stackpole Books, Mechanicsburg, PA. Copyright 2001.

Johnson, Tom A., *To The Limit: An Air Cav Huey Pilot in Vietnam.* Penguin Group (USA), New York, NY. Copyright 2006.

Joyce, James, *Pucker Factor 10: Memoir of A U.S. Helicopter Pilot in Vietnam.* McFarland & Co. Publishers, Jefferson, NC. Copyright 2003.

Krohn, Charles A., *The Lost Battalion: Controversy and Casualties in the Battle of Hue.* Praeger Publishers, Westport, CT. Copyright 1993.

Nolan, Keith W., *Battle for Hue: Tet 1968.* Presidio Press, Navato, CA. Copyright 1983.

Nolan, Keith W., *The Battle for Saigon: Tet 1968.* Presidio Press, Navato, CA. Copyright 2002.

Norman, Michael, *These Good Men, Friendships Forged From War.* Crown Publishers, New York, NY. Copyright 1989.

Oberdorfer, Don, *Tet!: The Turning Point in the Vietnam War.* Johns Hopkins University Press, Baltimore, MD. Copyright 2001.

Roberts, Chalmers M., *The Washington Post: The First 100 Years.* Houghton Mifflin Company, Boston, MA. Copyright 1977.

Santoli, Al, editor, *Everything We Had: An Oral Hisotry of the Vietnam War by Thirty-three American Soldiers Who Fought It.* Random House, Inc., New York, NY. Copyright 1981.

Smith, George W., *The Siege at Hue.* Ballantine Books, New York, NY. Copyright 2000.

Spencer, Ernest, and Murray, Toni (editor), *Welcome to Vietnam, Macho Man.* Presidio Press, Navato, CA. Copyright 1988.

Stanton, Shelby, *The 1st Cav in Vietnam: Anatomy of a Division.* Presidio Press, Navato, CA. Copyright 1999.

Storey, Robert, and Robinson, Daniel, *Vietnam, A Lonely Planet Travel Survival Kit.* Lonely Planet Publications, Footscray, Australia. Copyright 1997.

Weigl, Bruce, *Archeology of The Circle—New and Selected Poems.* Grove Publishers, New York, N.Y. Copyright 1999.

Wirtz, James J. *The Tet Offensive: Intelligence Failure in War.* Cornell University Press, Ithaca, NY. Copyright 1991.

Documents

Accident report and list of casualties, National Archives for the First Air Cavalry Division, detailing Camp Evans collision on October 3, 1968, between an Air Force C-7A plane and a U.S. Army CH-47 Chinook helicopter.

Captured document, Attack of Hue City, dated May 29, 1968, Combined Document Exploitation Center (CDC) Document IRR 6 027 4485 68. Combined Documents Exploitation Center, Washington, DC.

Department of Defense Files. After-Action Report, The Battle of Hue, February 26, 1968. A 13-page after-action report kept by the Command Historian of the United States Army, Vietnam of the Military Assistance Command, Vietnam.

Historical Study 2-68. Operation Hue City, prepared by Major Miles D. Waldron and Specialist Five Richard W. Beavers of the 31st Military History Detachment, Headquarters Provisional Corps Vietnam. August 1968.

Statistics from the Vietnam War, courtesy of the Vietnam Helicopter Pilots Association, Gary Roush, primary contact, Data Base Committee.

Vietnam War After-Action Reports, Lessons Learned Document, Battle Assessments, dating from May 1962 to March 1972.

First Air Cavalry Division publications

The *Cavalair,* the newspaper published by the First Air Cavalry Division, edited by Sergeant Dan Stoneking. Editions published in 1967 and 1968, used to confirm facts, details and basic information stemming from First Air Cavalry Division maneuvers described in the narrative.

The Air Cavalry Division, a magazine published by the First Air Cavalry Division, edited by Specialist Five Donald Graham. Published in July of

1968, used to confirm facts, details and basic information stemming from First Air Cavalry Division maneuvers described in the narrative.

Tolson, Lieutenant General John J., *Vietnam Studies: Airmobility 1961-1971.* Department of the Army, Washington, DC. Published in 1989.

Other publications

Gentlemen's Quarterly, January 1984 edition. Rudy Maxa article on Donald Graham, at that time publisher of *The Washington Post.*

Pearson, Lieutenant General Willard, Vietnam Studies: The War in the Northern Provinces 1966-1968, Department of the Army, Washington, DC, Copyright 1975. For sale by the Superintendent of Documents, U.S. Government Printing Office, Washington, D.C. 20402.

The Wall Street Journal, Wednesday, February 6, 2008, edition. Arthur Herman opinion piece on the 1968 Tet offensive in South Vietnam.

Time Magazine, Friday, April 12, 1968, edition. Article on the siege at Khe Sanh.

Time Magazine, Friday, October 31, 1969, edition. Article on the Massacre of Hue.

Mike Larson has collaborated with Jill Larson Sundberg on a number of books. These books include:

My Red Hat
My Red Hattitudes
Babes Remember
Cozy Cozy
Sunday Drives

Larson also has written:

There's Magic All Around Us
A Murder in Mundelein

Most of these books are available from Barnes & Noble Bookstores and on Amazon.com. For additional information, contact Access Marketing Systems Inc., 11025 Irwin Ave. S., Bloomington, MN 55437 or Phone Toll Free 1-877-788-1591.

Made in the USA
Lexington, KY
28 November 2014